When Is Enough, Enough?

When Is Enough, Enough?

What You Can Do If You Never Feel Satisfied

Laurie Ashner

Mitch Meyerson

HAZELDEN®

Hazelden
Center City, Minnesota 55012-0176

02 01 00 99   10 9 8 7 6 5

Library of Congress Cataloging-in-Publication Data
Ashner, Laurie.
    When is enough, enough? : what you can do if you never feel satisfied /
Laurie Ashner, Mitch Meyerson.
        p. cm.
    Includes bibliographical references and index.
    ISBN 1-56838-197-2
    1. Disappointment. 2. Satisfaction. 3. Self-actualization
(Psychology) I. Meyerson, Mitch. II. Title.
BF575.D57A84   1996
152.4—dc20   96-4892
                                                         CIP

Editor's note
Hazelden offers a variety of information on chemical dependency and
related areas. Our publications do not necessarily represent Hazelden's
programs, nor do they officially speak for any Twelve Step organization.
    The characters in this book are composites of many individuals. Any
similarity to any one person is purely coincidental

To Marcie and Howard Tilkin,
with love.

L.A.

To my wife,
who has given me more satisfaction
than I could ever have imagined.

M.M.

most about yourself.... How your symptoms serve you.... Ending the family legacy of negativity.

Generalized anxiety disorder—when you never really stop worrying.... Don't trust, don't believe, and other childhood messages.... Compulsive self-reliance: Are you the only one you trust?.... Are you setting yourself up for dissatisfaction?... Why it will never be enough.... How to reduce hypervigilance and other anxiety-provoking behaviors.... Creative stress management.... Building trust.

Psychological entitlement.... The pampered-driven child.... The truth about boredom and restlessness.... Boredom and self-sabotage.... Are you disregarding your greatest talents? Building a sense of competence.... Your prescription for changing boredom to energy.

When good enough isn't good enough.... Falling in and out of love.... Is it passion or paranoia?... Looking for love in all the wrong places.... Using relationships as mirrors.... When your best solutions become your biggest problems.... What your idea of a perfect lover tells you about yourself.... How to tell if you're overloading your relationships.... Finding lasting love.

Why is it easy to give others the credit?... The underlying fears.... A secret need for control.... Teenage trauma.... Transference.... Recognizing self-

We thank those who have contributed to this project.

First, we thank our editor, Steve Lehman, and all of the enthusiastic people at Hazelden.

Next, we are grateful to our professional colleagues, Dr. Michael Franz Basch, Dr. Frank Gruba-McCallister, and Dr. Ken Celiano for their insights and contributions.

For their support and inspiration, many special thanks to Jean Naggar, Mark and Martha Rubenstein, Neil Howe, George Potts, Ron Kaplan, Ellie Sigel, Lainie Garrick, Carol Ehrlich, Nancy Block, and Chuck Perrin.

Pam Berns, editor of *Chicago Life* magazine, for her unwavering support of our writing.

Most of all, thanks to all the people who were interviewed for this book and shared their most intimate experiences.

Hazelden Publishing and Education is a division of the Hazelden Foundation, a not-for-profit organization. Since 1949, Hazelden has been a leader in promoting the dignity and treatment of people afflicted with the disease of chemical dependency.

The mission of the foundation is to improve the quality of life for individuals, families, and communities by providing a national continuum of information, education, and recovery services that are widely accessible; to advance the field through research and training; and to improve our quality and effectiveness through continuous improvement and innovation.

Stemming from that, the mission of the publishing division is to provide quality information and support to people wherever they may be in their personal journey—from education and early intervention, through treatment and recovery, to personal and spiritual growth.

Although our treatment programs do not necessarily use everything Hazelden publishes, our bibliotherapeutic materials support our mission and the Twelve Step philosophy upon which it is based. We encourage your comments and feedback.

The headquarters of the Hazelden Foundation is in Center City, Minnesota. Additional treatment facilities are located in Chicago, Illinois; New York, New York; Plymouth, Minnesota; St. Paul, Minnesota; and West Palm Beach, Florida. At these sites, we provide a continuum of care for men and women of all ages. Our Plymouth facility is designed specifically for youth and families.

For more information on Hazelden, please call *1-800-257-7800.* Or you may access our World Wide Web site on the Internet at *http://www.Hazelden.org.*

Understanding the Mystery Of Chronic Dissatisfaction

This is not a book for people who count their blessings. This is a book for countless people who have met many of their goals but feel a nagging sense of dissatisfaction with themselves, their loves, and their lives.

When Is Enough, Enough? is about women like Laura, obsessed with winning a promotion to account supervisor at a major advertising firm. She thrusts herself into sixty-hour weeks, using every ounce of energy she can muster until she achieves the new position. Her joy lasts all of ten minutes. "I stood in my new corner office thinking, 'This is great, but I could be doing something much more *important.*'"

It's about men like Tim, a songwriter who spent ten years cutting demos and knocking his head against closed doors before a major artist agreed to record one of his songs. "I should be breaking out the champagne," he says, "but I can't stop worrying. What if my song hits and I can't do it again? What if this ends up being a twelve-week career?"

It's about Sandy, with a husband whom she loves, children whom she adores, and a growing feeling of despair. "Being with my children now, while they're young, is the most important thing. I know that. I had a career. It was no big deal. But I still feel I should be doing something more with my life. I'm torn in so many different directions. Have I been happy the last three years? No."

It's about Sal, veteran of a failed first marriage and hundreds of first dates, who always feels something is "missing"; Beth, pretty by most people's standards, who can't stop believing she's unattractive; Jim, working toward his third degree in a never-ending search for the "right" career; Carole, depressed for reasons she can't put her finger on; and a hundred other people who shared their stories for this book.

If you have ever wondered why no matter what you have, and no matter how hard you struggled to get it, you still feel little sense of fulfillment, chances are *When Is Enough, Enough?* is also about *you.*

Isn't it good to want what you don't have?

The feeling that it's never enough is not about workaholism, although the workaholic will certainly understand the feeling. Nor is it a feeling limited to high-profile overachievers who bottom out in the process. Anyone can fall prey to never-enough thinking.

We may believe that never feeling satisfied is the same as having ambition, but is it? There are some key differences:

♦ Ambitious people feel invigorated as they near a goal. Never-enough thinkers feel drained.

♦ Ambitious people take pride in their accomplishments. Never-enough thinkers become anxious with their success and obsessed with wondering, *Can I do it again? Was this a fluke?* Or, *So what? It's no big deal; anyone could do it.*

♦ Ambitious people make conscious choices and act deliberately. Never-enough thinkers act compulsively. Unsure about what they really want, they stay in constant motion.

♦ Ambitious people act out of passion. Never-enough thinkers often act out of paranoia: *What will they think if I fail? Why doesn't she realize I deserve the credit?*

That old familiar feeling

All of us feel dissatisfied or disappointed at times. But maybe it's the first moment we realize that we never feel rich enough, thin enough, pretty enough, or talented enough that we say, "When is enough, enough?" Or it becomes clear when we finally have everything we've wanted and still feel unhappy. We wonder what in the world is keeping us from feeling good.

As therapists we can assure you that many people come into treatment with the feeling that something is missing. We spent more than ten years of clinical work and research studying people who suffered from chronic discontent. We wondered: *Why do some people get exactly what they thought they wanted and are still disappointed? Why do others find it impossible to find the right career or the right relationship? Why do many of us want the one thing we can never have?*

What intrigued us most was discovering people who felt satisfied in spite of their failures, conflicts, and problems. What did they know that the rest of us should know?

What we discovered was that never-enough thinking bears little connection to what we have or don't have. Furthermore, we were able to isolate some glaring reasons why many people find the road to satisfaction so difficult. We stopped seeing dissatisfaction as the result of negative thinking but as a signal—a red flag that tells us we need to adjust the way we approach our goals. In other words, people who are never satisfied are unconsciously setting themselves up for disappointment, and there are startling reasons why.

A snapshot: What does it feel like to be a person who is never satisfied?

The feeling that it's never enough is a habit, a trait, and an outgrowth of the dominant drives that shape your personality. Eleven charac-

teristics were typical among the people we studied. If you feel chronically dissatisfied, chances are you will identify with these characteristics, too:

♦ Success doesn't bring you joy; it only makes you wonder, *Can I do it again?*

♦ You vacillate between feeling talented and special and having the nagging doubt of, *Who do I think I am?*

♦ You feel your efforts aren't recognized enough, yet compliments make you feel uncomfortable or put you on your guard.

♦ You're often the number two person: the vice president, the administrative assistant, the woman behind the man. You have a sense of being left behind, while others with less skill or ambition achieve their goals.

♦ It's not enough to be an average success; anything merely average fills you with a sense of failure.

♦ Having been taught not to depend on other people, you take more than your share of the blame for what goes wrong in relationships, at work, and in your family.

♦ You are drawn to situations that create the need to prove yourself.

♦ You unconsciously re-create past disappointments; your unfinished business with parents and friends replays itself in your current relationships.

♦ You minimize the anxiety and depression you feel about your life; you're so used to it, it feels like *you.*

♦ Because reaching out to other people is difficult, you try to bolster yourself with outward support systems (money in the bank, a secure job, community contacts).

♦ You are addicted to striving—and to emotional frustration.

If the definition of never being satisified fits you, you haven't developed these patterns or symptoms by accident. Much in your history set this pattern in motion, and much in your present keeps you stuck in it. But you do not have to go through life feeling you can never relax. You do not have to watch satisfaction slip through your fingers or throw happiness away with both hands.

In the chapters that follow we will explore many of the core issues that create chronic dissatisfaction. We'll discuss their origin and their remedy. You will hear the stories of people who have endured the feeling that it was never enough. Through their insight you will be helped to understand the patterns more clearly.

It will take more than "positive thinking" or forcing yourself to smell the roses to banish this lingering feeling of joylessness, but it can be done, and you can do it. To recover from this pattern requires a cognitive shift—a new way of looking at the entire problem—from the start. Such a shift begins with the following:

❦ *Realize that if you could "just do it," you would have done it.* We do not know what your particular struggle is. It may be an inner one. It may have to do with your self-confidence, your basic belief in yourself. Or it may have to do with your relationships. You may grapple daily with bitter feelings toward family members or disappointment in love. Or perhaps your struggle is with a rising tide of nothingness that saps your energy and makes you feel hopeless.

Whatever your particular struggle is, chances are you have expended a great deal of energy trying to overcome it. Maybe there's something you believe would change everything if only you could accomplish it: a new job, more money, a better marriage, a diet that worked, a makeover, a new plan. You believe this in your heart, but your feet just won't move toward this goal.

In the midst of your disappointment, your family and friends may have tried to point out all that's good in your life, all you should feel grateful for. Or they've offered you advice and solutions to what's troubling you by the dozens. You also have tried to pull yourself up by the bootstraps: *Stop complaining already. You have a million reasons to be happy. If you're not, then go out and do something about it.*

The first shift you need to make in your thinking is to understand that if you could just do it, you would have done it. Let's stop assuming for a moment that there is some mysterious something out there that is stopping you. If there is something you truly want, and you can't make yourself go out and get it, then there are excellent reasons why.

❧ *Stop wrestling with the truth.* As therapists we have come to recognize that it doesn't really matter that the client who comes to us complaining that she feels unattractive is really beautiful. It doesn't matter that the person who comes in complaining about a lack of success has a long history of triumphs. If you are dissatisifed, we aren't going to argue with you. We aren't going to tell you that you should feel satisfied. It wouldn't matter and it wouldn't help. More important, it becomes a moot point. What difference does it make if you are at the top of the hill if you don't believe it? What does it matter that you have a hundred achievements if they do nothing to dispel the emptiness? Beginning this book, allowing yourself to feel whatever it is you really feel, without argument, without guilt, without challenge, is the most important thing you can do to help yourself recover.

Fritz Perls, the father of Gestalt therapy, said, "What is, is." And nothing changes until it becomes what it is.

It is difficult and painful to be a person who is never satisfied in a world of quick fixes. One can barely get a problem out of his or her mouth before someone jumps in with ten things that could be done to solve it. It seems ironic that in a world of so much information, so much advice, there is so little real empathy.

We hear hundreds of problems in the course of our clinical work. They are all different. But they are all also the same at the core. We spend our entire lives trying to understand, but we never, ever really feel understood.

A client recently came to us after losing almost thirty pounds. Desperately she wanted to lose ten more; those ten pounds eluded her. Her husband told her, "Honey, you're beautiful. I love your body. You could never lose another pound and I'd still think you look terrific."

With the best of intentions and love, her husband gave her an entirely unempathetic response. He told her she shouldn't feel what she felt. It's the same response many of us get from those we love when we share our problems. This woman wasn't going to lose the weight she was desperate to lose for a reason at the core of the entire when is enough, enough syndrome. Ten pounds, twenty pounds wouldn't matter. It would never be enough. She would never feel understood.

The problem for many of us isn't that we lack solutions to our troubles. The problem is that we're lonely. Surrounded by people who tell us they understand, we feel misunderstood. We manage it through striving for something more, something different. We have so little experience with real empathy early on that we don't know what it looks like and we have no idea that it's missing. We have little empathy for ourselves. We only have plan A, plan B, and plan C, and the gnawing certainty that there must be something wrong with us because nothing makes us feel happy for more than fifteen minutes.

Empathy means that if you tell me you feel alone, I'm not going to tell you that you're surrounded by people and you have no cause to feel that way. I'm going to explore those feelings with you. I'm going to help you be courageous enough to take a sharp look at your aloneness and what it means to you, how it pays off for you, and where you learned it to begin with. I'm going to put to the side my own fears about the fact that I can't make you happy, because that is my issue, not yours.

Are we saying that discontent is good and that you should go around feeling miserable? Of course not. But as many therapists have said, you cannot heal what you refuse to feel. If you could banish discontent through the sheer force of your will, you would have done it.

❧ *Stop digging in the ashes.* When a situation—a career, a relationship, a lifestyle—gives you little personal satisfaction in spite of the energy you've invested, but you keep giving it more time, trusting that time alone will make it better, you're digging in the ashes. It's a tenacious kind of emotional limbo that leads to low self-esteem—and chronic dissatisfaction.

There are many of us who go to the same dry well daily hoping for water. We think we know what we want and so we try to get it. When we don't get it, we do the same thing louder and harder.

Time doesn't heal; it numbs. We have watched many of our clients valiantly try to adjust to a surprising number of disappointing situations they knew were bad from the start and then tell themselves that the trouble lay within them, rather than in the situation itself.

Stop digging in the ashes. In this book, we will ask you to continually challenge conventional wisdom about what is supposed to make us happy. For example: Never use your principal; never buy on credit; don't skip from job to job; don't spend more than a third of your paycheck on rent; don't improve your house beyond its market value are out-of-context rules used by many people. What's important to realize is that the purpose of these rules is to make money grow, not to enhance the quality of your personal life. You need to shape and apply these rules personally, so they further the larger goals of your life.

The same thing goes for such old saws as: Smile and the world smiles with you; cry and you cry alone. You may get a lot further with a few tears than you get with that stiff upper lip. Your admonitions to think postively may be the very thing that stops you from solving the negatives in your life.

To stop digging in the ashes requires that you set a boundary between yourself and people who encourage you to stay stuck. They might not want you to change not because of what could happen to you, but because of what could happen to *them*.

It requires realizing that what you want may be very different from what you need. You can be swimming in the wrong pond, and swimming very well. There's a saying in Twelve Step programs: Your best thinking got you here.

As you read the chapters in this book that pertain to your struggle, ask yourself: *What am I trying to talk myself into, in my life?*

❧ *Stop telling yourself that you expect too much out of life. Chances are, you expect too little.* We settle for stimulation, predictability, or comfort when we could have true intimacy and the excitement of feeling a connection with another person. We settle for salaries, security, and benefits when we could have the sense of well-being that comes from knowing our life has a purpose and a meaning. We believe that passion inevitably turns into a dull, depressing, even painful routine, so we want the new, the different, the never-tried.

There are a hundred self-help books that will tell you that your biggest trouble if you are unhappy is that your expectations are too high. But is wanting to feel in love too high an expectation? Are wanting money, a fit body, a good career, and happy children too high of expectations?

In our experience with people who are never satisfied, the problem didn't lie in having high expectations. Lack of motivation, yes. Lack of resources, sometimes. The wrong path to achieving them, definitely. Self-sabotage, often. A lack of vision or confidence in that vision, always. To give up our expectations means to settle for survival rather than growth.

❧ *Be ready to confront the core issues that create so much discontent.* For each of us who suffers from the syndrome, one or more core issues tend to dominate. *When Is Enough, Enough?* is organized around these core issues, phrased in the form of the nine most common questions clients bring into therapy:

♦ Why do I always feel that something is missing?

♦ Why don't I follow through on my dreams?

♦ Why can't I find the right person?

♦ Why do I always want the one thing I can't have?

♦ Why can't I stop comparing myself to other people?

♦ Why do I always end up getting less than I give?

♦ Why am I so bored and restless?

♦ Why can't I just relax?

♦ Why is it that nothing makes me happy for long?

The real challenge of recovering from the feeling that it's never enough lies in confronting these core issues. There are no shortcuts.

Change is an easy thing to decide and a difficult thing to do. Don't be too hard on yourself if change doesn't come easily. Make it your goal to not make the same mistakes too often.

We hope that for all of you who never feel satisfied, this book will help you confront the reality of whatever stands in your way. We will encourage you to redirect your energies away from whatever is defeating you and toward a more fulfilling path. We will offer tools you can employ to be able to exchange never-enough thinking for self-fulfillment. That is our wish for you.

❦ ❦

CHAPTER ONE

Why Do I Always Feel Like Something Is Missing?

The Search for Self

One faces the future with one's past.

—PEARL S. BUCK

"Finally I was having all of this success. My screenplay was optioned. I was getting calls from agents interested in representing anything else I'd done. I quit my job at the insurance company. I didn't even go in to clean out my desk."

The man who is talking just celebrated his thirtieth birthday. The screenplay he wrote hasn't made it to film yet, but his entire life has changed. People take his calls. They hire him to work on their projects. He's doing what he loves. He's making money. He can finally pay his bills.

Is he happy? "Funny. I bought a house recently. I find myself wandering around in it, feeling depressed, wondering, *Why does it still feel like something's missing?*"

The house is beautiful and the new addition adds space and charm. When Aimee walks through it, she remembers the nightmare of living without a kitchen for three months and how the dust that was everywhere made her eyes water. It's a rare hour she has to herself. Soon she will pick up the three-year old at preschool, do her shopping, and then fetch the five-year-old from afternoon kindergarten. "My husband had his friends over the other night to play cards and I had to laugh because they don't say, 'How's your career,' anymore. It's 'How's your Keogh?' They're all in a race to see who will retire first. Funny, but our whole lives have been about the next thing. We thought, we'll have a baby, then everything will be great. Then we thought what we really needed was a home, so we bought a house. Something was still not right, so we redecorated the house. Then we started a garden. Now we're down to all this talk about retiring. When we finally do, what if it's still not enough?"

Where does this feeling that something's missing come from, and why does it plague so many successful people? While restlessness can be caused by a failure to grow and change, many of us have climbed more mountains than we ever dreamed we would. As for changes, we're going through cars, clothes, friends, lovers, careers at warp speed, quickly disillusioned, but still hopeful that there's something out there that will allow us to feel good, once and for all.

It's a fill-me-up hunger that never really goes away. In *Beach Music,* Pat Conroy's semi-autobiographical best-seller, the main character sits among the splendor of Venice and muses, "I do not know why it is that I have always been happier thinking of somewhere I have been or wanted to go, than where I am at the time. I find it difficult to be happy in the present."

You, too, may identify with that panicky feeling of, What now, what next? or that sinking feeling of, Is this all there is? This chapter is about those of us who got much of what we wanted, more or less, and still feel something's missing. Let's begin by exploring the origin of that feeling and why it has so little to do with what we achieve or fail to achieve.

An adaptive self

When you talk to people who always feel something is missing, something becomes clear immediately. This feeling didn't suddenly appear unbidden into their lives. On some level, it's always been there. They search their minds for a time when they felt complete, and they come up blank.

It's five o'clock in the afternoon, and Michelle, thirty-nine, is in bed. On the nightstand is a spread of potato salad, a pound of corn beef, a stack of Oreos, and copies of the *Star* and the *National Enquirer.* Tomorrow she will be on the stairmaster for an hour and a half and the tabloids will line the cat box. But right at this moment propped up on her pillows, under her comforter, she is truly having a night *out.*

What generated a day in bed was a weekend visiting her parents. It's an annual event that used to send her to bed in white-knuckled, impotent rage for a week. This is progress.

Trouble started on the way home from the airport. "Seven of us were packed into Dad's Oldsmobile. He still drives with two feet, and it was making me so nauseous I thought I was going to have to tell him to pull over. My mother, the master of the-compliment-with-shit-on-it, turns to me and says, 'That's a great suit dear, but isn't the skirt a little tight?'

"My brother kicks me. He knows it's going to start, but I'm thinking, surely I'm beyond all this by now. I'm not going to let her get to me. 'That's the style, Ma,' I tell her, but there's an edge to my voice. Everyone can hear it. She puts on this hurt look and says, 'I just thought that for an outfit you've spent so much money on, the skirt should fit. You have so many flattering outfits, dear.' "

For Michelle, it's old ground. Her mother's incessant, veiled, well intentioned criticism has consumed months of therapy. Something in Michelle admires her mother's knack of killing two birds with one stone—she's been told she's too fat and she spends too much money, and she hasn't even been in the car ten minutes.

"Next we were treated to a lecture about how she used to dress for work, the best years of her life, the days of her Big Career. She was one of the few women of her generation to go to college, but she gave everything up to be a wife and mother of five children. No one mentions that she could have gone back to work long ago since her youngest child is thirty. My father's ears are turning red. I think he hates this particular story as much as we do. He turns off the air-conditioning and opens the windows—he can smell fumes in the car. My mother's hair starts to fly around. The woman works on her hair for hours, and part of me wants to pat my father on the back and shake his hand. We all love her, we all want her approval, and we're all reduced to petty revenge."

The weekend dragged along. The house was filled with relatives on the evening of Michelle's father's birthday. Michelle felt the darkness rise within her when her mother handed her a slice of birthday cake—a morsel, really, with only the thinnest suggestion of frosting. She gave her mother a withering look. "Do you want a bigger slice, dear?" her mother asked innocently. "You've done such a good job losing weight that I thought you were trying to keep it off."

On the plane Sunday night, Michelle sipped club soda and opened the carry-on bag that held last Tuesday's newspaper. Spreading it out, she turned to page twenty. On it was her picture and the announcement that recently she was made a partner at her company. The newspaper had remained in her bag all weekend.

That Tuesday had been a day of mixed feelings. She bought five copies of the newspaper on the way to her office. The item was already clipped and hanging on the bulletin board when she got to work. She stared at it feeling a mixture of pride and embarrassment. "I had this mad impulse to rip it down, to hide it. I mean, what if someone thought I hung it up there?"

People came in to congratulate her. "I never know what to say in those situations. I finally shut my door. Yes, being made a partner is great, but it's not such a big deal. It's not like I'm Bill Gates."

The man she's dating called her twice that day, and each time she thought he was calling to tell her that he'd seen the announcement. But it's a big paper. "I know he would have been happy for me. He'd say it was great. What's he supposed to say?" But she never mentioned it.

The incident goes to the heart of what has always been a mystery for Michelle. Criticism isn't as hard to take. She can answer her critics with a strong choice of words when she has to. But listening to someone tell her that they admire her accomplishments, that she's special, is another story. Believing it is almost impossible. There's so much more she wants to be.

Friends accuse Michelle of being a pessimist. She disagrees. "I'm a realist. People pull your chain. I do it myself. I've told people that their outfits are great, their babies are beautiful. I'm just as guilty as anyone else of telling people what they want to hear."

Ultimately, this is where she's stuck. True, there are people who pull your chain, so to speak. But there are those who tell the truth. Michelle doesn't differentiate. "I just don't want to be a fool," she says.

A fool. It's a revealing choice of words. It smacks of about a million experiences with Mom.

The trouble isn't that Michelle doesn't achieve enough. It's that praise goes over her head like it's meant for somebody else. She can't take in any admiration or allow it to nourish her. It would make her vulnerable. The rug could be pulled out from under her at any moment by something as simple as trust.

Time is running on. One wonders what it would take for Michelle to believe it when people tell her that her accomplishments, such as becoming the first female partner in a firm with a solid glass ceiling, are extraordinary.

What would be enough? She grins and glances at the tabloids that litter her bed, the huge color photographs of the stars. "Maybe if photographers from the *National Enquirer* were climbing on the tree in my backyard this minute to snap my picture, I'd figure I was someone important."

Maybe so. But maybe she'd be telling herself that it was only the *Enquirer*, not the *New York Times*.

Michelle felt depressed and lonely at a time in her life when she might have been happiest. Her depression cloaked growing feelings of rage and resentment that remained outside her awareness. No one can fault Michelle's mother for encouraging her daughter to be thin, financially solvent, and realistic. These were attributes Michelle wanted for herself. She dieted down to a size 10, money isn't a problem, but there are still "compliments-with-shit-on-them." Her survival strategy is what it has always been—to protect herself, even at the cost of happiness. She discounts herself before anyone else does. She hides her accomplishments.

"If it wasn't for you kids I'd be happy," is an enormously destructive message. It inflicts shame and guilt. Michelle's mother's jealous and competitive attitude caused her children to fear the bitterness their success generates in her. Michelle doesn't tell the family about her promotion because her mother cannot bear it. She loves her daughter, but she has little empathy for her feelings or needs. She cannot praise her daughter, because her daughter's life threatens the wisdom of the very choices she made in her own, choices which ultimately have left her feeling unfulfilled.

When Michelle's brother kicked her in the car, the kick must have felt like a gift. It was her brother's way of saying, "I know how Mom is," even as he cautioned, "Don't take the bait and spoil Dad's birthday." The kick meant, "I understand you; I recognize what you're feeling." That's the gift. In these types of families, there's so little empathy. Everyone knows the truth, but no one can say it. There's no room for vulnerability. Everyone is too defensive.

Today Michelle is a successful adult. Inside is a hungry child, one who has gotten creative in getting her needs met. Long ago this child asked, "How can I get what I want, playing by their rules?" Michelle survives by putting her needs back on herself and minimizing them, by achieving little victories over her mother.

The fact that she is devastatingly hurt by how few people recognize her achievements is something she minimizes, because, in fact, she sets it up. The spread of food on her nightstand nourishes her and gives her some semblance of comfort. The rigorous exercise the next day will give her a sense of control over her life. She'll bounce back and forth between control and comfort, but she won't allow anyone to help.

It's a Catch-22. Michelle's fantasy is that it will finally be enough when she accomplishes something so big, so grandiose, that it leaves no room for doubt about her capabilities, no space for compliments-with-shit-on-them. But in an envious world, who ever accomplishes that?

The narcissistic injury

In the movie *Pretty Woman,* there's a scene where Richard Gere serves strawberries and champagne to Julia Roberts, a prostitute whom he has solicited for the night. She looks at him, dazed, and says, "I appreciate this whole seduction scene you've got going, but let me give you a tip. I'm a sure thing, okay?"

Our parents' love was supposed to be a sure thing. Ideally there was one time in our lives where we felt loved, needed, and necessary to someone without having to do anything to achieve it. But those of us who had to seduce our parents to get their love—those who kept trying to meet the conditions of a very conditional love—we have a different view of the world than those who knew their parents' love was for sure. It's a feeling that something is missing that doesn't go away, no matter what we achieve or fail to achieve. We're hauling out the strawberries and champagne, hoping that this time, it will be enough and we'll finally be safe.

The self-help movement of the eighties, with its emphasis on Twelve Step programs and recognizing the effects of childhood trauma on adult behavior, was followed by a "Don't whine, deal with it" backlash in the nineties. In other words, don't blame your parents for a lack of adult responsibility.

But successful people who always feel something is missing hardly go through life blaming their pasts for today's misfortunes. They blame themselves.

When one searches the writings of the most eminent psychologists for the reason why so many successful people feel something is missing, one soon discovers the work of psychoanalyst Heinz Kohut. In *The Analysis of the Self,* Kohut proposed that high self-esteem—the feeling of self-approval not because of our accomplishments but just because we exist—is a product of the experiences in early childhood. According to Kohut, there's a period in the first year of life where it's necessary that we be adored, that we be told we're the most special person on earth, that we revel in a sense of our own importance. It's a stage of narcissism, a word that some people substitute for conceit, but which can also mean a healthy feeling of self-love.

Anyone who has had a child or spent time around children knows that children demand attention. We also know that it's difficult to give it every time, on demand. Some parents rise to the challenge. Others resent the challenge. No one will do it perfectly.

An infant who goes through a stage of healthy, primary narcissism, fueled by a parent's adoring looks, attention, and pride has the groundwork for a strong sense of self. Mother or father don't have to be adoring every second. They just have to do it "good enough." If we get a good enough "fix" of adoration and attention, we will be able to let it go. We will leave this stage no longer needing constant approval or being driven to prove ourselves. There will be a feeling of worth and security at the core. Without this experience, a narcissistic wound—a disturbing sense that one is not good enough to begin with—can occur. This wound can be the root of an adult sense that something is missing.

For many of us, Kohut's theories are alarming. There are those of us who sense (or perhaps even know, like Michelle) that our mother—a woman too busy, too absent, too disapproving, too wounded herself—did not give us what was required in this stage. Must we always suffer because of it? There is a second step in the building of the self, Kohut states. There are others who love us: fathers, siblings, grandparents, teachers. We can admire, idealize, and introject their qualities. Though not a substitute, they provide, in essence, a second chance.

Although our explanation of Kohut's theory is simplified, and an analysis of his work is beyond the scope of this book, something appears unarguable: We need as much love and attention as our parents can give us in the first years of life to achieve a sense of self-esteem. We need attention that is admiring without being smothering, all-encompassing but with the strength to let us go. If we don't get it, we may be forever looking for it.

You may have grown up with a father who felt he best prepared you for real life by pointing out all of the ways in which you needed to improve. Or perhaps you had overachieving parents who inadvertently caused you to feel that you weren't an integral part of their lives. Your parents' divorce may have left you feeling more like a pawn in their struggle with each other than a human being. A parent's addiction, career failure, depression, or illness might have consumed so much energy that you were left on your own to be your own parent. Or perhaps there were many experiences of love and acceptance in your family, but there were rejection and despair outside of it, perhaps in school or with peers.

Many of us do what Michelle did: We manufacture our own self-esteem. We do it with careers, accomplishments, babies, athletic achievements, and so on. It would all be great if it didn't still feel like something is missing.

The heart of the problem for those of us who go through life feeling that something is always missing is this: *Something in our ability to seek praise or to let it in has been damaged.* Something has gone awry in the simple process of accomplishing something, being praised or admired for it, and allowing that praise to nourish us without feeling we are "needy" because of it. The feeling of not enough is coming from the inside, not the outside.

We may be clever, self-confident, intelligent, and effective, but something inside is still vulnerable and insecure. We sense it the moment we make a mistake, get thwarted in a goal, or otherwise disappoint ourselves. That early need for someone to respond to us, to affirm us, might reassert itself, leaving us open to a repetition of the disappointment and, perhaps, humiliation.

Is what you want what you need?

The most important inner need people have is to be seen for who they are. Yet so much of what we actually do in life is hide this true self from other people. It's a paradox. We're tired of pretending; we wish we could just be ourselves, but the thought that this true self might be exposed to other people fills us with dread.

Dustin, thirty-eight, assistant principal of a highly rated suburban grammar school, is a hurried man whose day is composed of resolving teachers' schedule conflicts, arranging buses for field trips, managing databases of grades and transcripts, meeting with high school counselors, and showing guests around the school. He's the man next in line when the principal retires in two years, so showing Officer Friendly, spokesperson for the local police, to the first grade classroom where he's supposed to speak is both an annoyance and a responsibility.

One look at the officer waiting in the front office stops him cold. A voice goes off in his head and it says, "It's him. Grayer, heavier, but definitely him." He starts to sweat.

He was twenty when it happened. He had a fight with his girlfriend. She jumped out of his car. She wouldn't answer the phone and frustration and rage overtook him. He went to her apartment and she wouldn't open the door. They argued so loudly in the hallway, a neighbor called the police. He was taken away that evening for questioning. By Officer Friendly.

Will the police officer remember him? Dustin can barely meet the man's eyes, but the officer is much more interested in getting his speech over and getting to lunch than he is in Dustin. Dustin breathes a sigh of relief. "This town is pretty provincial," he admits. "They expect their school administrators to be model citizens." And Dustin is extremely cautious. No one knows that he smokes an occasional cigarette. Nor would they imagine that he has four Visa cards, each up to their limit, and a spending problem that borders on being out of control. It is as if Dustin has two personalities, a true self with real needs and feelings, and a public self made to order, which wears the right clothes, says the right words, showcases his talents, and functions in the way the world rewards with success.

In *New Passages,* Gail Sheehy explains why most people will develop a "false self" to some extent in their twenties and thirties: "We want validation, and in seeking it, we rely heavily on external measurements: the perks of our job, the size of our office, the feats of our children, the 'just right' clothes to wear to the awards dinner. Any of these become showcases for proving our worth. The thirties arc a serious dress rehearsal for how we will perform if and when we are given the leadership roles. There is nothing wrong with projecting this false self to the outside world during those early striving years, so long as it isn't too distant or disconnected from who we really are."

Distant. Disconnected. Those of us who have come too far from our true selves are most apt to feel that something is missing.

Where did we learn to dislike parts of ourselves? How did we develop a "false self" to protect ourselves?

As children, we tend to mold our personalities to adapt to our environment. If our environment is supportive, nurturing, and flexible, we are freed to express our individuality. If our environment is rigid, demanding, and conditional, however, we are forced to shape our behavior to meet the needs of others. We substitute our true self for a false self or adaptive self that is more acceptable to our parents whose love we need desperately, our peers whose approval we crave, our teachers, and others. In essence, we compromise who we really are and become what we believe others want us to be.

In the *Drama of the Gifted Child,* Alice Miller writes, "The tragedy is that of early psychic injuries and their inevitable repression, which allows the child to survive. In a broad sense, it is the tragedy of almost everyone: As children we strive, above all else, to accommodate our parents' demands—spoken and unspoken, reasonable and unreasonable. In the process, we blind ourselves to our true needs and feelings. In our adult lives, this is like trying to sail a ship without a compass. Not knowing who we are, what we feel, and what we need, even as grown-ups, we remain subject to the expectations placed upon us from the very beginning of our lives, expectations we fulfilled not for love, but for the illusion of love."

Guilty secrets

Reconciling who we really are with the veneer we show to the world is a major task of life, and no one can avoid it. All of us have an adaptive self. All of us have a self we show to the world that is better, finer, more together than the way we behave at times. There is no one without a secret, without some quality that doesn't live up to his or her ultimate, best expectations.

We give our clients a questionnaire after the first few weeks of therapy that they take home to complete. It's a fill-in-the-blank type of self-assessment. One item reads, "If you knew the real truth about me, you'd _____ ."

Clients often write: "You would be shocked!" or some variation of the statement: "You wouldn't believe it was me."

What are they hiding? Here, with their permission, are the guilty secrets, some from far in the past, some from last week:

♦ "My one-year-old daughter screamed, thrashed around, and crawled away while I was trying to change her diaper. I couldn't take it anymore. I threw a sock at her. It hit her in the head. But what if I had thrown something else?" *(Her home is spotless, her child outgoing and happy, she has the patience of a saint, and every night she provides home-cooked meals for her family because she doesn't want her child raised on a diet of fast food.)*

♦ "I did so many drugs in college, my nickname was 'Bonehead.'" *(He's a successful lawyer, a teetotaler, and a civil rights spokesperson who is often quoted in the press.)*

♦ "My son is seventeen. All it takes is for someone to do the math and come up with the fact that I was sixteen when I had him." *(She was chairwoman of the fund-raising committee for her son's* *school and raised more than $50,000, she was just promoted to group supervisor, and her husband is out shopping for a tenth anniversary present.)*

♦ "I forged my college transcript with the help of some Wite-Out and a Xerox machine. I was twenty, there were too many Cs in too many courses, and I felt my record wouldn't get the job. It made sense at the time, but I keep thinking someone's going to look into that file and notice and blow my cover." *(It's twelve years later. He achieved straight A's in graduate school, when he finally decided to buckle down.)*

♦ "I dress up, take off my wedding ring, and sit in the hotel bar, waiting for someone to pick me up. We talk, but it never goes further than that. Then I go home." *(She manages health care for corporations. She was a virgin when she married her husband at twenty-one. Her husband has had countless affairs since they've been married.)*

How shocking are these secrets, really? Not very. But the mistakes, the drives, the untamed cravings of the real self fill many people with shame. They cannot forgive themselves. Their self-esteem is dependent on unrealistic measures of performance. If they do good, they are good. If they fall short, they enlist survival strategies: avoidance, withholding, placating, covering up, blaming themselves.

Most of us have things in our past we'd rather not think about. But the people who constantly feel something is missing are often trying to deny their very "self." They may, in fact, have lost that "self" somewhere along the road to adulthood. These are people who

- feel hurt, but hide it.
- choke back normal feelings of anger and resentment.
- say everything is fine, when it isn't.
- never ask for help, even when they need it.
- are more interested in "showing well" than feeling well.
- believe on some level that if the real person inside of them is ever exposed he or she will be rejected.

No one would ever suspect how much more of us there is behind that mask of confidence and control, or how hard we work at that mask. The effort of it all can cause stress and a host of headaches, insomnia, backaches, fatigue, besides that ever-present feeling that something is missing. It's a defensive mask that hides who we truly are, what we really feel. When we put on the mask as adults, we're defending ourselves against deep hurt—a pain reminiscent of the first hurt we felt in childhood at not being fully accepted by people we needed and cared about deeply.

What's really keeping you stuck?

Call it a narcissistic wound or call it unempathic parenting, but as a result, the following feelings may haunt you as an adult:

❧ *You may never feel that you* **matter.** *I didn't matter enough for you to keep your promises, for you to overcome your addictions, for you to give up your vacations in Europe, for you to take better care of your health, for you to pay child support, for you to take my side, for you to listen. . . .I didn't matter enough to be chosen for teams, to be invited to parties, to be picked to help the teacher. . . .*These childhood feelings cause adult doubts about your own importance.

❧ *Your self-confidence fluctuates.* You feel special one moment, and wonder, *Who do I think I am?* the next. This is a re-creation of your childhood where you asked for recognition or validation, and ended up feeling shamed for it: "Don't be conceited. . . . Stop showing off!" This ambivalence about recognition is the root of the emptiness many people feel immediately after achieving a goal.

❧ *You are always searching for something more.* The adult search for meaning is often a re-creation of the childhood search for symbiosis—a psychological bond with mother and a first feeling of identification which is all-encompassing. This isn't to say that one wants to crawl back into the womb. But the desire to feel that you belong, that there is something out there that is bigger and stronger than yourself that you can rely on is a human drive. If you've never felt it, never experienced it, all you know are substitutes. You try to become your own source of everything you need. It's impossible. It's never enough. Self-esteem isn't built on achievements. Achievements are transitory. Self-esteem is built on the support and acceptance we get along the way.

❧ *You may be unconsciously pulled toward situations and people who re-create the feeling of longing or of not being good enough.* Freud called it the repetition compulsion. A choice of a career or a mate can be unconsciously devised to re-create this feeling of longing for something that's missing and resolve a childhood battle.

Adrian, a talented hairstylist, spent the first years of his career at a top salon. "They pushed innovation. That's what they stood for. But it was never enough. I was in my twenties, and it fit right in as a continuation of my experience with my father and his perfectionism. The salon was all bright lights and expensive fixtures, and everyone was miserable. Everyone would go out after work and get high. I would act out in those days, and then go back the next day and try to outdo the next person. No one really liked working there, but we stayed. They made us feel like we were on this path to greater enlightenment or something if we could only surpass ourselves. We were doing hair, not brain surgery, but there was no difference to them. I played the game. I worked hard. I guess I thought I'd win. It took five years of frustration to see that the whole place was dysfunctional. No one ever won.

"But I was used to the no-win. My father was a shoe salesman. All day long he'd hear, 'This pinches! The heel is too high. Do you have this style in black?' He'd run back for more shoes. I thought, *He's nuts. I'd never do this in a million years. What does he have to show for it?*

"I was different from him in every way; he has never accepted me. And I realized that those years at the salon felt so comfortable to me because it was just a continuation of everything I'd ever experienced with my father. I guess I thought when people care about you, they criticize you.

"I bought my folks a condo recently. They'd lived in this walk-up for thirty years, and it was hell for my mother after her hip replacement surgery. But all I hear from them is how the TV reception in the living room isn't as good as the last place they lived.

"I had an extra ticket to the Bulls playoffs, great seats I got from a scalper. I thought of my Dad. It might be his last chance. We were sitting at the game, and one of my friends mentioned how much money I'd paid for the tickets. My father started yelling at me. I was mortified. I wanted to shake him and say, 'It's never enough with you. You're breaking your back selling shoes, and you sit in judgment of me.' But I love the man. It's just the way he is."

❧ *You may spend your life striving to prove yourself—not to **be** yourself.* You may become obsessed with what other people think of you, on winning admiration; but admiration isn't love. It isn't necessarily validating, either, if we have to sell ourselves out to get it.

Your belief that you're valued for what you do, not who you are, may distance the people you want to be closest to. Shannon, thirty-two, was so successful marketing her husband's private practice that she brought him more than fifty clients in a single year. She was never conscious of how much she relied on her marketing skills to cement her marriage until an economic recession hit. For three months, Shannon was unable to bring in any clients, and one night she burst into tears and told her husband: "I feel like if I can't keep up, you'll find someone else." She was looking for comfort, but her husband turned on her, furious. "Do you really think I love you just because you help bring me business? That doesn't say a lot for me, now does it?"

If we view our achievements as leverage in love, it also means we see our partners as manipulative or dependent. They resent this. Or we attract people who are looking for a provider. Such relationships always feel empty because they reinforce the painful perception that we are only loved for what we do, not for who we are.

❧ *What you **want** may be different from what you **need**.* Your constant striving, jumping from project to project, goal to goal, may have very little purpose. For example, you have a master's degree in accounting, a certificate in social work, an article published on nutrition. Your achievements are like a roomful of uncatalogued museum exhibits. No one can find your gestalt.

❧ *You may be constantly indulging a fit of arousal.* By eating or drinking too much, gambling, overspending—all the things you do because you're so stressed out—you hide from yourself. You blur the feelings you need to experience and deal with directly. You dive into the comfort of addictions, looking for warmth or escape. The next day you berate yourself. This morning-after self-castigation is sometimes the real goal.

Why it will never be enough—and what you can do about it

Michael Franz Basch is a therapist's therapist. It is difficult to go through clinical training without coming across his books, *Doing Psychotherapy, Understanding Psychotherapy,* and his newest, *Doing Brief Psychotherapy.* He is professor of psychiatry at Rush Medical College in Chicago and is a training and supervising analyst for the Institute for Psychoanalysis.

In *Understanding Psychotherapy,* he wrote of a particular group of patients who appeared to have learned at an early age to offset traumatic disappointment by learning to rely on their own efforts. These patients responded to what the adults around them wanted or needed from them. Giving up hope of being understood, they opted instead for the attention they were able to recruit with their achievements. "The end-product is an outer shell of self-confidence based on cleverness, intelligence, and effective manipulation of the environment with a center that is vulnerable and insecure. Any threat to their sense of competence exposes them to the danger that their early need for responsiveness and affirmation will reassert itself, leaving them open to a repetition of the disappointment and humiliation that gave rise to the defensive self in the first place."

The patients Basch wrote about seemed so much like the people we were interviewing every day—confident people with many achievements, who still felt that something was missing in themselves. We were eager to speak to him.

With all his enormous grasp of theory, Dr. Basch is refreshingly down-to-earth. We asked him, "What would you do with a client, for instance, who by most people's standards is beautiful, but who complains that she feels ugly and unappealing? You try to be empathic, to tell her that she really is very attractive, but it gets nowhere."

"But that's not empathic," Basch points out. "If someone comes in my office and tells me they feel depressed, unhappy, unattractive, I'm not going to argue with them. The person is in distress. That's what matters."

What, then, would he tell this woman? "I'd say, 'It's a hard burden to bear because on the surface people probably react to you as a very pretty woman and that's difficult to bear when you really feel ugly in your own mind.' I would ask her if she's had such experiences. And then I'd listen to how she deals with the approach of men and women who find her attractive. I'd ask, 'In what way do you feel unattractive? What do you see that's so ugly? When do you feel this way? When you look in the mirror? When you're with other women or men? Have you ever felt attractive?' I'd explore these feelings with her. As she becomes more interested in exploring her self and is talking in a more insightful way, that's therapeutic."

Empathy. It seems so simple. Yet the successful person who feels something is missing gets almost none of it. "You've got so much going for you. Come on, cheer up." Or "How can you talk like this when you have everything in the world?" It's a completely unempathic response, like someone telling you to sleep when you're hungry or eat when you're tired.

True empathy—I understand you, I don't have to fix you, change you, rearrange you, or make you feel better—is a gift few people receive from others. It's the missing link for those of us who go through life feeling empty. Beyond everything, we have a compelling need to be understood, to be known.

RX: Your Prescription for Change

> *You, too, withhold the very things you complain are missing from the world.*
>
> —STEPHEN C. PAUL

What you need to understand about yourself

Given your history, it's understandable that you might feel empty at moments when it seems you have it all. But everything more you need is already inside of you.

The key questions

- Who am I without my achievements?
- How in touch am I with what I really feel?
- What do I need in a relationship? In a career?

Where you need to focus

- on your emotions and needs
- on rebuilding your true self
- on connection with others
- on learning to be empathic with yourself

The cognitive shift

- I can enjoy being like others rather than always having to be better.

> - Feelings can be strengths rather than weaknesses.
> - Everything that's missing is inside of me.

Thoughts and Exercises

❧ *What's really missing?* Maybe a clearer picture of yourself. Carl Jung divided life into halves—the first devoted to forming the ego and getting established in the world, the second to finding a larger meaning for all that effort.

"I don't know what I feel; I don't know what I want; I really don't know who I am anymore." We have heard countless people make this statement, and it's the core issue behind the feeling that something is missing.

We have met few high achievers who are immediately open to the fact that their family experience has anything to do with what's occurring in their lives right now. But something in our past has invited us to lose touch with ourselves.

"The past is over; it has nothing to do with me now." Unfortunately this statement too often comes from people who have raging migraine headaches, ulcers, chewed up cuticles, and circles under their eyes all stemming from painful, pent-up resentments. What they really fear is reprisal for their own feelings of hurt and resentment.

The objective of dealing with your feelings is to get to the point where you can understand the past and let go of it. But you can't jump to the finish line.

Blaming our parents is not a solution. It only keeps us tied to their approval. The key is to look at the adaptations we made to our families. The adaptive self is still behaving in ways that helped us survive the past, but these solutions are today's problems.

Ask yourself how the feeling that you're not good enough, or it's never enough, might be serving you. Is it familiar? Is it somehow comfortable? Is this the way your parents attempted to motivate you? Is this a pattern you are continuing?

It means you stop telling yourself you should be satisfied. It means you learn to recognize what you really feel.

❧ *Get back in touch with what you feel.* Emotions are probably the most important, yet most misunderstood, aspect of the human experience. Emotions are the underlying motivator of all behavior.

What feelings do you disown? The following is a list of feelings. Notice which ones you allow yourself to experience. Which ones do you avoid?

Irritated	Open	Detached
Resentful	Loving	Isolated
Angry	Free	Unloved
Frustrated	Energetic	Hopeless
Vulnerable	Anxious	Envious
Sad	Depressed	Confused
Guilty	Overwhelmed	Stupid
Scared	Paranoid	Inadequate
Playful	Silly	Indifferent
Alive	Outrageous	Hesitant
Joyful	Crazy	Self-confident
Happy	Spontaneous	Weak

If this list feels a bit overwhelming, think of the basic feelings of mad, sad, glad, scared, and hurt.

Feelings are experienced in your body not in your head. In which part of your body do you experience your feelings? Stomach, head, chest?

Reexperiencing your feelings may be a slow process. These feelings make you vulnerable. You believe—unconsciously—that vulnerability is a weakness and that keeping what you feel under wraps is a strength. But the emptiness inside never goes away until we are willing to expose the real person inside, including our flaws.

Many of us learned very early that our feelings were not okay.

Many of us have our feelings connected with shame (Boys don't cry; Girls don't get angry; Don't be happy when people are starving). As a result, we use a variety of defenses to keep "in our head" and not "in our gut." When feelings have been buried for a long time, sometimes it is necessary to find a good therapist to help you to identify and externalize these emotions.

As you look at your emotions with curiousity, you will begin to understand what they are trying to tell you.

When we suppress our painful feelings, we lose our happy feelings, too.

❧ *The feeling that something is missing can be a springboard into a much more satisfying life.* Reassessment of our lives is inevitable, especially after we've passed through the stages of settling into careers and family lives. At critical times in our lives, we are forced to ask, *Is my life satisfying and productive? Is it meaningful, or full of unrealized potential? What goals can still be achieved? Which must I reevaluate?*

These questions needn't throw you into a state of apathy. They are an opportunity to find a more reasonable definition of yourself and your needs, to give up a rigid perspective of life and widen your world.

Knowing what you want versus what you need is essential. Whatever you fantasize will finally make you happy—getting that promotion, buying that house, earning that raise, losing that weight, finding that person—may not make the difference you imagine. What one wants sometimes has little to do with what one needs.

To exchange a true sense of purpose in one's life for the frustration of constant striving, you have to connect with what you care about most deeply.

We ask clients, What do you really want more of in your career? and they talk about money, power, time off, better projects. When we say, What do you need in work? they talk about a sense of purpose, a sense of validation, a sense of connection with others.

We get a lot of what we want and little of what we need. No wonder we're so dissatisfied.

We use this fill-in-the-blank exercise with clients to help them clarify what they need:

♦ *The thing I'm really missing in love is* _____.

♦ *The thing I'm really missing in work is* _____.

♦ *The thing I'm really missing with my family is* _____.

♦ *One thing that would really make a difference in my life is* _____

_____.

❧ *Be empathic with yourself.* You cannot always find empathy in the world, but you can be understanding with yourself.

You do this by learning a new way of talking to yourself. First you listen, without trying to change what you feel. You feel it, so you can explore it in a more insightful way and move beyond it. As you read these examples, keep in mind that an empathic response is not advice. It's not a quick fix. It's an emotional validation.

Problem

"This dress is tight. I've gained five pounds and no matter what I do, I can't take it off."

Unempathic response

- "I look fine. The dress looks great." (*Even if it's true, if you don't believe it, it doesn't matter how much you say it to yourself.*)
- "I've got to go out and exercise. I'm so lazy. I've got to stop eating all that red meat." (*Now you not only feel fat, you feel inadequate. Not very motivating, is it?*)

Empathic response

- *"It's difficult to not be able to control my weight. I have every reason to feel frustrated."*

Problem

"I'm so depressed."

Unempathic response

- "That's ridiculous, look at all the wonderful things I have going for me." *(Perhaps true, but wonderful things don't always feel wonderful.)*
- "I've got to go out more. I've got to meet some new people and stop feeling sorry for myself." *(Now you not only feel depressed, but foolish and ashamed of self-pity.)*

Empathic response

- *"It's frustrating to feel depressed, and it seems unfair to feel this way when I can't point to a reason for my feelings. What do I need?"*

Problem

"I'm so angry, I could scream."

Unempathic response

- "Stop being such a baby." *(It isn't childish to feel angry.)*
- "Calm down. Count to ten." *(What we resist persists.)*

Empathic response

"I'm human. It's frustrating not to get what I want. It's hard to always be fair. It's a burden to go through my life feeling that I always have to be understanding or happy."

One caution about being empathic: This does not mean abdicating our responsibility to ourselves or coddling ourselves when the need to make some changes in our behavior is clear. Being empathic at its core means getting to the truth. Then, if need be, we can be tough on ourselves, or we can forgive ourselves. We can do neither when we deny ourselves.

❦ *Are you unconsciously waiting for someone to give you the signal that enough is enough?* Increased accomplishment leaves many people with a hunger for more and more. Each time we achieve a goal, a new set of options arises. There is no one to tell us when we have already done enough. Many of us unconsciously seek such a signal. Sam, a forty-seven-year-old, self-acknowledged workaholic tells the story of his heart attack and how his never-enough thinking came to an abrupt halt. "I thought, My partner can't complain if I goof off now; *I've had a heart attack.* My father can't give me that disappointed look because I can't turn my small business into a giant. He has to understand; *I've had a heart attack.* One part of me was all-consumed with morbid thoughts about death. The other was saying, Hey, this is great . . . now you can start *living.*"

You, too, may be looking for the signal that you can now start *living.* You don't need a heart attack—just a decision.

❧ ❧

Today I will accept myself just as I am. As I experience myself more fully, the process of change begins. My feelings aren't good or bad, they just are.

❧ ❧

CHAPTER TWO

Why Don't I Follow Through On My Dreams?

The Search for Purpose

Every artist was first an amateur.

—RALPH WALDO EMERSON

Have you ever vowed to update your resumé by January 1, but found yourself watching TV talk shows in February, your resumé untouched?

Realized that the man you're involved with is the mirror image of the last one: manic, self-absorbed, and commitment phobic?

Swore that this was going to be the year you write your novel, but spent your nights at the office, sifting through paperwork?

Wondered if you're sabotaging yourself?

"I knew I had talent," muses Lauren, thirty-nine, "and I had a great idea for a business. The problem was I didn't have time, or I couldn't manage to save anything for start-up costs." Suddenly one summer, Lauren found herself with both time and money. She had four weeks off and a small windfall left to her by her aunt.

What did she do? "Absolutely nothing," she admits. "I watched a lot of 'Oprah.' I got an urge to remodel my bathroom. By the time I was done, I'd spent the entire sum and racked up a huge balance on my credit card. There was nothing left to do but go back to my job, to the same trap. Why was I sabotaging myself?"

When Lauren came to see us, she had already read an avalanche of books and articles about procrastination and time management, without relief. She was about to learn three important things:

1. She wasn't lazy. By the time procrastination set in, *the decision not to move forward was already made.*
2. There were excellent, if not immediately apparent, reasons why Lauren went about the business of sabotaging herself.
3. There were no motivational seminars, no reward systems, no ten easy ways to eliminate self-sabotage that were going to work until Lauren uncovered the reasons behind her self-sabotaging behavior and dealt with them squarely.

You might identify with Lauren and her dissatisfaction and frustration. Right now, you may be saying, "I know exactly why I'm so dissatisfied with my life. It's because I'm not doing X or I don't have Y." And you may have found that every time you go about pursuing X or Y, you mysteriously find yourself in front of the TV. Or you may persevere until some crucial point, but in the end, you don't come through for yourself.

Regardless of the specific details of your story or struggle, whether or not your inability to do what's necessary to achieve your goals is a lifelong theme or a problem that has appeared recently, it's important to understand that this hasn't happened by accident. If you can't manage to follow through on your deepest desires, there are reasons that make sense to you.

Kyle, thirty-four, tells this story: "I heard a time-management expert's advice on a TV talk show some years ago. 'Make three baskets,' he said. 'Put in the first one the things that absolutely must be done today and refuse to go to sleep until you do them. Put in the second the things that are urgent but can wait. Put in the third all of those things that are necessary but not really urgent.'

"Excellent advice, I thought. I ran out and bought those little baskets. I labeled them: Do Now! Do Tomorrow! Do Later! After three days the lists were buried under a stack of paperwork waiting to find the appropriate basket.

"I learned a great truth from all these baskets: Whatever went into that first basket scared the hell out of me. I buried it, and then I no longer had to look at it. My problem was never a lack of organizational skills. Only later did I discover what was spooking me."

Are you willing to move forward? If not, why not? When you ask yourself that question with compassion and listen for the answers without judgment, you begin a process that will release you at the core of where you're stuck. This chapter will help you search for those answers and encourage the type of activity that will allow you to move toward your deepest desires with confidence and energy.

Do you have the courage to be you?

At thirty-four, Dan was a latecomer to success. Corporate downsizing had forced him out of two jobs in three years. He was wondering how he was going to finance another round of job hunting when the phone rang.

His neighbor was frantic. Her home computer screen had gone black in the middle of a spreadsheet and the hard drive was making a whirring sound. She would give Dan anything if he'd come and raise this file from the dead.

Dan was calmly replacing his neighbor's system files when an idea was born. That evening, Dan designed an ad. Doctor PC (alias Dan) would offer a series of home computer first aid lessons at a reasonable rate. As a bonus, clients would be eligible for twenty-four-hour emergency assistance.

For a week, the idea of having his own business was an obsession. He spent nights thinking of logos, business cards, and ads. He had energy he never dreamed he possessed.

Maybe it was timing. Maybe it was the photo in the ad: a man with a crazed look in his eyes waving his fist at a computer. Within a week, Dan was besieged by calls requesting the information packet he'd promised.

But when Dan sat down to write his brochure, he found it impossible to put his ideas into a two-page leaflet. He was unable, in fact, to write down a single sentence that sounded good. "I can't really explain it, but one day I was so excited, and the next I thought the whole idea was stupid. There were dozens of computer experts in town, already established. Who was I kidding?"

Still, he tried to motivate himself. He had an appointment one day with a friend of his father, a marketing expert who was going to help him design his direct mail package. The night before, Dan, a tee-totaler, drank three margaritas. He went to bed at midnight, one leg outside the covers, foot planted solidly on the floor to stop the room from spinning. "I woke up so sick, I had to cancel the appointment. I was too embarrassed to make another one.

"For the next two weeks, whenever I had a little time, I told myself I should work on developing my idea. I'd sit down at my computer and notice a spot on the window. 'I should clean that,' I'd think. Or, 'I bet I'm almost out of cat food; I should go to the store.'"

It was torture. In the end, Dan couldn't even look at his computer. The brochure was never written.

In therapy, Dan came face to face with an unconfronted truth: Something inside of him didn't want to have a successful business. The question was, Why?

The problem: Abandonment depression

Is it possible to obsess about losing ten pounds and not really want to lose weight? To practice your guitar hours each day and think you'd sell your soul to be a singer/songwriter, but not really want to succeed? To hear that a career opportunity is just a resumé away and unconsciously make a decision not to send it? To say you'd do anything to have a good relationship, but not really want to fall in love?

In a word—yes. What is it about those moments when we go from enthusiastic plans to a feeling of *This is stupid. I can't do this. Why waste my time?*

In his book, *The Search for the Real Self*, James F. Masterson wrote of his work with many individuals who were stopped in their tracks on their way to a goal by a sudden feeling of panic. According to him, when some people begin to pursue their goals, it isn't the action steps that are so confounding but the necessity of asserting themselves. The idea of saying, "This is who I am, this is what I feel, this is what I want," fills them with a feeling he termed *abandonment depression.*

To avoid the fear and the depression that would result if our real selves emerged, many of us restructure life and make it "safe." The unconscious thought is: *I'll give up being what would truly make me happy in exchange for never feeling the pain of abandonment.*

For Dan to move forward and change his life, he had to do more than set a goal and a timetable. He had to abandon a false self, a way of thinking and behaving that had restructured his life to make it safe. Not finishing the brochure provided an unconscious way for Dan to wound himself with more failure just as he was experiencing some success.

"It is the nature of the false self to save us from knowing the truth about our real selves, from penetrating the deeper causes of our unhappiness, from seeing ourselves as we really are—vulnerable, afraid, terrified, and unable to let our real selves emerge," writes Masterson. "Nevertheless, when the defenses are down and the real self is thrown into situations calling for strong self-assertion, situations that trigger the repressed memories of earlier separation anxieties and feelings of abandonment by the mother, the serious nature of the depression is glimpsed and felt. At this point it is not uncommon for the patient to panic and slide down to the very bottom from which he convinces himself he will never recover."

The false self is a disguise, a masquerade. Yet it is very convincing. It fools many people. It may even fool us.

A false self can take many different shapes: the quiet one, the rebel, the crazy one, the victim, Mr. or Mrs. Perfect. Dan's was the failure. All of these personas have one thing in common: They attempt to cover up parts of ourselves we feel are unacceptable.

The fact that all of us did not receive support for our emerging

sense of self from parents who could not or would not respond positively to our unique individual characteristics is central to
Masterson's thesis. Dan's attitudes, behavior, and experiences are
typical of a person who feels that being true to oneself means being
in pain. None of us become this way by accident. For most of us this
struggle mirrors our struggle growing up.

Dan, for example, has a stack of report cards with little comments from teachers that sum up the child he was thirty years ago:
creative, spontaneous, ambitious. "I was a little bit of a trouble-
maker, I admit it. That's what drove my father crazy. He'd tell me,
"Stop living in a dream world! Why don't you think before you act?
Don't be so greedy." I look through my class pictures and the pro-
gression is really interesting. In first and second grade I have this big
grin on my face. By fourth grade, that smile is gone. In sixth grade,
my eyes are on the floor. In my seventh grade picture, my eyes are
closed."

Dan recalls a vivid childhood memory of something that
occurred in a restaurant when he was eleven. "I ordered a cheese-
burger and my parents started arguing with me about it. They ended
up yelling at each other: 'He wants a club sandwich, don't you Dan?'
'No, he wants chicken salad, can't you see that?' Even the waitress
had to smile."

Dan's self-expression became unconsciously tied to a feeling of
being abandoned. "You couldn't fight my father, especially. If I had an
opinion, he stood there dissecting and analyzing it, telling me why I
should feel differently. It was better to say nothing at all." The only
choice seemed to abandon himself—his feelings, his needs, his
thoughts.

One can debate whether parents should go weeding in the gar-
dens of their children's personalities, root out those aspects that
seem dangerous, and cultivate those that seem safe for their own
good. But we'll never change a fact. The bigger issue is that we all
learn to adapt. Discovering how we adapt is more fruitful than being
stuck in the despair of wondering what we could have done if our
families were different.

Dan learned to censor his emotions, to comply. He learned to dis regard, even fear, those aspects of himself that threatened his parents to continue receiving approval from them. He believed that his father's constant criticism came out of love. He never lost the feeling that he should be more, do more. Nothing he achieved was ever enough.

But the emptiness Dan felt in those moments when he came closest to pursuing his deepest desires came from never feeling he had permission to be himself. "I have this feeling sometimes like I'd like to step out—step away from myself. It's as if there's another person inside, one who can laugh at himself, who takes risks, who's creative and in control. He doesn't sit around saying, 'You'll never make money from this,' or 'You'll never be able to do that.'"

A history of self-sabotage is almost always a key that we have some central conflict with our identity—a problem accepting our personality, our real needs and goals, and working with them, not against them. Our work must begin with building self-esteem. There is no shortcut.

The child who spoke but was never really listened to, who imagined but was told to be realistic lives inside most of us. Many parents want foremost for their children to be safe. This doesn't necessarily mean happy: Be an artist dear, but be a teacher first, so you'll have a pension and tenure. Don't throw out dirty water until you have clean. You're not happy? Who's happy?

These are arguments so logical, they're hard to dispute. Every dream is suspect, and every skill seems ordinary. If we can do it, everyone can do it. We're just not that special.

You may have learned early in childhood to stop going to that place inside yourself where your true creativity and impulses lie. You may feel full of shame, doubt, and panic when you go there. *Forget what I really think. Forget what I want. Will they be impressed?*

Whenever you receive admiration for your accomplishments, you feel a void inside. You feel these acknowledgments have little to do with who you really are. They're merely applause for the show you've starred in all your life. You long to be recognized for your true self. You long to have your deepest thoughts and ideas appreciated. You want to be validated for who you are, not praised for how well you can maintain the status quo.

Again and again we repeat the childhood drama of trying to become the child our parents praise. Even though we may be "showing well" to the rest of the world, if we aren't pleasing our parents, our peers, our partners, we never feel comfortable about it. We've lost the only thing that can possibly make us feel secure—a real connection with ourselves.

Recently a woman at one of our workshops confided, "I'd like to own a bed and breakfast place, but reality is I have two children and a husband who is about to lose his job. Am I supposed to make the whole family starve while I follow some fantasy?"

What makes us so sure that we'd fail if we pursue a dream? Surely it's not experience.

Why do we have these ambitions, these untapped talents, if we aren't supposed to use them? Could it be that if we moved forward, we'd be successful in a way we haven't yet tasted and have to throw our entire safety-made self-concept in the wastebasket? The sure thing, the sure salary, may not be about protecting our families but about protecting ourselves from our own self-expression and the frightening implications of our personal power.

Do you lack talent? Or is the idea of really expressing yourself, taking a stand on what you feel in your heart, the real block in going forward? Do your ideas fill you with a sense of opportunity one moment, and a sense of unaccounted for dread the next? This is the essence of abandonment depression.

Are you getting in your own way?

All of us need security in our lives; however, if you are constantly selling off your most significant talents or pushing aside your dreams to pursue something that seems more tangible and secure, you may stand in the way of ever feeling truly satisfied.

Here's why:

* *You spend your energies in wishful thinking.* You may cling to the hope that something will happen to propel you out of your current situation without having to take any real steps toward change. You believe that the "cure" has to come from the outside—meeting the right people, finding a more validating boss, the perfect diet, the perfect man or woman, a tutor who can get your child into prep school—because you have little faith in being in touch with your own feelings and allowing them to guide you. The energy that could be spent doing is spent dreaming.

* *You may become impulsive.* We all need to feel as if we have a purpose, some meaning in our lives. But when you couple that need with the fear of self-exploration, what you get is a tendency to be impulsive. You want to do something, anything, that makes it seem as if you're moving forward. One client, for example, admitted that her obsession with having a baby didn't stem from a need to nurture: "I'll finally have something to say to people who keep asking me what I'm doing with my life."

* *You keep digging in the ashes.* Because you tend to focus on things and people outside yourself to make you happy, you blame the boss's nit-picking for your frustration or your wife's nagging for your unhappiness. You concentrate on getting other people and situations to change instead of on expressing your talents. You try to make the best of things, and in many ways, that's a strength. Your weakness is that you don't know when to walk away.

Let's look at how these three characteristics work in tandem to sabotage success.

Lee was holding three job offers at established firms, so it was merely curiosity that drove him to accept an interview with a newer firm, one the business press referred to as a young upstart in the field.

When Lee was ushered into a corner office, his first thought was that the man who offered a huge smile and a hand thrust forward couldn't have been much older than he was. Moreover, he was dressed in blue jeans and cowboy boots.

A tour of the office turned up no one older than thirty-five. "You won't have to spend ten years working your way up to partner to earn six figures here," Steve told Lee as they chatted over Cokes. "In the next year we're going to introduce technology that no other company can match, and in two years we're going to be number one."

A salary offer 20 percent higher than what he was holding sealed Lee's future. Steve became his mentor and Lee moved steadily upward. In five years he was a vice president, occupying Steve's old corner office. And that, surprisingly, was the problem.

Lee was suffering from a bad case of number two-ness. The money, the travel, the shares of stock Lee accumulated couldn't make up for the fact that Steve was a defensive autocrat. Steve romanced new clients and did the creative work. He left Lee the job of administering and balancing the enormous egos of the technical wunderkinds who had turned a small company into a major player in the industry.

It was exhausting. "All day long people were lined up outside my office with their problems. They can't get along with this one. They want to fire that one. Joe down the hall has a credenza and a chair. They only have a chair. Why can't they have a credenza?"

At every annual review Lee spoke of his desire to move beyond his administrative position. He was told he was indispensable where he was. Lee tossed and turned at night, unable to sleep. He was beginning to sound like his employees: *Steve has a house in Telluride. Steve's salary package is double mine. All I do is spend hours explaining to furious employees why the Christmas bonus is low again.*

Worse, Lee knew something only the people closest to Steve would ever discover. Steve was not that smart. With his cowboy mentality and his burgeoning alcohol problem, he was becoming intolerable.

At that point, one of the company's main rivals made overtures to Lee. Impulsively, Lee entered Steve's office and told him he was accepting the position of vice president of a division of the rival company.

Steve made a counter offer. Bonuses, stock, perks, a presidency in the new division—all of it fell on Lee's dazed ears and it was six months later before he truly realized there was a catch. The work was still administrative. While Lee might be steering his own division, Steve was still navigating the company. Lee fought off a feeling of emptiness, wondering, *When is enough, enough?*

When we keep going to the same dry well over and over again hoping for water, we have to wonder if the real goal is staying thirsty. Lee was able to avoid his fears associated with independence and self-expression by tying the knot that held him imprisoned. Lee got some of what he wanted, but little of what he needed—a sense of creative control and a feeling of purpose.

When you compromise your dreams to pursue something that seems more tangible and secure, what you often end up with is the words without the music. On the outside, Lee had a career that looked perfect. But something essential was missing: an arena where Lee could validate his feelings and chart the course of his destiny.

What you need to know about self-sabotage

Why do many people get into the habit of backing away from their dreams, or otherwise sabotage themselves when they are on the brink of success? Four reasons are common:

❧ *1. You get an illusion of security from having all of these untapped talents.* When you have the ultimate business plan on scraps of paper in your drawer, or the Great Novel in your mind—but you never finish anything—you live in a world of endless possibilities. It's a comfortable kind of never-ending childhood. Put your ideas into action and it will soon be clear whether or not you really have that ultimate plan. With untapped talent, you are forever protected from knowing your own limits.

❧ *2. You solve a problem you may or may not be consciously aware of.* Take Carol, whose resolutions to begin a diet on Sunday become ancient history by Wednesday. Carol has no real voice in her relationships. Ask her what movie she wants to see Saturday night, and she'll ask what you want to see. However, when Carol allows herself to get close to a man, the weight she never manages to lose functions like a voice. It says, *Stay away. I don't want to compete. I can't handle being close. I don't know how to say no.*

Consider that, like Carol, you may be expressing something through self-sabotaging behavior that you can't otherwise express. Matthew, for example, was a man whose employer stated flatly that if he couldn't correct the problem of being late every other day to work, he had no future with his company. Yet, there seemed to be no amount of alarm clocks or wake-up calls that could unearth Matthew from his cocoon of blankets and propel him into the shower in time to make his train.

Matthew's rationale: "They don't really know how to evaluate good work here, so they hang you on stuff like what time you come and what time you leave."

Matthew was fired. He couldn't correct his pattern of lateness because it fulfilled a need. Matthew felt his contributions were unrecognized. He felt unimportant. By being late, he made a statement: "You don't notice my contribution. I can't express my frustration directly, so I'll frustrate you. I want to stand out. When I'm late, I show you that I'm an individual." Therapists call Matthew's behavior passive-aggressive.

One of the first things we ask clients like Matthew to do is to make a statement of their needs: What do you need in a relationship? In a career? From your family? From your children? It's surprising how many of us find making a simple statement of what we need difficult. Matthew, for example, couldn't say, "I need to be appreciated."

Think for a moment. If you have a pattern of feeling stuck, of avoiding going after what you really want, what do you get out of it? What fears might it soothe? What unrecognized goals does it achieve?

❧ *3. You get a secondary payoff from not moving forward.* Anyone who has ever been in a support group has had this experience. A person in the group spends twenty minutes recounting how he can't reach his goal, how he's tried everything, how he's beside himself and he can't imagine what the trouble is when all he wants in the world is this one *thing*. The group tries to help:

- "Have you made a list of things to do and numbered your priorities?"
  —"Yeah, but I never read it after I write it."
- "Have you tried imagining the worst that could happen if you don't reach this goal?"
  —"Yeah, but I still watch TV when I should be working."
- "Have you called a friend?"
  —"Yeah, but after I hang up the phone, I still can't get to work."
- "Have you tried to walk away and forget it?"
  —"Yeah, but I can't relax."
- "I think this has something to do with your relationship with your mother."
  —"Yeah, but she died in '65."

Eventually the group gets tired of making suggestions and they want to move on. This is the "Yeah, but" person's big moment. Not one of these people who have tried to come up with a suggestion brought anything to the table he hasn't thought of. Therefore, they're all inadequate.

Perhaps you recognize yourself as this type of complainer. Ask yourself, *Who do I make feel inadequate when I don't follow through? Who do I frustrate, besides myself?*

You may be surprised at the answers. Sean is a man who drifts from career to career. A marginal musician, he plays drums with a jazz band one night a week, his only source of income. He's barely on speaking terms with his parents. They can't understand why their son can't manage to get his life together.

Sean spends more energy avoiding his life than participating in it. His self-sabotage is more about rebellion than lack of skills. All his life he's had the suspicion that his overly controlling parents are waiting in the wings for him to fulfill them, to actualize their own ambitions and needs. He suffers from what therapists call opposi-tional enmeshment—he can't emotionally separate from his parents, and he uses his failures in life to make an unconscious statement: *You did this to me; now take care of me.*

His parents said enough was enough years ago. But when one of Sean's closest friends went to see Sean play in his band at a bar, he noticed something. Self-sabotage has a payoff for Sean. "By the end of the night, everyone was giving him things. People were buying him drinks, a customer gave him her business card. The bartender said, 'Sean, do you want to take home some food?' He gives out this mes-sage that he tries so hard, but things never work out for him. Everyone falls for it and wants to help. It's like that old joke: What's a drummer without a girlfriend? Homeless."

Some people come from families where there's a lot of failure and disappointment; everyone tries and tries but mysteriously things never work out. What we learn in these families is that if we give the appearance of trying, we never really have to *do* anything. Unfortunately, we're living in a world where there are surprisingly few A's for the appearance of effort.

What about the garden varieties of self-sabotage: the phone calls we don't make, the night we slept with a blind date without protec-tion, the leather coat we decided we had to have when our credit card debt was already too high?

We can think of several secondary payoffs. You set up a situation where you can scold yourself and be scolded by other people who are interested enough to oblige. Feeling bad gives you another reason why you're unworthy of success. Or you trap yourself in a situation where the necessity of digging yourself out means you can't take any risks right now—you have to stay where you are.

❧ *4. Whatever you're attempting to do has no meaning for you.* We know a man who failed the CPA examination three times and the reason was simple: He didn't really want to be a CPA. He was dancing to someone else's expectations.

Which brings us to a discussion of failure. Some of our so-called failures are really protective devices. They keep us from becoming someone we don't really want to be in the first place.

Tiffany was a woman with a vivid imagination and an impressive academic background. At each therapy session she bubbled over with plans. One week it was starting a catering business. The next it was training horses. Then it was opening a gift shop. She never followed through on any of these ideas. What became more obvious as she continued to come up with one idea after another was the occasional flash of anger in her eyes as she spoke, the edge in her voice. Therapy helped Tiffany discover why she was so angry. She was the daughter of an extremely successful father whom she barely knew. The only time she got his attention was on birthdays, her graduation, her dance recitals—when she achieved something.

Her mother alternately complained about his detachment from the family and then lectured Tiffany to be grateful for the many material things his success provided her with. It was a mixed message with disastrous results.

Tiffany found herself attracted to men who were very much like her father, men who could barely fit Tiffany into their schedules but told her she was unreasonable when she demanded more attention.

Because the only way Tiffany knew how to get love was to achieve, she was constantly fantasizing about some success scheme that would make others recognize her importance. She could not bring any of her plans to fruition because unconsciously she resented having to perform in order to be loved.

ying to prove something to someone? Perhaps you
oved it to yourself.

RX: Your Prescription for Change

> *When love and skill work together,*
> *expect a masterpiece.*
>
> —JOHN RUSKIN

What you need to understand about yourself

Given your history, it makes sense that you've stopped listening to your inner voice and, perhaps, believing in yourself. But you can get back in touch with your intuitive sense and let it guide you.

The key questions

- What would you do if you knew you couldn't fail?
- What do you fear you'll lose if you fully express yourself?

Where you need to focus

- on expressing your true self
- on finding and following your passion
- on working with your nature
- on managing the anxiety inherent in the creative process

The cognitive shift

- I can go for long-term respect from myself instead of short-term admiration from others.
- I have a right to define and develop my unique path in life.
- I can be appreciated for being myself.
- Every time I avoid something, I strengthen my bad habits, and every time I follow through with my plans, I strengthen my new, healthier habits.

Thoughts and Exercises ⚜⚜⚜⚜⚜⚜⚜⚜⚜⚜⚜⚜⚜⚜⚜⚜⚜⚜⚜⚜⚜⚜⚜⚜⚜⚜⚜⚜⚜⚜⚜

❧ *Learn to identify the first signs of abandonment depression before it knocks you off course.* You're full of enthusiasm. Some idea is kicking around in your head, keeping you up at night, and you feel you'll burst if you don't tell someone about it.

Stop. Give it a couple of days.

Notice if forty-eight hours later you're thinking things like, *I like the idea of graduate school, but it will take two whole years out of my life,* or *So what if I skip one exercise class? I don't want to overdo it and end up injuring myself.*

This is the beginning of the cycle. Next comes a mysterious period of acting out. You may find yourself eating or drinking uncharacteristically, sleeping twelve hours, having television marathons. One woman suddenly sprained her ankle, a tragedy that put her idea of being an aerobic trainer on hold for months. Acting out serves a function—it makes the depression and fear dissipate.

You are not alone. We all have lists of things we ought to do. Change is an easy thing to decide and a tough thing to do.

Ask yourself, *What is this binging, this avoiding, this procrastination trying to tell me?*

Creative discipline comes from pleasure. It's not a matter of throwing yourself against a wall repeatedly, as if the pain will suddenly motivate you. The most successful people are able to work hard at their goals because they love what they're doing, not because they're so good at holding the whip over their heads.

You have an important voice. You have something to say in the world that matters. When your work, your relationships, and your actions are an expression of that voice, you will feel and be successful. If you can't move toward a goal, perhaps you're trying to climb a ladder that's against the wrong wall. Perhaps you need a deeper connection with yourself, or someone, to help you clarify your desires.

Try the fill-in-the-blank exercise on page 54. Answer the first thing that comes to your mind.

♦ *If I achieved the goal I've been dreaming about, I'm afraid that*

_____ .

♦ *If I followed a new career path, I'd* _____ .

♦ *If I knew I couldn't fail, I'd* _____ .

♦ *If I took full responsibility for my life, I'd* _____ .

♦ *If I became suddenly rich and successful, my parents would*

_____ .

❧ *Soothe the anxiety that's a natural part of the creative process.* Your goal is to cope with the anxiety that occurs at the first stage of action, when you try to put your dream in motion. You do this by allowing yourself to feel it and believing that it will pass. Say these sentences to yourself:

- *I have a right to develop my unique path in life.*

- *Being safe and being happy aren't necessarily the same things.*

- *My best will be enough.*

- *Just because it's hard doesn't mean I can't do it. If it wasn't hard, everyone would do it.*

- *Anxiety is a natural part of the creative process. I'm breaking new ground. I can get through this.*

- *I don't need others to give me permission to speak. The most important words are the ones I speak to myself.*

- *Everything I need is inside of me.*

❧ *Take first things first.* Susan was a client who had gained ten pounds in the year after her divorce. She had invested $300 in a diet program that came complete with food, counseling, and motivational tapes. And she was sneaking out of her house in the middle of the night to run to the convenience store for chocolate doughnuts.

"I want so badly to lose this weight," she told us.

"But, are you willing to do it?" we asked her.

A week later, she told us this story: "I was clearing the table, staring at the half-eaten pancakes the kids had left on their plates, and I was reaching for a fork when I thought about what you said, *Am I willing?* Am I willing to be a little hungry, not for food, but for sweets and all the things I crave? That's when it hit me. I realized, *No, I'm not willing to be hungry. I'm just so hungry everywhere else in my life.*"

It was understandable that Susan felt so hungry. Reeling from the defection of close friends who found her divorce threatening to their own marriages, Susan found herself very much alone. Her finances were a mess, her lifestyle nothing like it had been before. If Susan's body wouldn't cooperate with her goals for perfection, there were excellent reasons why. The real goal behind all of this drama over dieting? To find a reason to love herself.

Abraham Maslow was the first to point out that human beings strive to fulfill their needs but that these needs have a hierarchy. First there are physiological needs such as hunger and thirst. Then come our needs for safety. Then a sense of belonging. At the top of the hierarchy are needs for self-esteem and self-actualization.

It's amazing how many of us are trying to go about the business of achieving power, success, the big deal, the perfect relationship, when we haven't taken care of the most basic of our needs.

A more productive goal for Susan was to feel healthy and gather the resources necessary to rebuild her life on a more solid foundation. A year later, when Susan had built a new network of friends, she had the energy necessary to cope with frustration and setbacks. This is not to say that we have to delay our goals until our lives are perfect. But we cannot jump to the finish line.

Before you start your climb to the top, ask yourself how sturdy your foundation is. How much support do you have in your life? How much reassurance? Where can you get more of what you need?

❧ *Stop digging in the ashes.*

> *Any path is only a path, and there is no affront to oneself or to others in dropping it if that is what your heart tells you.*

— CARLOS CASTANEDA

A woman we'll call Melanie had straight A's at a top ten university and a master's degree from the number one graduate program in the country. She scored a job with one of the top eight public relations firms in the Midwest. And what job did this prestigious public relations firm assign Melanie to do on her first day? Booking Ronald McDonald.

For giving another weary explanation for why Ronald would be unavailable to perform his magic show at some five-year-old's birthday party, for trying frantically to find two community events for him to appear at each day where people wouldn't throw garbage at him, she earned $18,000 a year.

"You have to pay your dues," Melanie thought. So she kept Ronald in constant motion and earned praise for her organizational skills. She tried to convince herself that there was the bigger picture: she was learning about children's marketing. She asked for a substantial raise and got it promptly after the first year. But at her second annual review she heard about agency cutbacks, the bottom line. She had topped out. She walked away with an increase that barely covered the cost of living.

She went back three times to argue for a better raise. The job was so tedious. She decided to wait for her next review. If only she could make a decent salary, it would be worthwhile.

We call this digging in the ashes. There was no raise, no promotion that was going to make her feel satisfied.

We told her, "Have you ever considered that if you're so good at promoting Ronald, you'd be just as good at promoting yourself? That if you can find audiences for his viewpoint, you could find audiences for your own?"

Her eyes lit up. Her depression vanished. She could barely

contain her ideas. She knew more about primary schoolers and intermediates than most seasoned parents. She also knew the types of performances that held kids' interest.

Today Melanie directs children's theater. She's written several books and she's tripled her salary.

If we don't have an arena where we can express our voice, we're going to feel empty. No amount of money or success is going to fill that emptiness for long.

When you begin to express your voice, amazing things happen. Bob was a client who had recently relocated his family to Chicago and felt lucky to find a position at an inner-city high school immediately. Because he was low man on the totem pole, they assigned Bob the distributive education class, a euphemism for work study.

Each day his students entered the building through metal detectors. He had to ask them to park their jackets outside the classroom because they reeked so badly of gasoline he'd get woozy. He'd open his book, give an assignment, and the class would bounce off the walls. One day a young man locked another in the closet and the maintainence men assured Bob no key was to be had. With the principal threatening to lower his rating, Bob decided enough was enough.

He wanted to apply for a job in the suburbs, but he was too tired to even write a resumé.

We weren't so sure that the suburbs were going to be an answer to his problems.

"These kids are really bad," he told us. "No matter what I say, they don't listen."

"What are you trying to tell them?" we asked.

"Oh, the usual junk. You know, general business. The curriculum's terrible, but they say I have to teach it."

"Maybe they don't listen because they sense you don't believe in what you're saying. You're their teacher. Didn't you go into this field because you thought you had something to say? What do you think these kids really need to know about business?"

It was food for thought, and Bob was starving. There was never a school system more adamant about teaching the prescribed curriculum, but Bob began to improvise anyway.

Each day he'd come into the classroom in a new persona: He was the customer who was never satisfied. The boss who was unfair. The friend who stole. He had been a star in his high school plays, and he was so convincing that his students begged to be chosen for a part in his roleplays. Because he believed strongly that knowing how to deal with these situations was essential, he had a new attitude. He wasn't beyond throwing the book down and getting right in some student's face with his teacher finger when necessary. He gathered trust. Eventually he got respect.

Today Bob is the head of his department. He revamped the work study curriculum, and no one stood in his way because no one was going to argue with success. He has more ideas, and he's implementing them. He's a man who has found his passion. He's also found a publisher for his textbook. He's no longer wondering why he can't follow through on his dream of getting a job in the suburbs. He wouldn't teach there for anything in the world.

❧ *Build a network of creative support.* How supportive are the people in your life when you talk about your dreams?

"I told her I wanted to go back to school and she accused me of being a lousy father."

"He laughed when I said I wanted to do voice-overs for television commercials."

"She hates everything I write."

There are probably a hundred people in your life who can tell you why you aren't going to succeed at whatever endeavor you dream up. Some of us surround ourselves with such people.

Here is a common scenario: You are drawn to successful people, very often risk takers. Your friends make a much greater income than you do. You have a constant sense of being left behind. Or you are drawn to people who need you to be stuck where you are. When you complain that you feel stuck, your friends bolster your confidence. You're talented, creative, they tell you. Why must you put yourself down?

Something interesting happens when you actually begin to move toward some goal. You start a new diet, for instance. "You can't exist on fruit!" your friend says, pushing the bread basket in your direction on the third day of your diet. Or you ask for a reference so you can switch jobs. "Of course I'll call that headhunter and recommend you, but I think you'll hate a career in sales. Don't you remember how you hate rejection?"

You have a significant role in this relationship. Because you seek advice and approval, because you maximize your self-doubts, you attract a certain type of person who thrives on feeling one-up and controlling you. It's not a question of what will happen to you if you take a risk; it's what will happen to *them*.

You don't need to feel guilty about trying to find a life that works for you. Nor must you be stopped in your tracks by other people's opinions about the legitimacy of your quest. Stop spending your energies trying to control what other people think. What they think may not matter. One successful author of children's books told us this key to success: "I stopped showing my work to anyone who couldn't buy it. That included my wife."

If your dreams are consistently squashed by someone else's lack of enthusiasm, it's time to look squarely at that relationship and the role you play in it.

Perhaps you have supportive people in your life. But are you supportable? Mark was a client who despaired of ever getting his wife to understand why he wanted to leave a group practice and set out on his own. But his talk of his plans always had a hidden zinger: "I'll be successful, and then I won't need you." It was no mystery that she was not supportive.

Some of us are constantly setting people up. Have you worn your loved ones out with so many dreams and plans you never follow through on that they say, "Oh, oh, here comes another one?" When they see you take the first step, they will be more apt to join your team.

Are you asking for money? Find a way to get financial support in one place, emotional support in another. They don't usually go together.

Are you accosting people with your new resumé when they walk in the door, exhausted? Do your conversations go like this:

YOU: So, do you think it's good?
HIM: Yeah.
YOU: Come on, you weren't even listening.
HIM: I was, too! It sounds fine.
YOU: Fine? What do you mean, fine?
HIM: You know, go ahead and send it out.
YOU: You don't really like it. Why can't you just tell me the truth? You don't care how much I hate my job. You're so damn unsupportive.

These little forays into self-defeat usually have a purpose. Ask yourself, *Am I really looking for support here, or disapproval so that I don't have to do what I'm afraid to do anyway?*

More often than not our ideas aren't poor or silly: we simply fail to find our audience. We lose confidence when others aren't immediately supportive of our ideas, and this says more about our skill in promoting ourselves, our ability to gather a supportive network of friends, and the level of our self-esteem than it does about the merits of our ideas.

Find your audience. If you feel something, a thousand other people feel it, too. Ignore those who tell you not to be yourself. Who else should you be?

❧ *Stop counting yourself out.* A man recently told me why he'd never tried to publish any of the songs he'd spent years composing. "There are a million songwriters out there, and most of them are starving."

It doesn't matter, doesn't matter, doesn't matter.

A couple of years ago we had lunch with a friend who was on the admissions committee of one of the nation's most prestigious universities. We asked him how many applications they'd received for the new degree program we'd seen advertised in the newspaper.

"Forty-five," he told us.

Our mouths fell open. Forty-five? We would have thought there would have been thousands.

"People screen themselves out," he explained.

They had advertised the program as an executive program, and people who otherwise could have applied counted themselves out because they didn't feel their current job qualified them as "executives."

Don't count yourself out. The job requires five years of experience and you only have three? Send that resumé anyway. The personal ad says he's looking for someone twenty-five to thirty-five and you're forty? Answer anyway. The manuscript is on hold because it isn't good enough? If you don't finish it, it doesn't really matter how good it is.

Some of us have spent so much time avoiding rejection and criticism that we rarely ever experience it directly. Now we have a full-blown phobia that keeps us tied in knots.

See rejection as an opportunity for growth and change. If you receive a poor evaluation at work or fail to get a raise you feel you deserve, look at it as feedback. Why have others failed to recognize your strengths?

If we set our goals high but make little effort, abandon careful planning, or fold at the first obstacle, we'll fail to reach many of our aspirations. Match your drive to succeed with the kind of action that encourages success.

※ ※

Today I will realize that I have a unique voice and the right to express it. I don't need to hear what others think. I need to hear myself think.

※ ※

CHAPTER THREE

Why Is It That Nothing Makes Me Happy for Long?

The Search for Validation

My grandfather used to make home movies and edit out the joy.

—RICHARD LEWIS

One day, something inside of Jeremy, forty-three, finally wakes up. He says, "Enough complaining. Enough suffering. Enough is enough."

He spends his weekend writing his resumé. He slips twenty of them in the mailbox on Sunday night. But he gets no calls, no response.

"I'm devastated. I can't sleep. Am I facing age discrimination, already? Am I going to be stuck working in this hell-hole of an organization for the rest of my life?

"Then, out of nowhere, I get an interview. I'm so happy. It's a good firm; my wife is impressed. Then it's like the walls turn black or something. My mind starts churning: *The last time you went on interviews was a hundred years ago, kiddo, and you can't possibly compete.*

"So, off to the bookstore, where I spend a fortune on books about job interviewing. I'm depressed because I was supposed to watch my kid play soccer, but instead I'm memorizing smart responses to interview questions. My old job is starting to look better and better.

"Next morning, the interview goes well. I leave with a good feeling. That lasts until about noon, when I'm back at my desk. I have so many friends in this company. If I leave, who will run the football pool? I've done it for ten years. I'm sitting there imagining Jack down the hall running the football pool, messing with the rules I created, when the phone rings. I've got a second interview!

"I can feel the adrenaline pumping. This is great. It's a coup for a guy my age to beat out young guys with their Big Ten college degrees. It's like I'm high. That lasts until the next morning. I'm sure I'm going to blow it. I can barely make it through my files, and I leave work early, my head pounding.

"I get the job. I hand in my resignation, clear out my desk, and realize the files in the cabinet are now someone else's problem.

"That's probably the longest period of happiness. It lasts about three days. The night before I start the new job should be a time to celebrate, but I tell my wife, 'What difference is a new job going to make? I'm still in the same low-paying field. I'm still doing the same old thing.' She gets so angry, she takes the kid and goes to a movie. I don't care. Life suddenly seems so exhausting, I go to bed."

Kendall, thirty-eight, lived in a two-bedroom walk-up apartment with her husband and their two children for twelve years and despaired of ever having the one thing she wanted: a house of her own like the one she grew up in. "The money came in the strangest way. I used to shop for an elderly woman who lived upstairs. I used to visit with her and take her to the doctor. When she passed away she left me a sizable amount of money, cash I never dreamed she had.

"I kept thinking that I'd finally be happy once we owned a house. Now we owned one, and all I could think was that the house was too small. We were barely unpacked and already I was saying things like, 'With the equity we build here, we can get a bigger house in a couple of years.'

"My husband threw up his hands. 'You know something? You're never satisfied. Nothing makes you happy.'"

It's a strange business. They want to be happy. They spend more money, more energy, more time trying to make themselves happy than most other people do. They spend even more hours trying to uncover the reason why they're not happy. Yet those who know them best will tell you that these people have little reason to be unhappy in the first place.

Why can't people like Kendall or Jeremy ever stay happy for long? Before you dismiss these people as unreasonable or impossible, consider this: It is emotionally devastating to go through life struggling hard to get what you want only to find out that it doesn't matter anyway, that it doesn't make any real difference. It's exhausting to repeat the process over and over again. It's frustrating to keep trying, hoping that something will change. It's painful to end up with the blues in moments when one should be feeling happiest.

You see other people enjoying life. Why is happiness something that keeps floating out of your grasp like wisps of smoke? It's doubly unnerving because the world has so little sympathy for you. People keep pointing out the reasons why you should feel grateful. You end up having to pretend that you're happy because there's a point when you've worn out people who try to help you out of this prison.

If you can identify with this, there are excellent reasons why you feel the way you do. Once you understand those reasons, you will begin to feel relief. The following chapter may help you recognize why your current strategies for overcoming this syndrome haven't worked, and what will.

Do you suffer from dysthymia?

If you can identify with the type of lingering unhappiness Jeremy and Kendall feel, ask yourself, *Do I lack energy? Is it hard to find anything I'm interested in? Do I feel vaguely unhappy, without any real reason? Do I put myself down all of the time? Am I sleeping too much, or having trouble falling asleep at all? Is it hard to concentrate? To make decisions? Is there a lingering sense of emptiness and sadness?*

If you answer yes, you may be suffering from a condition known as dysthymia, a chronic low-grade depression which affects an estimated eight million Americans.

What causes dysthymia? Some researchers believe all depressions are biologically based and possibly caused by a deficiency of neurotransmitters or brain hormones such as serotonin. This research led to the popularity of such antidepressant medications as Prozac, which balance the supply of naturally produced neurotransmitters.

Others believe dysthymia results from a psychological imbalance in thinking—distortions in the way we perceive the events in our lives, which lead to habitual negative thoughts.

The root of dysthymia may well be a combination of both factors. In any case, it is becoming more prevalent because of the current social climate—corporate turmoil, a flat economy, climbing rates of divorce, and strains from changing sex roles.

The tragedy is, only one out of five victims of dysthymia or other types of depression ever seeks help. As one woman tells it, "I went to work, I functioned, I just never got very much pleasure out of anything. But I'd felt that way for so long I thought, this is just me, the way I am."

The Diagnostic and Statistical Manual of Mental Disorders (DSM III-R), the American Psychiatric Association's manual of diagnostic criteria, defines dysthymia as "a depressed mood for most of the day, more days than not" for at least two years. In addition, at least two of the following must exist: (1) poor appetite or overeating; (2) insomnia or hypersomnia (i.e., sleeping too much); (3) low energy or fatigue; (4) low self-esteem; (5) poor concentration or difficulty making decisions; (6) feelings of hopelessness. What distinguishes dysthymia from a major depressive episode is the severity of symptoms. In many cases of major depression the onset is identifiable, and the symptoms indicate a marked difference in the person's normal functioning. People diagnosed with dysthymia, in contrast, often state that they "have always felt this way" or sometimes assume that their symptoms are part of their personalities, as in, "I'm a moody person." Because the sufferer may not have any seriously debilitating symptoms, he or she may cringe at the idea of therapy or even medication for what seems a simple lack of get up and go.

Many dysthymics try to adapt to the depression, and it is these adaptations that sometimes catapult the person into treatment: "I was drinking a glass or two of wine, never before six, to cope with the stress of working all day, and then having a second shift at home," admits Karla, thirty-two, a real-estate agent. "Then it became three or four glasses, and it was starting to get scary. I've learned that the alcohol was a depressant and there are more effective ways to deal with depression than with a bottle of chardonnay."

Others find temporary solace in food, nicotine, marijuana, gambling, television, or sex. Next comes fear. Fear that it takes more and more of whatever it is to chase the blues away. Fear that creativity and motivation seem to be slipping away. *It's four o'clock; only two more hours until I can get out of here and have a smoke, a drink, something to make me feel better.*

The problem: A depressive retreat from feelings

For many people, chronic low-grade depression is a retreat from feelings such as anger, hurt, or sadness. In *Understanding Psychotherapy,* Michael Franz Basch explains that when one tries to cope with such feelings and fails in spite of mobilizing all of his or her resources, depression occurs as a protective way of restoring some sense of order. "Depression indicates that the self system has had to retreat to a lower level of functioning in the face of its inability to meet higher goals. Depression also serves as a communication, a message to the world at large that the self system can no longer be counted upon, that it has ceased to function in some significant degree, that one has lost hope, and that help must come from the outside." In other words, the self says, enough is enough, and retreats away not only from the feelings that are most troublesome, but all feeling in general. It's a concept that goes far toward explaining why depressed people often feel, "What's the use?"

Jonathan, a sales rep who landed a line of gift items, can identify. He found himself unable to make the calls or build the connections he needed to establish the line in his territory. When he'd get new leads, a voice inside of him would say, "Why bother? Why drive a hundred miles and end up writing fifty bucks worth of business?" Sluggish and confused, he retreated into shuffling paperwork, and overservicing the few clients he did have.

"In therapy I learned that I saw everything in black and white—I was either a total success or a miserable failure. I was such a perfectionist. Doing the simplest thing was exhausting. My depression came from feeling overwhelmed." With support, Jonathan learned new skills for looking at each day, each incident, more realistically without generalizing everything.

Suffering: Is yours self-created?

Psychologist Frank Gruba-McCallister, associate dean at the prestigious Illinois School of Professional Psychology, and one of its most popular instructors, has been fascinated for many years with the study of human suffering.

"Are there people who choose to suffer?" we asked him.

"A lot of people suffer because they're suffering," he told us. "They're upset about being upset."

He explains, "Most people cling to the wish that they can be free of suffering. The message that we often receive is that suffering can be conquered by some magical solution, such as some miracle cure or drug, some material possession, or some special relationship with another person. All of these eventually prove to be false promises. Because life is a process of constant change, it is also a process of constant loss. For that reason, suffering is an inescapable part of being alive. When we can't accept that, we suffer more."

It seems a depressing notion in itself. But Gruba-McCallister's point is that maybe 25 percent of life contains this inevitable suffering. The other 75 percent we create ourselves.

For example, suppose you are in your car driving to work on a snowy morning and you stop for traffic. Another car skids into you. Anyone would be upset. This is Gruba-McCallister's 25 percent.

Some people will feel angry, call the insurance company, get the car fixed and move on, because suffering is a time-limited process that eventually goes away.

But some will stew and ruminate. *How can a person do something like this? This isn't fair. I shouldn't have to have my life rearranged now. I shouldn't have to endure experiences like this. I'm going to get this person. I'm going to sue.* That's the 75 percent of self-created suffering. As Gruba-McCallister puts it, "When we meet suffering with such resistance, we only suffer more. For then we end up suffering because we are suffering."

What fascinates Gruba-McCallister most about suffering is its potential. "We need suffering because it provides us with the challenge we need to grow and develop as human beings. By disturbing our need for security, suffering is a necessary ingredient in stimulating us to grow and improve ourselves. Progress does not come when we are feeling content and comfortable. We need loss, and the suffering that comes with it, to get us started on the process of growth."

If it hurts so much, why do you do it?

The people who suffer from depression may be trying to protect themselves and restore a sense of order by shutting down emotions. Those who suffer because they cannot accept their suffering are trying to gain some sense of control over their world. Our symptoms often serve us.

If you often grapple with the fact that something inside of you will not allow you to stay happy for long, then you, too, have an excellent reason for suffering. Consider the following reasons why people do it:

❧ *To appease superstitious fears of reprisal and the unconscious belief that you don't deserve to be happy.* "If I relish my success, or enjoy it, something terrible will happen." This fear is like a dash of cold water on any feeling of pleasure. Fear of reprisal usually relates back to childhood fears of omnipotence —the belief that we somehow control it all and nothing happens at random.

In *Necessary Losses,* Judith Viorst writes, "[Some people] may have a need to believe that 'Someone Up There' has control, that terrible things do not happen without a cause, that if they are struck by tragedy and devastating loss, they are struck because in some way they deserve it." If bad things happen to good people at random, then what control do we really have over our lives? It's better to believe we caused it than to accept that we can't have all the control over our lives that we'd like.

Given this view, it's crucial not to tempt the fates with too much self-satisfaction, lest the rug be pulled out from under us. Such believers in the celestial scoreboard think, *When something good happens, something bad is just around the corner.* One man told us, "My parents taught me that everything evens out in the end. Someone is counting: *He's making a list, checking it twice; he's going to find out who's naughty or nice.*"

Rebecca, fifty-four, remembers hearing the word *kinehori* when she was growing up. "It's a Yiddish word that means something like a hex. One time I wanted money for a prom dress. 'No boy has asked you yet,' my mother told me. I said, 'Ma, Stan and I have been going steady for a year; of course he's going to ask me.' My mother got very upset. 'Are you crazy?' she said. 'Do you want to put a kinehori on the prom?'"

We're not stupid. But steady doses of that kind of reasoning leave their mark. Given that history, it's understandable why one might think that to be happy, to feel confident is a setup for disaster. You're logical enough to laugh at your superstitions. You're emotional enough to hedge your bets.

Suffering becomes a means to an end rather than a result of anything that happens in your life. It's protective: "I'm already suffering, as anyone can see; I get no enjoyment out of my life, so there's no need to hit me again with bad news, thank you."

Happiness is a vulnerable state. If no one knows you're happy, maybe the celestial scoreboard won't notice and send you something bad to even the score.

One of our clients was devastated when her father was killed in a car accident when she was sixteen. The man her mother remarried was resentful of providing for what he thought of as another man's children.

She learned a lesson from her father's death: Happiness and security can be whipped away from you in an instant. She is a woman who feels it is safer not to be too happy or to dwell on any of her successes because if she never experiences any highs she might not miss it so much when they are gone.

❧ *To feel loved in a problem-focused family.* "You got a promotion? That's nice dear, but did Billy get over his cold?" Some of us grow up in families where the blue ribbon gets a fleeting smile, but if we develop a headache, our parents are still concerned about it three weeks later. The lesson is: When you're troubled, people care more.

Evelyn, forty, complains: "Every time I talk to my mother, all she talks about is my brother Alan. She's given him more time, more money, more therapy, and he's still on drugs. He still doesn't have a job. Now she's upset because he's in a snit about something she said and he's not speaking to her. 'Why don't you go where you're wanted, Mom?' I ask her. 'You've got two grandchildren here who'd love to see you. I'm cooking a roast; why don't I tell Jerry to pick you up on the way home from work?' But she's too depressed to leave the house. Besides, Alan might call. It's like an obsession."

Evelyn is the product of a problem-focused family. It's predictable that her brother Alan isn't getting any better, for all of the attention lavished on him. "For my mother, I really believe it's about power and control. She can't control me because I'm not dependent on her. Alan, with all his craziness, makes her feel needed, makes her feel powerful. I truly don't believe my mother wants Alan to get better. If she did, she'd let go and make him take some responsibility for his own life."

What's troubling Evelyn lately is that her own depressions are becoming startlingly like her mother's. "It's like I have a cap on my emotions, like I'm stuck in neutral or something. I don't feel happy, I don't feel sad. I just feel nothing."

When we're around negativity all of the time, we become negative. In the problem-focused family, negativity is rewarded with attention. It becomes a whole style of relating to people we are close to. Voicing our fears and problems is our way of seeking a bond with others. Evelyn's depressions are calls for a sense of connection in the only way she's learned people connect.

☙ *To get your needs met indirectly.* Sandra was a woman who complained bitterly about her relationships with unfeeling, manipulative men who pursued her and then quickly abandoned her the moment she became emotionally involved.

Sandra's father left when she was a young child. Sandra's mother never admitted that there might have been anything she had done to cause the split and reviled her father at every opportunity.

Sandra saw her mother as a victim in life. She is often compelled to become a victim herself. She doesn't see that she participates fully in the games that go on between herself and "unfeeling, manipulative men." Sandra will look at her watch to "catch" her boyfriend being ten minutes late, just to validate the fact that he can't be trusted. She discounts his compliments to keep the status quo that no one ever really cares about her. When we think we can gain some satisfaction from the victim role, we are constantly scanning to find validation for this perspective.

The victim role originally stems from real life events where our needs are not met. In most families, there's no way to talk about these unmet needs. So our adaptive self finds ways to negotiate this problem. The victim role is one of these ways where we try to get our needs met.

In Sandra's case, it's significant that her father wasn't there for her. Rather than dealing with the pain of that, she manipulated others through guilt or withdrawal or indirect aggression to try to get their attention and to try to get her needs met. She did very often pull in people who said, "What's wrong? How can I help?" But no one likes to be foisted into the role of persecutor or told again and again that they are inept. Every man she dated eventually broke off the relationship with Sandra. Then she felt she really was a victim.

Although the victim role was once a survival strategy, it fails to help us achieve lasting, healthy relationships today. A lot of people will head in frustration in another direction from the depressed, negative victim. But because it worked so well in childhood, we're reluctant to give up the role and we're short on alternative methods for meeting our needs.

❧ *To survive a dysfunctional work environment.* There are toxic work environments where to show you're satisfied is to court disaster. One woman maintains, "Whoever got a raise by saying they were happy? You tell my boss that your sales for the month are up, and he cuts your territory in half."

A man told us that in his organization everyone bonds over mutual misery. "They handed out the Christmas bonus checks at a luncheon, and half of us got up and ran to the john where we tore open those checks. Picture ten executives standing over the urinals having a bitch session about how cheap this company is. It was the high point of the holiday."

❧ *To protect yourself from further disappointment.* In some families, a child's happiness is threatening to other people. Tracy, forty-five, says, "My stepmother would be most abusive when I made a team or got a good grade. She was jealous of my relationship with my father. She had to tear me down in his eyes." The feeling that her happiness or self-confidence somehow harms other people or creates conflict is baggage she's never fully been able to relinquish.

❧ *To get revenge.* Can a person go through life refusing to be happy out of spite? "My whole life has been one big 'F- - - you' to my mother," discovered Barry, thirty-two, who sought therapy when his own self-sabotaging behavior resulted in a series of low-paying jobs he lost for being late. He would soothe his underlying anxiety—*Am I really good enough? Am I really important to anyone?*—by eating or drinking too much, but this only gave rise to feelings of shame and self-recrimination, which made him even more bitter.

Barry's past provided a clue to his behavior. "My mother has no respect for men. When my sister speaks, she hushes everyone, afraid to miss a single word. When I speak she interrupts, rolls her eyes, or walks off into the kitchen to put the finishing touches on the salad.

"She has no respect for her boss, either, because he's also a man. Take last week, for example. I met my mother for lunch at her office. We were walking out of the door and she said, 'No one is supposed to leave the building for lunch, you know.'

"I stared at her. 'Why didn't you say something?' I asked. 'Let's go back in. I don't want to get you in trouble.'

"She kept walking toward my car, talking over her shoulder: 'I do it all the time.'

"If I was forced to name just one thing about my mother that drives me crazy, this would be it: She thinks she's above the rules everyone else has to live by. She thinks she's always right. Her criticism is relentless. I never do anything right.

"Six months into therapy, my mother and I were in one of our circular arguments:

"'Why do you pay some stranger all that money to tell you what your problem is? I'll tell you what it is for free: You're too sensitive.'

"'Ma, he doesn't tell me what my problem is.'

"'Then you should ask for a refund.'

"I try to explain. 'We talk about my feelings.'

"My mother snorts. She explains how she doesn't have feelings. I tell her psychiatrists call that denial, but even then I don't win. 'Denial is good,' she lectures me. 'When a person feels depressed, they should get busy and forget about it. When you're angry, you should calm yourself down. How are you going to get over your feelings if you keep talking about them? It's unhealthy.' The fact that I'm in therapy drives her crazy."

Which, of course, is one of the unconscious reasons Barry is in therapy. People like Barry often believe that being successful or happy is giving in to their parents. The only way to get back at them, to win the old battle over who was right, is to stay unhappy. Despite its negative results, Barry is the one making these decisions.

The daily wear and tear of negativity

It is so easy to shame ourselves with our problems. If we grow up in a critical family, we learn the language of criticism well. If we spend our time around negative people, we learn to be negative. However, attempting to gain satisfaction through criticism and negativity only serves to recycle the problem. We turn the sword on ourselves like it was done so many times in the past. To break this pattern, we need a shift in perspective.

The shift we suggest is this: Rather than seeing negativity as a maladaptive, dysfunctional aberration, see it this way. Our current struggles are adaptive and creative solutions.

You aren't a negative person. You are a person who thinks negatively because you believe it will help you achieve a positive goal. This goal is often validation. But, you may, in fact, only be creating more negatives in your life:

❧ *You can grow so accustomed to feeling chronically depressed that you no longer recognize it as a problem.* It simply feels like you. But a loss of interest or pleasure in activities, the fact that you don't feel better, even temporarily, when something good happens—weight loss or gain, constant fatigue—all are warning signs of depression.

❧ *You tend to attract other people who are at the same level of pain you're at.* In other words, if everyone we are close to is chronically dissatisfied or depressed, we may feel we have a lot of support. But our painful thinking is constantly being reinforced. Change is preceded by a state of dissonance or incongruity. This is something we don't find in homogeneous groups.

Why it will never be enough

The person who can never be happy for long doesn't enjoy misery, but seeks two objectives by focusing on the negative: protection and validation. He or she gets neither. This is why it will never be enough.

Here is a typical scenario. Trying to protect yourself from reprisals, envy, whatever, you begin to see the dark side of a recent accomplishment. Yes, you clinched a better job, but you have to work longer hours. True, you're finally getting married, but you're going to lose all of your freedom. For a moment you feel safer, just thinking like this. By fettering out these negatives, you beat the world to the punch. You cannot be disappointed or taken by surprise.

But it's scary and frustrating to dwell on the negatives. You talk to people about your unhappiness, wanting validation, wanting relief. Instead you become surrounded by people who tell you, "No, the world isn't coming to an end; think positive!" Or they give you advice which you don't want and don't take. To them, this is cheering you up. But it's a completely unempathic response. People keep telling you why you shouldn't feel the way you feel. You dig in your heels. Craving understanding, you get more unhappy, more negative, as if to prove a point. It's never enough. You just get more of what you don't want.

There was a moment in David's life when he realized it would never be enough: "I opened my own consulting service, and in the beginning, when there were few clients, I panicked. At the moment I thought I was going under, a friend recommended me for a big project. Soon more clients came. But there wasn't a moment when I stopped to pat myself on the back, to think how incredible it was that I had really made it. I was stressed out, complaining how I had no personal life. All my friends could see was that I was making money hand over fist, and they thought I was the luckiest son of a bitch in the world.

"One day a close friend told me, 'If you're going to go through the slow times miserable because it's slow and the busy times miserable because it's busy, you're going to spend your life miserable.' I walked away from that conversation angry. People just didn't understand. Nothing anyone said made me feel any better.

"Walking past a store window I caught my reflection. It almost made me jump. I looked so much like my father. The lines in my forehead were deepening just as his had and it was from the same bitterness. Suddenly I understood how my mother's attempts to make him happy, her complaints that nothing ever satisfied him, had only created a man who felt lonely in the deepest sense."

In a search for an empathic response, some people get so depressed, so unable to function, they spiral further and further down. We'd like to save you the pain of that experience.

RX: Your Prescription for Change

Pain is inevitable.
Suffering is optional.
—M. KATHLEEN CASEY

What you need to understand most about yourself

Given your history, it's understandable that you feel the future won't be bright and that you feel a need to protect yourself. But protection need not come at the cost of your happiness.

The key questions

- What do I fear I'll lose by being happy?
- What do I believe I'll gain by being unhappy?
- What am I bitter about? Who am I angry at?

Where you need to focus

- on facing depression or dysthymia and seeking treatment, rather than believing this is just your personality

- on overcoming your bitterness from the past
- on building a healthy "family of choice"
- on expressing your emotions
- on finding things that bring you joy
- on learning how to play again

The cognitive shift

- If I relish my success and enjoy it, I'll have the energy to create more of it.
- My current unhappiness doesn't pay other people back for the past.
- Misery is not a lucky charm that protects me from bad luck.
- I deserve to be happy.

Thoughts and Exercises

❧ *Get a professional assessment.* You may simply call what you feel burnout or a bad mood, and it may be. But it's difficult to assess the level of depression when you're in it.

Get it checked out. If it turns out that you suffer from depression or dysthymia, you are not at fault. It can happen to anyone. This idea that we should be able to pull ourselves up by the bootstraps keeps more people stuck than any single factor. Such thoughts aren't necessarily signs of strength. Often such a mind-set springs from compulsive self-reliance caused by a damaged ability to trust.

In our practice we've often seen a simple evaluation dispel fears and bring people a new sense of hope. An objective person can help you confront the underlying questions: Are certain events in your life making you unhappy? Or is the problem your distorted, inner reaction to those events, which is something that you can change with some new skills? Could you suffer from a biochemical imbalance that hasn't been diagnosed?

Harold H. Bloomfield, M.D. and Peter McWilliams offer powerful, empathic words in their book, *How to Heal Depression:* "You didn't do anything to become depressed. Your failure to do something didn't cause your depression. Depression is an illness. You are no more at fault for having depression than if you had asthma, diabetes, heart disease, or any other illness."

Don't blame yourself. Don't blame anyone else. "Where your depression came from isn't important," Bloomfield and McWilliams maintain, "how to heal it is."

With the right kind of treatment, nearly everyone can experience relief from dysthymia or depression. You have a right to enjoy your own life, to feel alive, to have a vision and the energy to go after it.

❧ *Identify how your symptoms serve you.* Once you've ruled out depression, you are the only one who can assess whether your inability to stay happy for long has some inner goal. More important, does it work? Is there anything ultimately validating in this struggle?

We've had many clients do the following exercise. We've asked them to list on paper anything they think they might be able to achieve by suffering, being unhappy, or staying depressed. Then we ask them to make an assessment. Is it working or isn't it?

Here are some of the answers we've gotten:

GOAL: I don't want to set myself up for disappointment. I want to be on top of problems.

REALITY: *There's no big surprises. I generally see things coming. But I also think I see things coming that never happen and worry about a lot of stuff that never occurs. For five minutes of panic I'm trading hours of worry.*

GOAL: People listen to me when I'm unhappy. I feel cared for. Sometimes they have good suggestions.

REALITY: *Sometimes I feel that people treat me like a child, with no respect. Some of my friends are pretty messed up themselves. But I think that people who have it all would never*

> *have anything to do with me. Maybe it's just an excuse, because I don't want to face rejection.*

GOAL: I'm not happy because I truly don't have what I really want. I think it motivates me to see the glass half empty.

REALITY: *If it was motivating me, I'd be doing something besides watching TV, too depressed to go out. I'm overwhelming myself by thinking of what's missing instead of what's there. Instead of the feeling of,* What now? *It's,* What's the use?

GOAL: I want someone to come along and make it all better, I guess.

REALITY: *In my last relationship, I felt smothered. At first I thought it was great that she had all these ideas for how I could go back to school, how I could make more money. But that's all she talked about. I felt like her project. I finally had to say, "Listen, I'm really not here for career counseling."*

Like these clients, you're the only one who can say whether you get anything out of your behavior. Make a cost/benefit analysis.

❧ *End the family legacy of negativity.* Awareness is vital here. You've got to recognize the family legacy of negativity. People don't always see it in their families, because they're so entrenched in it. It becomes a worldview or a way of life.

One of our clients was able to see his own legacy clearly when he attended a wedding with his family. "They sat at the table, saying how the bride looked fat in her dress, the flowers were overdone, the chicken was overcooked, the speeches were stupid. It went on and on. And I finally saw why I had always felt ugly as a child."

Criticism of others begets self-criticism. This man no longer involves himself in family "roasts" of family members, friends, and others. He gets up and goes in another room. He catches himself in his own tendency to be critical of others, including his parents.

❧ Break the superstitious connection. Stop beating yourself into recovery by suffering. This belief that if you suffer enough in life you'll be vindicated is an illusion.

Many people believe that putting themselves down is a magic charm that they need to motivate themselves to higher levels of achievement. Test it to break the cycle. The next time you achieve something, catch yourself thinking of the remaining negatives in your life and shout, "Stop!" See if the walls come crashing down when you no longer give in to those superstitions. Watch other people who revel in their achievements. Why aren't they punished by the celestial scoreboard?

Some need for protection in your past gave rise to these superstitions. That protection may no longer be needed. You don't need the anxious energy of fear and self-doubt. You have many more resources than you did in the past. You can let go of what's no longer viable or helpful.

❧❧

Today I will realize that I have the right to be happy. The past is over. I can change my perception in this moment.

❧❧

CHAPTER FOUR

Why Can't I Just Relax?

The Search for Trust

*It's an old ironic habit of human beings to run faster
when we have lost our way.*

—ROLLO MAY

This is Karen's most vivid memory of a seminar she recently attended: "There is a group of us, maybe twenty-five, and they hand out these forms. Everyone is writing and I start to sweat. The forms say 'use number 2 pencil only.' I dump out my whole purse, but the one pencil I have says number 3. I see other people writing in ink. The woman next to me is scribbling away with a marker. She grabs a cigarette, and I think, *Here's a person who doesn't even question whether she's allowed to smoke in this place but just lights up. Why am I sitting here, in a panic, like I'm on a job interview or something?*

One might wonder why Karen, who wrote her master's thesis on something so complex it's difficult to spell, would still dig through her purse, upset because some meaningless forms call for a number two pencil and hers is a number three. What does it matter? Why should she care?

She learned to care. She cares for a reason. If you can identify, then you, too, care for a reason.

You hear people talk about anxiety. You think, *They don't know the half of it.* For you, it isn't a case of cause and effect, like you have a speech to give, so you feel anxious about it. You never really relax. You have an emotional thermostat turned high to nuances, a sensitivity to a lot of surplus information other people filter out and disregard. This sensitivity is your strength at times. But it has an enormous cost.

Psychiatrist Michael Franz Basch has successfully treated anxious patients for decades. In *Understanding Psychotherapy,* he explains his patients' anxiety this way: "Overstimulation leads to distress. When replaying problems doesn't reduce overstimulation, anxiety results. Rapid heartbeat, sweating make you feel out of control, increasing the anxiety. There's anxiety from anxiety."

Overstimulation. For those of you who can never relax, this is a key concept. But the smallest things stimulate you. You feel anxious from the moment you wake up until the second you drift off at night. "It's how I think," one client told us, "and what am I going to do about the way I think?"

The problem: Generalized anxiety disorder and a deep ambivalence about letting it go

The woman who sat in the seminar feeling panicky because she doesn't have the right pencil doesn't suffer from a hopeless sense of insecurity, but from what therapists term *generalized anxiety disorder.* People like this feel tense all day long, regardless of what they're doing, and their symptoms persist continuously for six months or longer.

There's no question that anxiety as a psychiatric complaint is on the rise. In today's fast-paced competitive world, more and more people are reporting symptoms of stress and anxiety. Sales of prescription tranquilizers have never been higher.

Yet there are people who handle the same challenges that reduce others to a white-knuckled alarm-state.

The *DSM III-R* lists the following as a symptom of generalized anxiety disorder: "Unrealistic or excessive anxiety and worry (apprehensive expectation) about two or more life circumstances, e.g., worry about possible misfortune to one's child (who is in no danger) and worry about finances (for no good reason), for a period of six months or longer, during which the person has been bothered more days than not by these concerns."

In addition, organic factors such as hyperthyroidism and caffeine must be ruled out to qualify for this diagnosis. The person must also be suffering from at least six of the eighteen symptoms. You may be familiar with them. The symptoms are: trembling, twitching, or feeling shaky; muscle tension, aches, or soreness; restlessness; getting tired easily; shortness of breath or smothering sensations; palpitations or accelerated heart rate; sweating or cold clammy hands; dry mouth; dizziness or lightheadedness; nausea, diarrhea, or other stomach problems; flushes or chills; frequent urination; trouble swallowing or "a lump in the throat"; feeling keyed up or on edge; exaggerated startle response; difficulty concentrating; trouble falling or staying asleep; irritability.

Anxiety serves a useful purpose when it calls attention to the presence of an unresolved issue and brings one's resources together to solve it. But when anxiety is prolonged and intense, it becomes the problem in itself.

What if anxiety has overtaken so much of your life you can't remember the last time you weren't worried about one thing or another? Is this something you have to live with?

Why can't I relax?

Diana is a woman who wonders if she has been given some kind of inexplicable sixth sense. "I can walk into a room and immediately know who is depressed, who is angry. It's like I have radar for other people's feelings."

Trouble is, this sensitivity throws her off balance. She'll go into a year-end review expecting to be fired and come out with a promotion. Relationships turn her into a bundle of nerves. "What did he mean by that?" she'll think after a date makes an offhand comment. "I analyze everything. My mind is always churning."

Hypervigilance—the type of anxious scanning that gave Diana so many difficulties—often develops in childhood as children try to create safety in a chaotic environment. Since she was a toddler, Diana knew the signs that her father was about to explode into one of his rages. "His eyes would narrow, the light would go out of them. He'd speak in a soft voice, with a terrible patience. It marked the crossing of the line which we all learned to recognize immediately." Diana would try to get her younger sisters out of the way and pray that her mother could calm him.

People who endure this type of unpredictable environment often develop sensitivity to other people's moods and feelings, a perception that seems uncanny to the rest of us. They are prey to constant overstimulation, and hence, anxiety.

The person who is always scanning other people's faces for information is trying to avoid being taken by surprise. However, this creates even greater anxiety.

If you are always scanning, chances are you rarely interpret what you see positively. You act on your assumptions—and these assumptions are often misleading. For example, Gordon, forty, was in the middle of his second job interview when the head of the division walked in. She said to the woman interviewing him, "You have another person waiting to see you, so you might want to wrap this up."

Scanning both women's faces, Gordon concluded that they were moving him on because they weren't interested in hiring him. For the remaining five minutes, Gordon answered questions in depressed monosyllables.

Gordon spent an anxious evening trying to figure out where he had gone wrong. In truth, the division head had already made a decision—to hire Gordon. She cut the second interview short because she felt making him jump through any more hoops was unnecessary.

You are exhausted by the end of the morning. You are trying to protect yourself from disaster, prepare yourself for the worst possible scenario. That's part of the reason why you are trying to assess what everyone else is thinking. But hypervigilance is a tremendous drain on the nervous system.

Don't trust, don't believe

How much do you trust other people? Think for a moment.

Twenty-six-year-old Jeffrey was in a training seminar on cooperative learning and the trainer asked the audience to write down a number between one and ten to indicate how trusting they felt they were of others. Jeffrey wrote down two and then folded his paper in half and put it in his pocket.

But the seminar leader wasn't just throwing out a random question. She asked, "Are there any tens?" and a bunch of hands went up. Jeffrey started to feel anxious. She started putting people together in groups based on the number they wrote. By the time she got to six, the room was emptying out fast. When she got to five, Jeffrey raised his hand. "So I was in this group with these other fives, a congenial bunch of people," Jeffrey remembers. "At the end of the day I told a guy in my group, 'You know, I really shouldn't be here. I wrote down a two, but I was embarrassed to say it.' The guy starts laughing and shows me the sheet of paper he wrote his number on. It said, 'one.' "

To stand up and say, "I don't really trust anyone, so make my number zero," seems a shameful thing.

You may have an excellent reason for your lack of trust. Trust, which often takes years to build, can be snatched away in an instant. Without a basic feeling of trust, we are constantly scanning, reading into situations what may or may not be there. Gayle's story is a case in point.

It started during the summer before eighth grade. Gayle met Lisa at an overnight camp. They passed the test to become junior lifeguards the same day. Both girls sneaked away from their cabins, snagged a powerboat that was loosely tied to a pier, and cruised the lake while the other campers and counselors slept. It was an evening that cemented their friendship. When they found out that a change in school boundaries meant that they would be going to the same high school, they were ecstatic.

Gayle learned something the first day of high school. She watched Lisa in the lunchroom automatically gravitate to the most popular crowd. Gayle trailed behind her friend, anxious and over-whelmed. She backed away to find another table, and Lisa grabbed her arm firmly.

"I was definitely in her shadow," Gayle says. "She had everything, and I mean everything. Brains, looks, talent. She was the type of person you want to hate, but you can't because there's no arrogance in her; she genuinely cares about other people.

"Every school dance, Lisa would say to her date, 'Bring along someone nice for Gayle, would you?' I'd go to the dance and try to distract my date from lusting after Lisa."

Then, at a basketball game sophomore year, Gayle and Lisa met George. Gayle remembers, "He obviously went for Lisa, but he didn't make me feel left out. We had common interests. Lisa had no interest in basketball at all—she went to games to meet guys—but George and I could really talk sports. We became friends."

But it was Lisa who George asked out. "It was pride, I guess, but I didn't let Lisa know how I felt about George. She would have stopped dating him. But I wanted George to notice me on his own, without Lisa pushing us together."

Then it happened. George called Gayle one Saturday night and asked her to see a movie with him. She told herself that it wasn't really a date, just two friends going out together, but the entire night her heart hammered in her chest so loudly she was afraid he would hear it.

He asked her out again and again in the following weeks. "Lisa was genuinely happy for me. She suggested that the four of us go out together."

So they did. They went bowling, Gayle with George, Lisa with her man-of-the-moment. Ten minutes into the evening, both girls knew the score. George ignored Gayle and gave all his attention to Lisa. He tried to show Lisa's date up. He tried to coax Lisa away for a serious conversation. Gayle watched, feeling like her heart would break.

"He's an idiot," Lisa told her later as Gayle cried in her arms. "He's not worth it."

"It didn't matter. For two years I'd been obsessed with George and the moment that I thought he was finally interested in me, I learned the bitter truth: He was just trying to make Lisa jealous by showing interest in me."

One single childhood incident of disappointment can hardly be blamed for a lifetime of mistrust. The trouble was, what happened afterwards cemented the feeling that Gayle couldn't trust anyone. "With every man afterwards I tried to read his face for signs. Was I making the grade or not? If he said he would pick me up at seven, and it was seven-fifteen, I'd think, *What does that mean? If he really liked me, wouldn't he be early, not late?* I was constantly analyzing, trying to stay one step ahead. And I was so jealous. I've had men swear to me that they aren't interested in some other women. I'd think, *They just don't know it yet. I see the signs.*"

For much of her life, Gayle has had issues with trust. When a man says he loves her, she feels a sudden fear. When someone says, "Come join us," there's never pride. There's only a sinking feeling. She expects to be disappointed, she expects that being close will mean getting hurt, and to defend herself against disappointment or humiliation, she is constantly scanning her environment for clues.

We have often asked clients who complain that they always feel anxious: Do you really want to relax? It's a question that stops many people in their tracks. Many people are ambivalent: "I feel if I don't keep pushing, pushing, pushing, I'll come to a complete standstill. I'll have no motivation at all."

Anxiety feels like action, but is it?

To worry, to ruminate, to obsess—it often gets us nowhere, but the payoff is we feel we are doing something about the problem. Worrying makes us feel like we're taking action. It's hard to see that it's an illusion.

David, thirty, suffered from dyslexia and attention deficit disorder, a combination that made school a formidable challenge. "I couldn't concentrate long enough to focus or retain anything in class. My memory wasn't very good. There were all these things standing between me and what I had to learn. I was always trying to get caught up. I always felt I was behind. After a while the ball got so large as it was coming down the hill that I couldn't even try to catch up. So I would pretend like I knew what was going on. It translates to my present-day life in that no matter what I'm doing I always think there's something else that I should be doing, or something I haven't done. No matter what I do, there's still that thing, that cloud following me. I can't relax."

David feels he has good reason not to relax. If he lets up for a minute, he might fall behind. But he's not in school anymore. Everyone who knows him tells him to relax, that he's doing fine. David can't believe it. How could doing the opposite of everything he learned about being successful in life ever work? He does voice-overs for commercials. Any vocal coach will tell you how important it is to relax your jaw, relax your vocal cords, transcend yourself. David's strategy is paralyzing him.

We're often protecting ourselves from challenges that no longer exist in our lives, with so much energy, so much angst. We're digging in the ashes.

Alexandra is a woman who says, "I don't care what you worry about. It's nothing next to the thought that your child won't come out all right."

She has never hired a baby-sitter, and her children are in pre-school. She told herself she would relax when her children were old enough to be able to talk and express to her what goes on when they're away from her. By now both children are articulate enough to tell the truth, and she realizes there is more to her reluctance to hire baby-sitters than fear for her children's safety. "Raising these children is my job. If I leave the kids with someone else, it's like I'm not doing my job." This makes perfect sense given the perspective of a woman in the work force for ten years who never once called in sick.

You can't trust others. You have to do it all. You won't be hurt if you don't set yourself up by relying on anyone else. You're pushing,

pushing, pushing. It's the beginning of what psychologists call compulsive self-reliance, the biggest anxiety producer of all.

Compulsive self-reliance: Are you the only one you really trust?

Imagine this: Your supervisor introduces you to a capable-looking young woman who will be an intern in your office for the summer. The intern brightens when she meets you. She wants to help you. You think

a. *Great chance to get rid of some of this busywork, and hand her a stack.*
b. *No thanks, by the time I explain it to her I could do it myself.*
c. *Forget it. They hang people on stuff like this. Next they'll be thinking an entry-level person can do my job, so why pay me?*

You and a friend plan to take a ski trip this winter, and she suggests Vail because she's been there twice before and her travel agent is marvelous. You want to know

a. Who you write the check out to. Once you agree on a ballpark figure for what you're willing to spend, you trust her to make all the plans.
b. Who her travel agent is. You want to hear the rates, the flight times, and the accommodations firsthand.
c. The conditions at all of the ski resorts in the Rockies, what the options are, and the name of another travel agent. You're not sure your friend is getting the best advice.

You're taking a class at a local college. The instructor tells you that you will do the final project in groups of four. Your first thought is

a. *Great. It's fun to work together and share ideas. It'll probably make it easier.*
b. *I hope we each get to do our own section and get graded accordingly.*
c. *No way! How long do I have to drop this course and still get a refund?*

You're driving to meet a friend at a new restaurant and after twenty minutes of driving around you have to admit that you're completely lost. You

a. Roll down your car window and yell to the man walking his schnauzer, "Hey, do you know how to get to Peter's Pasta Place?"
b. Drive to a gas station to ask for directions—you don't bother strangers on the street for anything.
c. This would never happen to you. You demand such explicit knowledge of streets and thoroughfares before you step inside your car, you could draw maps for Rand McNally.

An ominous-looking notice requesting a parent conference regarding your eight-year-old arrives in your mail. Your spouse offers to go so that you don't have to cancel a sales call you spent weeks setting up. What do you do?

a. Tell your spouse, "Great, I owe you one," and wonder if your mother would be willing to take this kid and bring him back to you when he's twenty-four.
b. Cancel the meeting and go with your spouse. Even if your spouse brought a tape recorder, you'd feel more comfortable hearing what the problem is yourself.
c. Cancel the meeting and tell your spouse that there's no reason you both have to go. Your spouse is the impatient type, and you don't want to make a bad situation worse.

You and your friends rent a powerboat at a resort. You listen attentively as the harbormaster tells your group how to restart the engine if you have to. An hour away from the harbor your friends want to beach the boat, shut the engine off, and catch some rays. You think

a. *Great. This is a real vacation!*
b. *Gulp. He said to push the red button to restart the engine, didn't he? They wouldn't rent boats that don't restart, would they? There's a coast guard on this lake, isn't there?*

c. *Not in this lifetime.* There's no ship-to-shore radio, no paddle, no coast guard that makes you feel comfortable at sea. The whole time on the boat you're thinking, *Isn't it time to get back to shore?*

Are most of your answers B's and C's? If so, you may suffer from what therapists refer to as compulsive self-reliance. Your favorite saying is, "I'll handle it." The fear isn't that others might survive without you. Unconsciously, you simply don't want to become dependent on anyone, or incur any form of emotional debt, or tie your fate to anyone else's. You want to be the giver. The giver is always in control.

To relax means to let go. But the person with compulsive self-reliance can never let go. There is never anyone else to rely on.

It's an anxiety-provoking way of going about life, a cognitive proclivity to go it all alone. It's based on fear. But you see no other choice. You lie in bed with a 102-degree fever and the phone jammed to your ear, firing instructions at co-workers until your head aches because your work habits are such that no one really knows how you do your job. You make thirty phone calls to let friends and relatives know that your mother has passed on. Your sister begs you to let her assume part of this burden, but you believe this news must come from you. You cringe if you have to ask someone for a ride, a favor, or advice, yet you offer your soul to other people without a second thought.

One might think at first that compulsive self-reliance is just another term for people who are "control freaks," but there are differences:

♦ The controlling individual expects that others will succeed if they do it his or her way. The compulsively self-reliant person has an expectation of being disappointed no matter how well others might follow his or her directions.

♦ Controlling people often initiate contact with other people who can help them accomplish their goals. Overly self-reliant people avoid delegating. They work around people.

♦ Controlling people are impatient with other people's weaknesses and complain that people don't try hard enough. Compulsively self-reliant people are grudgingly accepting of anyone else's faults but their own.

♦ Controlling people will raise their hands in lecture halls, pester the boss, stand up in a meeting, make a dozen phone calls to get clarification, but they will not accept responsibility until they are given adequate information. Overly self-reliant people will quietly plug into the Internet, read the textbook, figure it out themselves. They take responsibility, even when it isn't theirs to take.

♦ If a controlling person has to work in a group, he or she will gravitate to a leadership role, do only his or her part of the task, and demand that others do the same. The overly self-reliant person will stay in the background, his teeth set on edge by all the "small talk," and know the answer to everyone else's task by the time he hands in his own report.

♦ Controlling people will blame others for making the mistake. Overly self-reliant people will also blame others. Then they'll be up nights, kicking themselves, because they should have known this was the way things would turn out and done something about it.

♦ Controlling people admit they're often anxious, buy self-help books, seek treatment. Compulsively self-reliant people are ambivalent about giving up their anxiety. "If I take a Xanax, I won't really be me."

How compulsive self-reliance develops

In *Necessary Losses,* Judith Viorst writes: "By blaming oneself, we can believe in our life-controlling powers. By blaming oneself, we are saying that we would rather feel guilty than helpless, than not in control."

A persistent sense of overresponsibility (It's my fault that it rained; it's my fault that he's in a bad mood) is the hallmark of the person who survived a painful childhood, colored by a parent's alcoholism, toxic criticism, or neglect. These people share the unwarranted guilt that comes from never being able to fix their families. The feeling that they should be more and do more colors everything they do. They were adults long before they were even adolescents.

Lois's parents, both top-achievers in high-level careers, traveled frequently. They left Lois and her two younger brothers in the capable hands of Helena, their housekeeper. Then Helena developed a drinking problem. "I was too young to understand the changes I was seeing," Lois remembers. "She was sleeping all of the time. I asked my mother, 'Could Helena have cancer?' My mother told me I was watching too much TV. When my parents left for Europe, Helena passed out at the table. I couldn't wake her. I was terrified. I couldn't reach my parents. They were on a nine-hour flight."

At eleven years old, Lois was seeing that her brothers made the school bus on time, that the shopping was done, that there was food in the house. Lois was seeing to it that her parents were free to travel without worry. Her trust in adults eroded. She'd learned the lesson of relying solely on herself. She's taken far more responsibility than she needs to take at every crossroad in her life. And she can never relax.

Are you setting yourself up for disappointment?

Our solutions to childhood challenges often become problems in themselves in adulthood. The protection from disappointment that self-reliance is supposed to provide backfires for the following reasons:

✣ *Self-esteem isn't just based on achievements but also on the reassurance and support we get along the way.* Many popular theories purport that self-esteem comes from within. You can sit alone in your room, repeating positive affirmations, and raise your confidence in six weeks. But a person cannot be his or her own sole source of validation. It is a combination of inner acceptance and outer validation that results in feelings of self-satisfaction. Compulsively self-reliant people cannot get what they need to nourish themselves on their own even though they desire it, which is why a sense of emptiness often follows their achievements.

❧ *You may unconsciously make others feel invalidated and unimportant.* People see the compulsively self-reliant person as aloof, bored, detail-oriented, hyper. Many people hold the idea that if they are independent enough, if they are never a burden to anyone, this, in the end, will make them more lovable. But it's vulnerability, not perfection, that makes one person seem emotionally available—and therefore lovable—to another. It's also letting a partner know you have faith and trust in him or her that encourages intimacy.

❧ *You attract procrastinators.* These people are drawn to the help they know they will receive from someone who can't bear to see a half-done job. "I guess I'll return my son's library books; if I wait for him to do it we'll have overdue fines the size of a mortgage payment. . . . Let my wife do our taxes? She can hardly balance her checkbook." The people around us grow more and more helpless. In the end, we never get appreciation for our abilities, only resentment.

Why it will never be enough

We have met many people in the course of our practice who come to therapy wanting relief from anxiety. At the same time, they are deeply ambivalent about giving it up. If they stop scanning, if they let go, if they follow a plan that helps them relax, what guarantees are there that the other shoe isn't going to drop right when they least expect it?

Are you trying to guarantee your survival by never allowing yourself to relax? Amanda, forty, learned that no matter how on guard she was, it wasn't enough. She is a public school teacher. The beginning of the school year always threw her into a panic. New faces. New parents. New problems. She would come to school in the middle of July, work in the heat, moving desks, putting up bulletin boards, planning activities for the first month.

"You want to be prepared. You want to be in control. So I'm standing at the Xerox machine on a hot day in August. Public schools have no air conditioning. They have no ventilation. I was dripping sweat.

"The machine jammed. I was almost in tears trying to get the jammed paper out. You can't imagine how important I thought these papers were. I was thinking that I'd have to run out to Kinko's and pay because I couldn't get through the first day without these worksheets. Then it hit me. A voice in my head went, *It will never be enough. You can run off a pile of these papers, you can plan for that first week like you've never planned for anything, but it won't make a difference. It will never be enough because you don't trust. You don't see that those kids aren't out to destroy you. That the principal really wants you to succeed, not fail. That the parents of these kids won't rise up when you're shaky in seventh grade math because all they want is for their kids to have a good year, with less problems for them.*

"For one small moment, I realized that until I learned to trust, to see the bigger picture, there was never going to be enough preparation, enough Xeroxing, enough standing on my head, to make me feel secure. I was going to go in with all these papers and still feel like a fraud at the end of the day."

RX: Your Prescription For Change

The art of being wise is the art of knowing what to overlook.

—WILLIAM JAMES

What you need to understand about yourself

Given your history, it is understandable that you feel that trusting others is setting yourself up. But knowing when to let go of control can also make you strong.

The key questions

- Why am I afraid to trust?
- Am I re-creating the drama of my family?

Where you need to focus

- on connection
- on understanding and managing your anxiety
- on asking for help
- on eliminating black-and-white thinking

The cognitive shift

- Colleagues can be resources, not just competition.
- I can choose to be a member of a group, not always the exception.
- There can be rewards in being a team player.

Thoughts and Exercises

❧ *Let enough be enough.* A certain amount of anxiety in life is inevitable. To feel anxious every moment is not. Distinguish ordinary ups and downs from more serious mood problems. Rule out physical causes of anxiety by visiting your doctor for a checkup. Excessive caffeine, medication side effects, a thyroid disorder, low-blood sugar, and so on, can cause that shaky, sweaty feeling. Eliminating stimulants and increasing your physical exercise can be immediately beneficial.

If anxiety is debilitating, seek treatment. Anxiety disorders are among the most easily treated of psychiatric problems. "I felt so tense all the time, I thought it was just part of my personality," one woman admitted, explaining why until recently, she never sought treatment. "My friends used to tell me to stop being so sensitive. It took an objective person to point out that this wasn't something I could control automatically and I didn't have to live like this."

Neither do you.

🦋 *Stress management can be fun.* Take a walk in the woods. Play tennis. Lunch with a good friend. Listen to music. Pet your cat. Read a story to a child. Play Monopoly. Relaxing, like anxiety, is a habit.

🦋 *Recognize that you might be ambivalent about giving up anxiety and the compulsively self-reliant lifestyle that fuels it.* You're the only one who can assess whether this protective strategy helps more than it hurts.

♦ Fill in the blank: If I let myself rely on other people,_____ .

Take your answers seriously. Do you really need so much protection? Or are you still responding to a past that's gone? Are you choosing people who can't be relied upon to play the biggest roles in your life? Why do it? What do you gain? What are the costs?

🦋 *There isn't one stress-management strategy, but many.* Find one tailored to your nature. Anyone can tell you to go out jogging, but if that's not something you're going to follow up on, it's useless. Sean, thirty-seven, recalls going to a meditation seminar years ago. "They told me all I had to do was chant a mantra for twenty minutes. I was so tense, I couldn't sit still that long. Subsequently, I did nothing about my stress for the next five years, feeling I'd failed."

Take a searching self-evaluation. What are you struggling so hard to control in your life? A relationship? Another person's actions? Someone else's problems? How everyone else feels about you? What would happen if you let go? Do you believe that anxiety and worrying will help you? In other words, if you turn yourself into a nail-biting wreck over a presentation you're working on, do you believe this will ensure a better job? Has it?

❧ *Reduce scanning and hypervigilance.* If you are often anxious it is a good idea to build some boundaries by avoiding anxious situations if possible. For example, you may start by avoiding the ten o'clock news if it seems filled with tense stories of murder and violence. Or perhaps there are certain people in your life (the ones who tend to constantly pour all of their problems onto your plate) whom you would do well by avoiding or setting time limits with.

❧ *Take a tip from the Taoists who believe that moderation leads to balance and harmony.* Struggling to meet extravagant expectations for months at a time, then giving into dismal do-nothing despair is hardly a middle way. This is what happens when we become over-stimulated, overwhelmed. You can't do it all, but you can do your best. Your best is good enough.

❧ *Express your feelings.* Perhaps you are angry at someone, but fear their reaction. So you hold it in much like a pressure cooker. This "bubbling" inside is experienced as anxiety. Let those feelings out. Write a letter. Put your thoughts on paper. Express yourself.

❧ *Be a friend to yourself.* David Burns describes in his book, *Feeling Good,* ten "cognitive distortions" (i.e., all-or-nothing thinking, mini-mizing, generalizing, and so on) that tend to make things look worse than they are. For example, if your father was abusive you may fear all men. Or perhaps you catastrophize by thinking a small sensation in your chest is a heart attack. Cognitive therapy encourages you to debate these assumptions and find a more reality-centered truth.

❧ *Integrate spirituality into a holistic schema of health.* One common way used in the Twelve Step movement is to declare powerlessness over your anxiety and to turn it over to a higher power. For many people, this is a remarkably effective solution. It immediately disengages our controlling ego and triggers a relaxation response.

❧ *Try a deep relaxation exercise.* One of the most powerful ways of achieving a consistent sense of relaxation in your life is through the practice of deep relaxation. There are many techniques that can lead you to this result, including meditation, hypnotherapy, and guided imagery work. The bottom line is essentially the same: Deep relaxation of our minds and bodies isn't something that just happens, but something we can create.

The daily practice of twenty minutes of deep relaxation will produce the following results: (1) a more generalized sense of relaxation each day; (2) an increased level of energy and production; (3) more restful sleep at night; (4) a reduction of psychosomatic illness such as headaches, high blood pressure, ulcers, and so on.

Here is a relaxation exercise that many of our clients have found helpful.

Find a comfortable place where there are no distractions. Take the phone off the hook or tell your family not to disturb you for a half hour. If possible, put on some soothing peaceful music. Have someone read the following script to you or record it into a tape recorder for playback.

Imagine yourself breathing in relaxation and breathing out tension . . . with each breath feel a wave of relaxation come through your body . . . see yourself at the top of a beautiful staircase with ten steps . . . design this staircase any way you like . . . as you slowly walk down you feel calmer and more relaxed as you go deeper and deeper into a wonderful state of relaxation . . . calmer and calmer . . . your body feels heavier as your muscles let go and feel limp and relaxed . . . imagine a golden light passing through your body filling you with a sense of peace and contentment . . . as you arrive at the bottom of the staircase, you open a door to the most scenic spot you can imagine . . . feel the breeze . . . smell the air and flowers . . . use all your senses to see, hear, smell, feel, and touch the beauty . . . absorb yourself in the splendor and relaxation

of this scenic spot . . . see yourself just as you'd love to be . . .
notice how healthy you look . . . you feel healthy . . . you are
relaxed . . . you see your life exactly as you wish it would be
. . . everything is easy . . . everything works out and makes
sense in a way you never imagined before . . . you can relax
because you know that you don't need to do anything right
now . . . you don't have to be anything . . . you are enough . . .
this moment will strengthen you . . . you are nourishing yourself . . . you are getting stronger as you relax and let go. . . .*

You will find that each time you go into a state of deep relaxation, it
will become easier to access this state.

❦ *Give trust another try.* When we are compulsively self-reliant we feel
as if the whole world is on our shoulders. There is no one we can
trust enough to seek out help or reassurance. This increases anxiety.
While it is understandable, given some of our family histories, that
we don't trust others, there are ways to work through this.

One effective method for learning to trust is in a group therapy
setting. One client admitted, "When I first joined a group I was convinced that I would be gone in a matter of weeks. They were all talking so openly, I felt very uncomfortable. In my family I was the one
who was teased and made fun of and I was convinced that this was
what would happen in this group. I kept expecting people to criticize
and humiliate me, but it never happened. Over time I became more
open and their continued support and reassurance amazed me. Over
time I was given feedback about how I had a tendency to push away
others and actually leave them before they could leave me. The process was not overnight, but over a period of about a year. I found
myself turning to others for help and support when I needed it."

You have to risk some vulnerability by being more open. This will
feel uncomfortable at first. You are changing a habitual pattern. You

---

*To request a tape of this and other meditations, write to the authors at the address listed at
the back of this book.

must determine who is safe and who is not. Who is truly interested in us enough to want to hear our story and care about our feelings?

If you are unsure, ask yourself: Do these people seem to listen when I talk or call the attention back to themselves? Do they seem to listen closely to others? Are they open themselves?

Remember also, trust begins with ourselves. Embracing and accepting the truth of our own feelings and needs makes it possible to trust others. The world is a mirror of our inner life.

❧ ❧

Today I will see my anxiety as a message to set appropriate boundaries with others and do something nice for myself.

❧ ❧

CHAPTER FIVE

Why Am I So Bored And Restless?

The Search for Competence

Hope is a good breakfast, but it is a bad supper.

—FRANCIS BACON

At thirty-three, Jerry is a man who feels that his life hasn't really started. Out of college at twenty-two, with a half-dozen rejection letters from prospective employers, Jerry began what he refers to as his "decadent year."

There were days when he slept until noon, woke up yawning, and planned his evening: a new club, a party, a game of pool. There was the night he was driving around with his girlfriend, working his way through a six-pack, when he got the idea that they should just continue down the highway two hundred miles to Florida.

His girlfriend begged him to let her out of the car. He drove off to Miami alone, where he survived by spending the night with women he met while playing pool and eating out of their refrigerators. He discovered gambling in Miami and a thrill that had little to do with winning. There was excitement in having everything at risk. For the first time in years, Jerry felt alive.

His father's threats, his insistence that Jerry come home and work for him, settled him down for a year or two. "But I felt like I was choking," Jerry remembers. "From the first day, he refused to listen to any of my ideas. He said I had no experience, but how was I supposed to get experience if he was always telling me what to do? I finally quit after three months to start a business of my own."

The business never materialized. He went back to school to study computer science and dropped out, bored. There were ideas for franchises, home businesses. His most recent girlfriend split after realizing he could not persistently carry out any of his plans. Watching her go, something snapped inside of him.

Today, his decadent days are past. Jerry completed a real estate course and passed the state exam. He has a respectable sales record, but his interest in real estate has begun to wane. He dreams of going back to school for a master's degree, but catalogs of graduate programs are gathering dust on his nightstand.

"My friends are settled into their careers, working their way into middle management positions, and it's depressing," he admits. "I keep thinking, 'This will finally make me happy' or 'That will change everything,' but it ends up being the same old thing. I think there's got to be something out there, somewhere. But I don't know what it is."

The problem: Psychological entitlement

When Jerry came into therapy, he was confused. "I don't know why it's so difficult to keep motivated. I don't know why I never get a break." There was no abuse, no neglect in his background that he could point at to account for his failures. If anything, his experience appeared to be the opposite. "My parents were always saying, 'You're so special, you're so bright. You can do anything.' But nobody trusted me to do it.

"I remember getting a C on a theme I wrote my junior year at high school, which meant a C for the course. With college applications already in the mail, waiting for my transcripts, my mother was livid. She marched right into school. 'I'm an English professor,' she assured the head of the department, 'and I can guarantee you that my son's analysis of *Tale of Two Cities* is very insightful.' Funny thing is, I never read *Tale of Two Cities* and she never read the paper. She probably scanned the first page, but she figured if I wrote it, it was outstanding. After all, I was her son."

Jerry's father was a brilliant man with little empathy for those not similarly endowed, who assumed his children were being obstinate if they couldn't comprehend an algebra problem or analyze the causes of the Civil War. One of Jerry's mistakes was asking his father to teach him to drive. "He got in the car, gin and tonic in hand. It was a stick shift, and the car kept jerking, and he was screaming, 'Watch it! I'm spilling my drink!' He stepped out of the car dazed and disappointed and angry at me. His son, after all, should have been able to get behind the wheel of a car for the first time and smoothly drive away."

Rude awakenings

Together, Jerry's parents drove home the message that he was a special child, and they expected him to accomplish great things. But the coupling of the messages "You're special and therefore should accomplish great things in your life" and "When things go wrong you're either not concentrating or it's someone else's fault" becomes a firm foundation for a lifetime spent feeling entitled to a lot and feeling emotionally devastated when it doesn't happen for you immediately.

Jerry suffers from something psychologists refer to as psychological entitlement. Entitlement is a set of projected expectations that the world will automatically treat us specially, rescue us, provide for us, appreciate us. The experience of having people tell us we are exceptional without having to provide any evidence to sustain it has far-reaching ramifications. With all Jerry was given, he never got what he really needed: motivation to gain a sense of competency through experience and permission to fail on the way to success.

Jerry felt entitled to many things. He felt entitled to have his girlfriend drop her life and accompany him to Florida. Once there he felt entitled to room and board in exchange for his company as a pool player. He felt entitled to his father's respect for his business acumen from the first day on the job. He felt entitled to immediate recognition, service, and respect.

Unfortunately, feelings of entitlement do not spring from self-confidence or an inherent ability to wrest the best from others. Feelings of entitlement are defenses against feelings of inferiority and shame. To avoid these feelings, we unconsciously pretend just the opposite. We overinflate ourselves to convince others that we are okay and that others should give us the praise and admiration we need. High expectations are foisted on an unsympathetic world. When people fail to respond the way our parents did, life becomes a rude awakening.

People like Jerry are bored and restless because they spend their lives waiting for something to happen. They've grown up being told of the talents, intelligence, beauty, and charm mother and father see in them, often overestimated because of their parents' own needs. They are disillusioned and bitter when this miracle life they are supposed to have doesn't materialize. Often they find themselves drifting through life, unable to find a meaningful career or a satisfying relationship, because the merely mundane, the day-to-day struggle that finally results in achievement is something they've never been willing to accept. Emotionally, they feel devastated. People like Jerry blame themselves and feel like failures even when they are quite successful.

Arthur Miller's famous play *Death of a Salesman* is a primer for anyone who has had the family role of the strong one, the bright one, the shining family star foisted on them. Willy Loman, the salesman, has struggled all his life for minimal success, and all of his dreams are wrapped up in his oldest son, Biff. Biff is going to be the one to make it. Biff is the "special" one. But Biff drifts through life, unable to work for anyone who gives him orders or who doesn't appreciate him the way his father assured him they would. After years of lies and despair, rage wells up inside. He tells his father: "Why am I trying to become what I don't want to be? What am I doing in an office, making a contemptuous, begging fool of myself, when all I want is out there, waiting for me the minute I say I know who I am! . . . I'm not bringing home any prizes, anymore, and you're going to stop waiting for me to bring them home!"

The pampered/deprived child

Some of us are immobilized by our parents' expectations. Others are immobilized by our parents, period.

"My father was teaching me to build a tree house," Bill, twenty-four, remembers. "I was hammering away, and he yelled, 'Hey, you're making half-moons!' He grabbed the hammer out of my hand. Soon he was building the tree house and I was inside watching TV. Almost everything was like that. I struggled and someone took it out of my hands and did it for me."

A curious thing happens in this kind of family. Fathers don't say, "Listen kid, this is your tree house. Don't leave me with the whole thing." Instead the whole family goes out to admire the tree house. "Look at the wonderful thing little Billy built," they say, and everyone pats Billy on the back. Billy smiles uncomfortably, feeling a deep sense of shame.

Bill is typical of the pampered/deprived child: pampered with attention, deprived of a feeling of competence. His mother and father saw it as their duty to solve their children's problems with whatever resources they had at their disposal. When it came to Bill's problems, they didn't just provide the solution—they became the solution.

Children like Bill become adults who have little faith in their own competence. These feelings stem from the reality of the experience with overly controlling and protective mothers or fathers who unintentionally robbed their children of feelings of competence by giving too much. Excessive doses of attention, money, and time in childhood deprive us of something very basic: a sense of competency, self-esteem, the drive to initiate, to persevere, to rely on ourselves. A childhood spent hearing that you're entitled to a lot, yet never being trusted to do much to get it, leaves people with pronounced dependency needs.

Parents do this with the best of intentions. Convinced that any childhood trauma will result in a lifetime of trouble, parents who love too much protect their child. Their sons and daughters will have an easier life than they did and never know frustration, sickness, loss, want, or unhappiness if they can help it. The overall message, "You mean everything to us and we pamper you because you deserve special treatment," is internalized through constant repetition and then projected onto the rest of the world.

The experience of having the people we love drop everything to rush in to solve our problems leads to problems in intimate relationships and careers, as well as nagging depression and joylessness. Bored, restless, and expectant, people like Bill drift through life, moving from job to job, relationship to relationship, waiting for something to make them happy. Such expectations lead to frustration and depression when the world doesn't pay attention to them, appreciate them, forgive them.

Gail, twenty-seven, hired a personal trainer after the birth of her second child. He was a popular trainer who was reluctant to take on more clients, but finally made an exception for Gail. His one stipulation was that she give him a twenty-four-hour notice before canceling or pay for the session. Gail's older daughter went to bed with an earache, and Gail phoned the trainer to cancel twenty hours before the session. The trainer insisted that she pay. "I was pissed as hell. I mean, what was the difference, twenty hours or twenty-four hours? I threatened to quit. I pulled out all the stops. I told him I was in the position to send him many more clients in the future, and if I quit it would be his loss."

The trainer never gave in. Gail never quit. In fact, this man has her grudging respect. "In my family there were no boundaries. There was never a rule without some exception. You just had to plead your case. Do I think I deserve special treatment? Probably. I feel impatient when things don't happen real quick. The doorman doesn't buzz me in right away and I'm angry. Customers who chitchat with the cashier while I'm waiting in line make me want to scream. Only lately, when I watch my daughters do the same thing and I'm the victim, do I start to see the costs."

There's a difference between entitled and spoiled

It's easy to confuse the concept of entitlement with being "spoiled." As therapists, we're constantly amazed at how unspoiled some people who suffer from entitlement really are. Spoiled is getting everything you want. Entitled is getting everything someone else thinks you need to become what they want. The entitled child may open a slew of Christmas presents and find nothing inside that he wants. He doesn't get the Power Rangers because Mom and Dad don't want him to grow up with violent fantasies. But he gets a top-of-the-line computer because his education is his parents' priority. He's being honed and groomed and the message is, he'd better produce.

The truth about boredom and restlessness

Let's take a closer look at boredom for a minute. Boredom is often a response manufactured to cover feelings of awkwardness we experience when we find ourselves out of the familiar role of being the special one, the one everyone pays attention to, the child everyone is fascinated with. The simple act of listening without jumping in to interrupt may be a formidable task if you were raised in a family where everyone was captivated by your point of view.

We have seen clients unconsciously try to create a crisis in their lives, just to get back in the spotlight where they are comfortable. These crises only create more entitlement and more discontent.

Entitlement plays the most havoc in our most intimate relationships.

"My husband is so boring," a client recently complained. She had good reasons. All he talked to her about was work. She's struggling with the nausea of a first pregnancy, consumed with plans for the arrival of their baby and a thousand ways her life will change. She's bitter because her husband wants her to continue working part time.

Her two best friends gave notice the second after they stood in their bathroom testing their urine against a home pregnancy test. Why should she still have to work? "I want to share the details with him, because I want him to share the experience with me. I want him to be a real father to our child."

A reasonable and realistic request. But what's really going on here?

Her husband felt that she shared so many details of her pregnancy, for hours at a time, that his eyes glazed over. She cut him off midsentence when he mentioned anything about his own life that didn't directly concern her and the baby. As far as her working, yes, she has a point considering how tired she gets, how much responsibility lies ahead of her.

What's really hard for her to see is that he would gladly agree that she stay home if they didn't both want so many things for their child. He talks about his work not because he's needy or isn't excited about their baby. He really values her opinion. He wants to know what she thinks. No one else matters as much.

This woman's entitlement feelings didn't come from being overly protected and nurtured. She's had a difficult past. There was a voice in her head that would go off at times and it would say, "I suffered so much; I deserve something in return. It should all equal out; I'm entitled." She spent many years doing little with her life, avoiding opportunities. In some ways it was an attempt to have the childhood she'd never had. The men she was attracted to in those days gave her everything—except credit for having a brain.

Thinking back on those days while she spoke about them in therapy put a whole new spin on what was happening in her marriage. "I'm starting to see that my husband is exactly the kind of man I need. He won't let me be his baby. He doesn't want to play daddy to a child and a wife. He isn't going to solve every one of my problems like some genie in a bottle. I was so bitter about this until I understood what it meant. I'd finally found a person who believed in me, who trusted me as an equal."

It's so hard to see. When someone won't rise to our highest expectations, it's easy to think that they're wrong, selfish, insensitive, stubborn. But maybe we're being asked to give a little more because someone else has finally seen that we have a valuable contribution. We have some competence in life. We have something to give. We don't need a provider. We are our own provider.

Boredom and self-sabotage

There is probably nothing on Earth that many of us feel entitled to more than money. You may be reading this chapter thinking, *But I really am entitled to more. Look at what I contribute. Look at how hard I work.*

We aren't going to argue with you. There are millions of people who are simply not paid what they are worth. And then, there are people like Robert.

"I had four jobs in five years. Each time I left for more money, more opportunities. I was bored to death; I'd come home from meetings so mad I was ready to bite huge chunks out of my living room sofa. Everything moved so slow. Everything was politics. Everyone was trying to save face. I was ready to take the ball and run with it, but these companies were so provincial. I was sitting at a computer, crunching numbers until I thought I'd die.

"I'll tell you the truth about those jobs. I left every one of them right when I was about to be promoted. Those promotions didn't seem to be enough. The road ahead seemed too long. But that wasn't really it. When I mastered my job—and I did it quickly—I'd get restless. When they'd give me better projects to work on, it just didn't seem enough. I saw some grand flaw in the company structure. Some compelling reason why I was in the wrong corporate culture. I could be doing so much more with my life. That's what I told myself. Then I'd mess up or quit.

"The truth is, I got restless because I was scared. Scared that people were counting on me. Scared that I was going to become a slave to the company. Scared that I'd have to produce at even higher and higher levels, all the time, and it would never end. I admit there were times I thought, *I shouldn't have to work.*"

The restlessness that comes from feeling entitled to more, may, in fact, be a sign that you're underchallenged, or overlooked. But boredom is often a defense against anxiety. It's an emotional coasting, a shutdown of feelings while we go through the motions. And some of those feelings may be doubts about our own competence—not only in our skills but in our fortitude. *Do I really have what it takes? Am I willing to give up the dream of the quick fix, the easy ride?* What scared Robert was doubts about his own capability. He wanted more money, more power, but he ran from it.

Think about the last time you were in a meeting and you were really bored. Was it your meeting? Were you in charge? Probably not. Did you say much? When the meeting went off track, when people began to speak just to hear themselves talk, did you try to get the meeting back on track? Or did you sit there fantasizing about what you'd really like to tell all of these people? Were you anxious because you felt you couldn't say what needed to be said, and then bored because your only choice was to stare at your watch?

Analytic abilities get rusty from lack of use. A lifetime as a special child convinces us that everything we undertake must be special. This is immobilizing.

"I remember Statistics 401," says a woman who suffered through one of the nation's most rigorous MBA programs. "The professor spoke English he learned off a Berlitz tape. And the content of the course was inane stuff like: There are twelve goldfish in a bowl, and some are blue and some are red, and what is the probability that the one who floats to the top, dead from lack of food, is a red goldfish?

"I decided from the first day that I would have to find some hungry grad student and pay him to get me through this course. Proficiency with statistics had nothing to do with any future I could foresee for myself. But there were people in that class who raised their hands every minute, asked a thousand questions, made the professor go over those goldfish again and again. Couldn't they see that it didn't matter? *Just get through it, idiots,* I thought. I sat there bored out of my mind. I resented those people, mostly because they thought they could get this man to say something comprehensible. I was so restless I sat through the midterm, cracking my gum, until the girl across the table gave me a look that could kill."

This student has a valid point. To her way of thinking, she's right. Professors should make the content understandable to students. Statistics as a body of knowledge means little to a vast number of students who have to study it. But there's an old saying: You can be right or you can be happy. And this habit of feeling entitled to more but not believing in her own competence to achieve it had more vast ramifications in her life than any subject matter.

Boredom is a defense. She decided she couldn't understand the class from the first day. She saw no option but to read magazines during class and watch the clock.

If you're bored and restless, chances are you also feel powerless over your present circumstances. This is the key issue. Until you solve it, you end up thinking, *When is enough, enough?*

Do you set yourself up for disappointment?

If boredom is a defense, restlessness and the cranky behavior that follows it is an offense. Entitlement is hard to give up because it seems like a solution rather than a problem.

Often one hears how we must feel we're truly deserving of happiness to have it; "If I believe it, I'll see it." One would think wanting so much would drive us to achieve more, or try harder.

The important thing to understand is that entitlement isn't active. It's a passive response to the world, and that is why it's a setup for disappointment. Consider the following statements made by clients who suffered from an unconscious sense of entitlement, boredom, and restlessness and see if you can recognize the passivity:

♦ "I realize that the type of woman I want is attracted to guys who make big bucks. That's why I don't date."

♦ "I'm not going to work for $20,000 a year. That would barely pay my bills."

♦ "I'm fascinated by the law, but it takes six years to become a lawyer and then you end up writing briefs."

♦ "I know I could have my own business—not some little coffee shop, but a chain that would give Starbucks a run for its money—but I just can't discipline myself."

♦ "Work in a bookstore while I'm working on my novel? I think it would break my concentration. What I really need is a collaborator. Someone who will go fifty-fifty: I'll tell the story and they'll write it."

Why it will never be enough

Unfortunately, things don't just come to us because we feel we deserve them. While dreaming is a strong tool for working through a creative process, it does not make relationships, careers, or money appear, automatically, in our lives. The belief that all of your fantasies will come true, that things will always work out for you, that you deserve it automatically, that others are at fault if you can't achieve it, is part of the baggage you carried out of your past.

It's never enough, for the following reasons:

❧ *You may miss opportunities while you're waiting to be noticed.* Further, you spend much of the time waiting for something from the outside to make you happy. As Ruth, thirty-four, explained: "When I was a kid and I was unhappy, I would sit at the dinner table, pushing the food around on my plate, and everything would stop. My mother would beg me to tell her what was wrong, until she finally got it out of me.

"The first time I went into group therapy, I came in depressed. I sat quietly, playing with the button on my shirt. People just kept on talking. When I didn't say anything, someone stepped in and took my twenty minutes! I paid for those twenty minutes. The therapist didn't stop her either, and I thought this was so unfair I almost quit the group. But this is my problem. I keep waiting for someone else to jump in, tell me what's wrong, and fix me."

You, too, may find that you have unconscious expectations that others should be stronger, give you more, and be overly sensitive to your needs. You may feel frustrated because other people so often let you down. You may feel that you're endlessly searching for the right relationship. The perfect job. Friends who will really understand you. The tutor who can motivate your son to learn fractions. When it doesn't happen, you're stubborn. You walk out of the parent-teacher conference. You take your little red wagon and go home. You make your point. But you come home to, *What now? What next? When is enough, enough?*

❦ *You may disregard your greatest talents.* We have watched clients throw away opportunities to use and enjoy their real talents because those talents weren't "enough." For example, a pianist who was unemployed shook his head in disbelief at the suggestion that he might find work playing background music in restaurants. Unless he was playing with the symphony, it wouldn't be enough. What if one of his friends came in and saw him playing jazz standards in a bar? Never mind that he might have enjoyed it. Joy wasn't the point.

Too often entitlement feelings cause us to sabotage our own success. It's rare for people with the type of family experience that fosters entitlement to fashion their careers around talents or instincts. More often they spend their time scanning the trade papers for the next big opportunity, the ten best-paying careers, the deal that will allow them to jump to the finish line.

❦ *You may suffer from "demand resistance."* Demand resistance is a chronic negative response to obligations or expectations. It is almost always unconscious. You make daily lists of things to do, then grow angry and anxious when it's time to get moving. You resent anything that smacks of being told what to do, even returning a phone call or asking a friend to dinner.

Controlling parents and teachers foster demand resistance: "Take out the garbage, now. I said, *now.*" What sweet revenge to leave the lid off the can so the trash flies all over the alley. Do it often enough, and you won't be elected for this particular job anymore.

Demand resistance has at least four possible functions we can think of. Others may stop making the demands and do it for you. By withholding what another requests of you, you assert your power. You can avoid doing things you're afraid to do, on principle, and avoid coming face to face with possible failure. You avoid letting other people overrun you, without having to engage in more active types of conflict.

There's a tremendous cost. Pleasurable activities, such as working out at a health club or taking a class in Italian cooking, must be performed outstandingly or given up completely. You find yourself constantly setting goals and sabotaging them, making demands of yourself and resisting them. You are always angry at yourself.

The more sure you are of yourself, the more you work on building a strong sense of who you are, the less you'll feel vulnerable to being overrun or resisting your goals just to prove a point.

❧ *Feeling entitled keeps you on the periphery of life.* Marianne Williamson, author of *A Return to Love,* says that the reason so many of us are obsessed with being stars is that we're not yet starring in our own lives. Competence in childhood grows into adult self-confidence. But being rescued by our parents leaves us with few resources to deal with frustration. We become adults who avoid challenges. And being abused by our parents leaves us with even less. We feel entitled to more, and don't have the least idea of a way to go about getting it.

But would being acknowledged as the star soothe the anxieties that drive us into so much self-sabotage? There is an exercise we do in our groups that often brings one particular cost of entitlement into focus. We give a member of the group the assignment of "Prince" or "Princess." That person has a special seat, away from everyone else. There's much laughter and kidding as each group member bestows gifts and special greetings. The Prince or Princess doesn't have to participate in any work. If he or she does, everyone nods and automatically agrees.

Everyone asks to be taken off this assignment after a couple of weeks. They learn that it's tedious not being a real part of the group. The praise and presents aren't earned. Therefore, they have no value.

❧ *You may try to escape your emptiness and boredom through addictions.* Drinking, gambling, and eating may be used to alter your mood. You seek stimulation, and these activities provide it momentarily. Obtaining your drug of choice, driving yourself to the track, preparing a feast takes up hours of your time. Many people in recovery talk about how amazing it is to have hours and hours to fill now that they're no longer filling time servicing an addiction.

RX: Your Prescription for Change

Responsibility means not blaming anyone or anything for your situation, including yourself. It is the ability to have a creative response to the situation as it is now.

—DEEPAK CHOPRA

What you need to understand about yourself

Given your history, it's understandable that life seems unfair and that you might be unconsciously ambivalent about success. But when you conquer self-doubt, you will unleash enormous energy.

The key questions

- How much do I really believe in my abilities?
- Do I expect people to cater to me?
- When people request things of me, do I instinctively resist, against my own best interest?

Where you need to focus

- on building your competence
- on developing empathy
- on learning to tolerate frustration
- on overcoming demand resistance

The cognitive shift

- I can accept that no one owes me anything in life.
- Other people's needs and opinions needn't be an imposition.
- I can tolerate unpleasant feelings.
- My life is of my own making; I can provide for myself.

Thoughts and Exercises

❧ *Take a self-assessment.* You may have had experiences in your family that are similar to those of the people you've read about in this chapter. Or, your experience may have been quite different. How can you tell if your boredom and restlessness result from entitlement? Try the following quiz.

1. You're telling a story about a strange thing that happened to you last Saturday night. You're in the middle of your story when someone interrupts you, and you realize no one is interested in hearing the end. You feel

   a. Amused. You think, *I guess you had to be there.*
   b. Irritated. It's rude to be interrupted.

c. Angry. It's a great story and this is the kind of thing that can ruin your evening.

2. Your company is allowing you sixty dollars a day for expenses while you are on a business trip. You skipped lunch and ended up having fast food for dinner. You've spent a total of twenty dollars. Back in your room you

   a. Watch TV. You don't need to spend every dollar of a business expense.
   b. Find a way to spend a little extra.
   c. Order a massage or a bottle of fine wine. It's your obligation to spend it all.

3. You and a friend are waiting to be seated at a table in a popular restaurant. The host directs you to a table for two. You spy a table for four in the corner, but the host says the policy of the restaurant is only to seat larger parties at larger tables. You

   a. Sit at the table for two not too unhappily. Restaurants have a right to make money.
   b. Tell the host that you feel this is a bad policy and have a hard time enjoying your meal.
   c. Ask to speak to the manager and demand to be seated at the table for four.

4. You've been seeing a therapist for a problem in your marriage and this is your fifth session. When you sit down, your therapist says, "How are you?" What sounds most like something you'd say?

   a. "Fair. How are you?"
   b. "Not good. We've been fighting all week. Let me tell you what she said to me last night. . . ."
   c. "I don't think this therapy is doing any good. It's been five sessions and I still feel depressed."

5. You're boarding a plane with your spouse and the flight attendant points to your seats—one aisle, one middle. There's a rather large gentleman sitting in the window seat. Where do you sit?

   a. Depends. My spouse and I negotiate.
   b. Definitely the aisle. I get claustrophobic and I have long legs.
   c. This wouldn't happen. You'd have the flight attendants rearrange the plane until they found you a more comfortable seat.

6. You're dining with four of your friends. When the check comes, you grab it to

   a. Pay for everyone.
   b. See how much you owe.
   c. See how much everyone else owes; you don't trust other people to do the math.

7. When you get angry

   a. You try to be fair.
   b. You can usually get people to do what you want.
   c. You won't give in until you get what you want.

8. Your date suggests a movie that you don't want to see and she doesn't want to see the one you want to see. You

   a. Keep suggesting movies until you find one you both want to see.
   b. Go to see her movie and pout all night.
   c. Demand that she see your movie and suggest that if you don't have the same tastes the relationship is probably doomed.

9 Which of the following choices best describes you?

    a. An achiever
    b. A procrastinator
    c. An underachiever

10. You want a big screen television, and your spouse thinks it's a waste of money. You

    a. Try to compromise. You'll get the TV and your spouse will get something he or she wants.
    b. Tell your spouse it's unfair, that you work hard, and that you deserve to buy whatever you want, and keep whining about it until he or she gives in.
    c. Buy the TV no matter what your spouse thinks. After all, you deserve some things in life.

11. You are being asked to work overtime four nights in a row, even though you aren't going to be paid for it. You feel

    a. Not thrilled, but this is part of the job.
    b. Angry and used. You complain to management.
    c. Justified in not staying overtime, so you say you have an emergency and can't stay.

12. Your closest friend is angry with you. What do you do?

    a. Find out what's wrong, explain your intentions, and apologize if necessary.
    b. Avoid your friend until he or she gets over it.
    c. Make a list of reasons why you're equally angry at your friend, and fire away the second you're accused of doing anything wrong.

If the majority of your answers are Bs and Cs, suspect that entitlement plays a role in your life. Suspect it even more if you're also bored, restless, disappointed, yet immobilized.

❧ *Concentrate less on goals and more on building competence.* There's no mystery to building competence. It just takes fortitude. You stop being the "idea person" and start being the "doer." You stop waiting for such things as more time, more money, a relationship, for your children to be grown, and realize that everything you need is here right now. You get out of your head and into your life.

Understand that boredom and restlessness is often protective. There's an underlying vulnerability from not trusting your competence. Your basic sense of self-confidence and independence has been damaged and your primary focus must be on rebuilding it. This will dispel your feeling of boredom and restlessness more than any single thing. Taking ownership of your thoughts, emotions, and interpersonal patterns is what is needed here.

❧ *Take on the list of tasks you typically avoid or delegate.* These might include the laundry, taxes, finding your keys, planning your vacation. Determine the benefits and costs to delegating.

Jim, twenty-seven, discussed the costs and benefits to having his father do his income taxes:

JIM: My father is an accountant. He's also a perfectionist. When he does my taxes, I know I won't miss any deductions.

THERAPIST: You're right. That's a definite advantage. Are your taxes complicated?

JIM: Not very. Nothing much has changed from last year. The deductions are the same; I could probably pretty much copy last year's form. But he enjoys doing the taxes.

THERAPIST: Do you enjoy having him do it?

JIM: Well, I enjoy not having to do the work. I hate forms. But, you mean, do I enjoy going over there and sitting down with him and all those papers? To be honest, we end up arguing. He hates the way I keep records.

THERAPIST: Are you happy with your record keeping?

JIM: Not especially. But it's my life, you know? I don't appreciate being lectured like a ten-year-old. And then there's something uncomfortable about having someone like my father know my whole financial picture. He rants about how little I'm saving, how I'm not planning for retirement.

THERAPIST: So, by having your father do your taxes, you save the discomfort of dealing with forms. But you gain the discomfort of being treated like a child.

JIM: I never looked at it that way, but, yes. And I wonder if it's worth it.

❧ *Pick one new task each week to take on yourself and finish it.* Competence is built through experience and no one can teach you that. You can have a library of self-help books, but without action steps, you will stay stuck. Remember that change is an accumulation of small successes. When you hear that demand-resistant voice in your head, quiet it by firmly telling yourself, "I can finish this regardless of how I feel." Acknowledge yourself at finishing—you will have a strong tendency to minimize this accomplishment.

❧ *Be wary of impulsiveness.* When we're feeling bored and restless we can use it as an excuse not to finish something, or to quickly jump from career to career, relationship to relationship, seeking that feeling of being alive. Don't use restlessness as a cue that it is time to move on. Ask yourself, *What else might be going on here? Am I afraid of something? Am I anxious? Do I feel hopeless about having any impact on this situation?*

June, forty-two, was told at her year-end review that her consistent tardiness had been noticed and that it could stand in the way of her promotion. June was livid. "They didn't take into consideration that I stay late every day. They all have children, so they're in the office at seven so they can leave at five. But that's not my lifestyle and I don't see why I should be penalized for it." The next morning, she was late again. She was late for the next two weeks until she finally realized what was happening. "It was my old entitlement—you can't tell me what to do. But I suddenly saw that I was making an issue out of a nonissue. I was giving them a reason not to give me a promotion, because, frankly, I felt that if they valued me as an employee, they'd cater to my schedule."

You have value. You do not have to prove it by being late to show you are above the rules. When others aren't noticing our strengths, it's often because we aren't accepting them either.

❧ *Notice how you may be attracting codependent rescuers into your life.* "I was thirty years old and still taking $800 a month allowance from my parents," one man told us. "It was like a ritual, Sunday brunch and a check. As my father would hand me the money I would gaze downward and mumble thanks. Not another word was said.

"My therapist pointed out that the money was taking a significant toll on my self-esteem. I told her, 'But they can afford it; they have over a million dollars in the bank! I don't have anything.' She asked how I felt when I took the money. The truth was I tried not to think about it. I felt ashamed.

"The greater truth, however, was that I didn't feel like I could make that kind of money on my own. I never had an experience of providing for myself financially. My parents had helped me every step of the way. They paid for college through a master's degree and sent money along the way. Taking money was the familiar thing to do and they didn't seem to mind at all.

"A part of me agreed that I should stop taking the money, but it took a year and a half of therapy to actually tell my parents to stop giving me the money. It was incredibly hard to stop rationalizing, 'But they have so much more!'

"As my own income started to increase, I took the leap. We cut back to $400 a month, then eventually to nothing. I felt a sense of pride in paying my own bills. I started feeling better about myself."

What's hard on your self-esteem these days? What compromises, shortcuts, relationship situations are taking a toll? Isn't it time to say, enough is enough?

❧ ❧

Today I will look to myself for the answers, and I will believe in my ability to find those answers.

❧ ❧

CHAPTER SIX

Why Can't I Find
The Right Person?

The Search for a Mirror

When I was on the search for the cosmic mate,
I tended to exclude people like myself.

—ANN WILSON SCHAEF

"**I**'m not looking for much," Vanessa, a thirty-nine-year-old architect, says when asked about the kind of man she'd love to meet. "Just
someone who's intelligent. Independent. Good looking. Exciting. It
wouldn't hurt if he had money, either."

Does Vanessa ever meet anyone like this? "Sure. There was Jack.
He was smart, successful—a CPA. He looked great on paper. But after
six months, something was missing for me."

Is she frustrated? "Sure, at times. But what am I supposed to do?
Just settle for anyone who comes along?"

Mark, thirty-four, would agree. He met Cheryl in Chicago's
Belmont Harbor at the sandy spot dog lovers call Doggy Beach. Mark
was tossing a Frisbee into the water to his black Labrador when a
golden retriever splashed into the game and took off with it. The two
dogs were growling ominously on the beach when a young woman
leaped into the fray. By the time he got his Frisbee back, Mark knew
two things: The dog's name was Adonis, and his owner was sexy as
hell. Tall. Confident. Thick, chestnut brown hair swinging almost to
her waist.

From a strange beginning, Mark and Cheryl hit it off immediately. There was something earthy about Cheryl, almost elemental. Mark, who was used to dating MBAs, found himself on unfamiliar turf. Cheryl did desktop publishing on her home computer to pay the rent, but her passion was ceramics. He'd come to her door and she'd be covered in clay. By July, their dogs were buddies. By August, he was thinking he was in love.

By September, she was talking about relationships. He was suddenly noticing that it took her twenty minutes to order food in a restaurant. And she read romance novels by the truckload, books he considered trash. Worse was the way she managed her business. He took a look at her accounts one evening. When he suggested that she lean a little harder on the people who owed her money, she balked, and the argument that followed was heated. "And she wasn't going anywhere with her ceramics either, for all of her talk about being an artist. She had talent, I guess, but most of the time she starved. I wondered, am I going to end up taking care of her?"

He picked and picked and picked. Sometimes he made her cry and then he'd feel terrible. Consumed with guilt, he'd buy her flowers.

One night friends from work invited him out. There were pitchers of margaritas and in the tequila-infused camaraderie, Mark grabbed the hand of an assistant account executive and held it to his lips for a long moment. "It meant nothing to either of us, but it meant everything to Cheryl who knew about it by nine the next morning and told me she'd had enough."

Mark tried to talk to her, but she wouldn't listen to him. "'I never lied to you,' I reasoned. 'I never talked about marriage.' In my own ears it sounded self-serving. My head was aching and I thought, 'I'm making the mistake of my life letting her go.'"

It wasn't any easier when his friends heard the news. They looked at him in wonder and said: "What possessed you, man? She's beautiful. She's creative. She's crazy about you. When is enough, enough?"

Mark was philosophical. "I don't know why her income became an

Issue. I have more money than I need. I kept thinking that she wasn't smart enough and that it would bother me over time."

That was eight months ago. He's had two relationships since. One lasted two months and the other two weeks.

The other night he was standing in a line at the movies when he saw Cheryl and her new boyfriend. Mark went up to her. The three of them chatted until it was time to take their seats. Mark barely watched the film. For two hours his eyes were constantly drawn to the row ahead where the couple sat. "The guy seemed like a nice guy. He kept looking at Cheryl like she was the most incredible woman in the world."

Something about it hurt. All he ever met, it seemed, were women who were wrong for him. Too fat. Too short. Too sensitive. Too aggressive. Obsessed with marriage. Obsessed with their careers.

"My expectations might be high," Mark concluded, "but what should I do? I keep thinking, if I keep searching, I'll finally get it right." Yet there are moments when Mark is home after another worthless evening and wonders: "Why can't I like this person? Why can't I find someone? What's wrong with me? Why am I never satisfied?"

When good enough isn't good enough

If you identify with Mark, dissatisfied with love and searching for more, chances are there has been a moment when you've asked yourself a pivotal question: *Is there really something missing in this relationship? Or is it me?*

In *Perfect Women,* author Colette Dowling writes about people who are involved in what seems like an endless search for the right person. She calls it "shopping for a star." It involves much more than looking for a person who will truly care about us, Dowling believes. Often it's searching for perfection in another person. "The wish for a perfect lover is connected to a deep sense of inferiority and a need to compensate for that feeling," Dowling writes. Although Dowling is writing about women, her theory holds for men as well. Although star searchers point to a lover's faults for why the relationship never got off the ground, it is often the shortcomings they perceive in themselves that cause them to quickly perceive others as "not good enough." What they are looking for in a lover is someone who will complete them. It may seem that there is never anyone attractive, intelligent, wealthy, or exciting enough to give us a feeling of self-worth and compensate for what we feel is lacking in ourselves.

The unconscious goal of a star search is to find a "mirror"—someone to define us and tell us who we are. Why should we need this? It's because we have a vague sense of our identities.

In childhood, we needed our parents to mirror us in order to gain a sense of wholeness and separateness. In the simplest terms, mirroring is a reaction of another person to us which gives us back information about ourselves. In childhood, it's this simple: "Look how big you're getting. I know you're excited, but hold still. You really love applesauce, don't you? Hello, beautiful."

Statements such as these are the rudimentary beginnings of a sense of identity. If all goes well, we'll get a thousand messages that tell us we're unique and special.

Mirroring doesn't end in childhood. People are constantly mirroring back to you information about yourself as you interact with them.

In the best of circumstances, we have a core so strong that it isn't constantly shaken by the reactions of other people. With a solid identity, we have the tools to assess other people's responses to us. We say, "This fits" or "He doesn't really know or understand me, which is why he reacts that way." That core, or foundation, is strongest when our parents were good mirrors.

But some parents are inadequate mirrors, to put it mildly.

A woman we'll call Linda phoned in one day when we were doing a radio talk show in Detroit right after *When Parents Love Too Much* was published. "Are you doing a sequel? I think you should do a chapter on my mother," she said.

This is the story she told us: "I always wanted to be an artist, and finally I talked her into letting me take art lessons one summer. I brought home my first painting, something I was really proud of, and my mother took one look at it and said, 'Bring me a brush, dear. Let me fix it.'"

At that point the phone lines lit up. The calls continued to pour in as she spoke about a lifelong love/hate relationship with her mother's advice. "I'd tell her to mind her own business, but it didn't matter. If she didn't agree with something, I couldn't do it and enjoy it. Like when I begged to go to overnight camp. 'You'll hate it,' she told me. 'They sleep in tents and there are bugs.' I won that battle, but do you think I enjoyed a moment of camp? I sat in the tent scratching my mosquito bites, making up stories in letters home so I wouldn't hear my mother say, 'I told you so.'

"And I always knew how she felt about anyone I dated in an instant. I'd have a guy over and when he left, I'd go up to her. Carefully keeping my voice casual, hating myself, I'd say, 'So what did you think?' She'd say, 'He seemed nice. Were his parents born in this country?' That would be it."

Four years of being away from home at college seemed to loosen Linda's dependence on her mother's advice. "And I fell in love. Really in love. I never imagined any other life after college that didn't include Vincent." But it all fell apart a week before graduation when Vincent stunned Linda by telling her he'd decided not to go into his father's business. "He wanted to be his own man. He didn't feel he could respect himself if he just followed in his dad's footsteps in a business he had no interest in.

"I couldn't believe he'd walk away from a vice presidency at a major company for some silly idealistic nonsense.

"He told me I was beginning to sound like my mother, and that really stung. I knew exactly what she'd say about marrying a man with no prospects. I looked at him in disgust. He was a dreamer." On that note, it ended.

Linda's in her thirties now, and it's a decision she still deeply regrets. Vincent was close to being everything she wanted, but marriage to a man who seemed to be searching for himself didn't fit in with her expectations about the type of person she should marry. For Linda, love and affection with someone who really cared about her wasn't enough, and for good reason. Little in her history encouraged a strong sense of self or competence. She was subtly encouraged to be dependent on her mother, taught that she should disregard her own judgments. Her mother had tremendous expectations for her, and especially for the type of lifestyle a husband should provide her with.

One can argue that everything Linda's mother did came out of love and her desire for Linda to be happy. But there was another emotion deeper than love that drove Linda's mother. It was fear. Fear that Linda couldn't make it on her own. Fear that Linda would end up deprived. When Linda looked into her mother's eyes, these fears were mirrored back.

Linda internalized these fears. It became essential to find the "right" person who would be so strong, so wealthy, so stable, that he would fill in the missing places within herself and allay her fears.

When we grow up under an avalanche of expectations and fears that have more to do with a parent's fantasies than our reality, it has vast ramifications for our relationships with others. We meet someone and make a quick assessment of their strengths and weaknesses. *She's my age, but I think I'd be happier with someone younger. . . . He's got a great career, but he's not creative.*

If our parents failed to be adequate mirrors because they saw us as extensions of their own needs and wishes, we gained a shaky sense of separateness. We feel incomplete within ourselves. Our feeling of wholeness depends on linking ourselves to someone who makes us feel whole, who has what we think we lack. The extent to which we went unmirrored in childhood determines how "perfect" a person we'll have to find to make us feel complete enough to fall in love.

Falling in and out of love

Some people who struggle with these issues never date much. They know within ten minutes over coffee that this person is not the one, and they feel, why bother. But others fall hard, and sometimes, often. Brian's story is a case in point.

When Brian's parents divorced, he was six years old. His parents argued over his summer vacations, custody rights, and child support. "But it wasn't because they were all that concerned with my best interests, although I wanted deeply to believe that. They were much more interested in hurting each other.

"The truth is, my mother fell apart without my father. She didn't know how to do anything. Every time I'd come home from a weekend with him, she'd pump me for information about who he was seeing. There were times I took a certain joy in telling her. I wanted her to get on with her life. It was killing her, and I wanted her to forget about my father. My father had certainly forgotten about her. You'd have to see him to understand. He's what you'd call powerful looking, and he knows it.

"Once he dated a woman who was in her early twenties. He invited her to dinner with us. I was thirteen. I don't think I said a word the entire evening. Later he said to me, 'I just wanted to let you know that I can still get prime stuff.'"

Somewhere along the road of childhood, Brian became his mother's confidant and emotional support. And Brian became a responsible, adult-like teen, quiet and conscientious, ever wary of his mother's moods.

He was fifteen when it happened for the first time. At a party he met a friend's older sister, home for the weekend from college. Two nights later they made love in her car. "I don't know why I did it. The challenge I guess. And she told me I was different and wonderful, and I guess I wanted so badly to hear someone say that. It was only afterwards that I realized I wasn't even remotely attracted to her."

The young woman fell completely for Brian. "I should have ended it there, but instead I let it go on, and when I finally broke it off it not only cost me the girl but her brother who was a good friend."

It was the beginning of a pattern for Brian, stimulating sex followed by a total loss of interest. "She'd want me to meet her folks and I'd suddenly be thinking, 'This is definitely not the *one.*'"

Still, Brian often stayed months in a relationship he was ambivalent about. He was reluctant to end it because he hated to hurt another person. He often behaved so poorly that the other person eventually rejected him.

People like Brian receive distorted mirroring in childhood that gives them the impression that they are supposed to fill in the void of the missing parent. It's an impossible scenario for a child, but many children try to fulfill this role. They feel obligated to make people feel better, to accept a host of other people's problems as their responsibility. And many believe, often unconsciously, that if they were really lovable, the missing parent wouldn't have left.

Brian, as a separate person with feelings and needs of his own, was practically invisible to both of his parents. Stimulating sex made him feel "alive." But once it was over, he re-created the drama by taking too much responsibility in relationships and later seeing the relationships as engulfing. His relationships were a spiral of too much responsibility, resentment, guilt, and a need to distance the other person.

Is it passion, or paranoia?

People like Brian often complain that what's missing in their relationships is passion. "I care about her, I really do; but I don't feel any passion. Maybe this sounds ridiculous, but I want someone to dig her nails into my back and scream when we're making love."

What's impossible to miss about many of the people who share this complaint is their tight shoulders, their quiet, almost passive voices, their shallow breathing. Sometimes they speak of passion with virtually no expression in their voices at all.

If you're currently in a relationship where you are discontented because you want to feel a little passion for the other person, we ask you this: Are you feeling passion anywhere else in your life? Is your work exciting and involving? Is there a purpose in your life that thrills you? Do you go through your day feeling fully alive?

Many men and women complain that they can't feel passion in a relationship, but the real problem is that they don't feel passion, period. They're bored to tears by their careers, bored by their friends, and the things that make them feel alive are few and far between. They're looking at life waiting for something to happen, for something they can care deeply about to appear on the horizon so they can cast off this emotional numbness. They exist in some neutral territory where life isn't so bad, but isn't really very good, either.

Brian describes the last time he felt passion. "It was with a woman named Ann. I couldn't concentrate at work. When she'd finally return my call, my heart would beat faster. She seemed so distant at times. She was still carrying a torch for a guy she dated in college. We'd make love and it would be incredible."

Trouble is, that queasy feeling, the wondering—*Will he call? Does she like me?*—the heightened excitement Brain felt when she seemed distant wasn't passion. It was paranoia.

Those of us who grew up invisible, as Brian did, have such a hunger for a response from a distant, uninvolved person that we've confused passion with the intensity of our need for validation. Real unconditional appreciation of our truest selves was lacking in childhood. Love wasn't a given but a battle that resulted in short-lived victory or defeat, and passion became confused with suffering and frustration. Intimate relationships that move past the stage of second-guessing seem boring and empty because the thirst is more familiar than the water.

Looking for love in all the wrong places

Sarah grew up in a family where people had few aspirations, where bills were paid to collection agencies, and everyone spent hours arguing over television channels. "In my family it was a big deal when May rolled around and they could blow up the plastic pool. They spent the summer drinking Meister Braus and eating double-stuffed Oreos."

Her parents never gave her one reason to hope that she'd ever have some other kind of life. The entire family used to call her Miss High and Mighty for her habit of sitting in her room studying at night and dreaming of going to college.

Sarah never went to college, but she did make it out. She earned her high-profile job in one of Chicago's top advertising agencies by being strong, being driven; and there's no vulnerability about her.

Sarah dates driven guys, success stories, like herself. She's looking to get married, but she is often disappointed and bored with whatever man she's seeing after only a few dates. Her friends have started to tease her that she'll never be happy with anyone. "I think the trouble is that I don't like corporate types, and that's all I'm meeting. I think I'd be more attracted to an entrepreneur, who made it from nothing, like I have."

Sarah may think that she's found the antidote, but in truth she's never satisfied because she's climbing a ladder that's against the wrong wall. Sarah's been possessed for years with a driving need to show her parents, "See I've succeeded." They never notice. Though Sarah believes it's because she's not yet successful enough, it's really because they don't understand Sarah's type of success and never have.

No matter what a potential lover offers Sarah, it will never be enough because she consistently chooses men who can't give her the one thing she craves: a feeling of intimacy. What Sarah needs from a relationship is what her family denied her—a feeling that she's not an outsider. Why can't the men she dates give her that? They are die-hard workaholics. Most know little about intimacy, and even if they did, it isn't a priority. Their work is so all-encompassing that they alienate anyone who tries to come close.

So what does one do, beyond looking for the next fish in the same pond? You deal with the wound. You stop doing the same thing hoping for different results. You put the mirror on yourself.

Why it will never be enough

Obviously if you've dated five or six people in your life and you haven't found the right person, what you really need is to give your self time. It's those of us who meet many potential partners and who are never satisfied who need to suspect that something more is going on here.

It's so difficult to see, but the answer doesn't lie in finding a person with more external achievements. The "not enough" is coming from within you. In some ways, you don't want to buy that someone really is enough. You get too much mileage over the whole drama of it not being enough.

Underneath the drama is a lot of ambivalence about intimacy, fears of engulfment: *Will I have to give up all my freedom? Will this person smother me? Will this person devour me with so many needs that there will be nothing left of me?* Or fears of abandonment: *Can I really depend on anyone? Can I ever be sure enough of someone's love?* Sometimes the fear is of exposure: *If they really knew me, they wouldn't love me.* If one has these fears, it's very human to want to protect oneself by being the first to leave.

If you don't feel you're enough inside, it's difficult to accept anyone else. They're going to feel too good, triggering a fear of abandonment. Or you're going to think, *There must be something wrong with them if they want to be with me.*

All of the men and women whose stories you've read in this chapter were ostensibly looking for the right person, but searching for something else. Sarah wanted to rid herself of the feeling of being an outsider and prove to her parents that she was a person of value. Brian wanted to shake the feeling of being invisible, to have someone mirror back some sense of individuality. Linda wanted a sense of competence and, ultimately, security. Each of them set him or herself up for disappointment by focusing on relationships as a means to an end.

The key question isn't *What do I need in another person to make me fall in love,* but *What am I avoiding developing in myself?* You shift the focus away from finding the right person to building your own self-esteem, to becoming your own provider, rather than searching for a provider.

The best relationships bring two people together who both have a strong sense of self. This self has boundaries. Those boundaries aren't so rigid and protective that we can't allow another person's influence to help us grow. They aren't so fluid and weak that we take in other people's opinions of us as fact, and rise and fall according to their approval.

You don't develop this sense of self alone in your room, hoping that if you say enough nice words to yourself you'll wake up one day and feel whole. Yet you can't allow other people to define you and hope that they'll tell you who you are. You need to look at your relationships as mirrors, and instead of running from any of the information you receive, embrace it, and begin to read those reflections for what they tell you about yourself.

RX: Your Prescription for Change

You can only see others as clear as you see yourself.

—STEPHEN C. PAUL

What you need to understand about yourself

Given your history, it's understandable why you look for much more than love in a relationship. Love has let you down, but it's possible to learn to believe again.

The key questions

- What am I avoiding developing in myself?
- Where did I stop believing in love?

Where you need to focus

- on accepting yourself more fully
- on becoming your own provider, rather than searching for a provider

- on tackling hidden fears of intimacy

The cognitive shift

- My relationships mirror my own self-esteem.

Thoughts and Exercises

❧ *Notice how your relationships mirror your own self-esteem.* When people finally find love, it's generally because they have taken certain steps in order to do so. Foremost, they made a cognitive shift from thinking, *I never meet anyone I can be happy with,* to *This says more about me than them.*

Make a list of the last five people you dated or became involved with. Under each name, list what went wrong. List what was missing for you.

As you look at your list, consider that everything on it in some way is a mirror of something you desire to develop in yourself.

Many of our clients have done this exercise. Here are some of the things they wrote:

"He was too self-centered."

MIRROR: I don't acknowledge my own needs. I have a hard time putting myself first. I'm drawn to people who are self-absorbed because I'm so selfless at times. I'm self-centered in that I expect other people to read my mind.

"She's too needy."

MIRROR: I have a hard time dealing with vulnerability. I hate it in myself. If I was vulnerable around my father, he squashed me like a bug. I figured the best way to deal with it was to have no needs. What I really want is for someone to listen to me. Maybe I want to be the one catered to. In that way, I'm needy.

"He's no fun."

MIRROR: I feel guilty when I'm not working. Even when I play golf I'm so competitive, the fun is gone by the second hole. I need a six-pack to relax, then I punish myself with guilt for this sick attempt at having fun.

"He left me the second he knew I loved him."

MIRROR: I abandon myself the second I know I love someone. I try to be what they want. I put my life on hold.

"She didn't turn me on."

MIRROR: I choose safe women. I don't ask out the ones who really turn me on, because they intimidate me. It takes a lot of stimulation to turn me on, because I'm never emotionally involved. Women tell me I'm a selfish lover. I don't turn them on because I don't want to deal with the aftershock.

"He's not successful enough."

MIRROR: There are graduate school catalogues gathering dust on my nightstand. I'm late every day for work because I hate being there. I've stopped believing that I can make it. I've sat through too many year-end reviews, too many cost-of-living raises. I'm tired. I want what I can't have and I don't know how to stop wanting it, other than find someone who has it.

These revelations didn't come at once for our clients. The process wasn't easy. But once they knew what they really felt, they accepted it. It wasn't bad, it wasn't good. It just *was*. Because these feelings were within them, they had the power to use the information to change their lives.

❧ *Notice when your best solutions are becoming your biggest problems.* Although early, accurate, mirroring gives people a strong sense of self, if our parents couldn't provide it, we do better to move away from blame and despair and move toward discovering how we adapted. In truth, children have no other recourse than to adapt if they want to survive. The adaptive self has a full arsenal of solutions to the problems of getting love and acceptance, often from people who couldn't give it or who only gave it after we jumped through hoops to get it.

A woman who carries a burden of anger against her father for his neglect, his verbal abuse, his authoritarian ways, and so on, is prone to project mistrust on every man she meets. A man who is still bitter about his mother's attempts to run his life, her way of treating his father, and so on, is prone to project mistrust on women he becomes involved with. Psychologists refer to this as *projection*.

Think for a moment. How did your parents communicate? Was someone's voice always listened to while the other person's was ignored? Did they give up on communicating and merely shout threats at each other?

Were you allowed to have your own voice in your family? Were your feelings taken seriously? When you said, "I'm hungry," did anyone listen? Or did they say, "How can you be hungry, you just ate?" When you said, "I can't understand this math," did they say, "Sure you do, you just don't study."

What was your role in the family? Were you allowed to be a child, or coaxed into being a small adult? Were you kept a child, long after you should have been? Were you the scapegoat? The caretaker? The hero?

How are these patterns repeating in your life? Your solutions as a child, quite effective, may have become your problem today. For example, your father was domineering and he had a hundred questions about where you had been and who you had been with the moment you walked in the door. Your solution was to say as little as possible and retreat to your room. But now your lover asks, "How did things go at work today?" and you feel the hairs rise on your neck. You say "Fine," which leads to a battle about how you never tell him anything.

We had a client, a beautiful, talented woman, who made so little of her accomplishments. She would tell her boyfriends her inner-most fears and insecurities. She'd complain about how out of shape her body was, how poorly she was doing in her career, how lazy she was. Not one word of it was true. Her boyfriends would try to re-assure her, but eventually they began to question their own eyes. They became critical. Eventually they'd leave her, often in search of something better.

Her self-effacing manner made perfect sense given her history. When she was eleven, her father remarried a tyrant of a woman who had barely unpacked her bags before she instituted rules for everything: how her stepdaughter's drawers should be organized, how many soft drinks she could consume a week, how many phone calls she could make in a day. The only way to avoid con-flict was to become extremely self-effacing. That her stepmother liked. In fact, the more she put herself down, the kinder her step-mother treated her.

You, too, may have found ways to protect yourself. Perhaps such protection is no longer necessary.

❧ *Your idea of the perfect lover can tell you about yourself if you let it.* Make a list of everything you really want in a relationship. This is no time to be humble or realistic. Just write quickly, without editing out your fantasies.

When you've finished, take a good look at this list. Our hunch is you have a list of everything you want to be, yourself.

Finding out what needs to be developed in yourself and learning to work toward it is a process. It takes time and it takes courage. But it's so much more rewarding than the obsession with a lover's faults and the endless search for the right person.

We meet the right person when we become the right person.

By no means are we saying that you should settle for just anyone, anytime. But there's a moment when we stop looking for the momen-tary thrill of arousing and being aroused in favor of something deeper.

We've finally found ourselves. We stop looking at other people as providers of what we lack but as a loving presence in our lives, people who don't have to do anything or be anything more than they are. We forgive and learn how it feels to be forgiven. We might fear being exposed, but not as much as we desire to explore the mysteries of another person. Suddenly relationships aren't a battle of success or defeat but an adventure of knowing and being known. We can give our deepest selves because we accept our deepest selves.

 Before you end the relationship you're currently in because it's "not enough," talk to an objective person. How many bad relationships does it take until we see that there's something self-defeating going on here? Just one. This one. The last one. It doesn't matter. If you can never find the right person, you've got a reason. Enough is enough.

Tell your relationship history to an objective person. This may be a friend. This may be a therapist. Therapy isn't a process of showing you how you're wrong. No competent therapist is going to coach you to accept someone who is unacceptable.

You may learn that you're right to feel that the current one isn't the right one. Salena was a woman who came to therapy in the middle of a tortuous relationship. She met him at a Valentine's Day party. "Everyone was in a sport jacket and tie, he was dressed in sloppy jeans, smoking a cigarette, and letting the ashes fall on the rug. My first thought was, *This is someone I wouldn't take home.*"

But that night she felt adventurous. She put her doubts aside. "He took me home; we made love. There's a moment, you know, when you feel safe in relationships like this. I mean, I thought, he's never going to mean anything to me. If he doesn't call tomorrow, so what. This isn't real life."

Breakfast the next day turned into lunch, into dinner, into more love on the couch. He gave her a foot massage. She massaged the knots in his back. They did it again. They did things she'd never done with a man. She was appalled by what he asked her to do, but, still, she did it all. It was all very confusing.

"He didn't call the next day. I thought, 'So what? I'll move on.'"

Maybe she would have. Then he called. They spent a night at his apartment, not making love, but watching a movie on cable. They ordered out food, and he never even suggested that he should pay for half.

Before she knew it, she was waiting for his calls. She couldn't believe he was treating her this way. She obsessed about it.

She's not alone in her experience. It's the experience of any of us who aim low, never admitting that we're aiming low. We can walk into a room of people and find the one person who's hopelessly insecure, the man who is manic depressive and won't admit it, the woman whose life is a mess. The big draw here is that we know from the beginning that there is something unacceptable about this person. We meet this person and the music starts to play. The tune goes, "He has a drinking problem, so it won't matter that I never went to college. She has so many problems with her divorce that she won't ask me why I've never been married." He's *this,* so it doesn't matter that I'm *that.*

That's what these relationships are ultimately about. There's a flaw we have that we believe is so hideous we have to find someone with an even bigger flaw to feel comfortable enough to give ourselves. And we let go with abandon. Surely we have the power here. Surely this person realizes how much better we are than he or she, comparatively.

When he or she doesn't appreciate us, we're devastated. This is the ultimate proof that we're really not good enough. Someone we don't really admire doesn't admire us.

What's really going on here? He or she didn't appreciate you because that person couldn't even comprehend you. This is the lesson many of our clients learn in therapy. A swan might admire a bear, but they aren't going to make love.

Go for help if you find yourself caught in these binds. Give up the idea that you can handle it alone. If your love life is getting worse, not better, realize that your best thinking got you exactly where you are,

❧ *Be wary of overloading your relationships.* Kristen, twenty-eight, spent only six weeks with Keith—five dates, to be exact. When he spoke of vacations he was planning without her, she felt hurt. If he went out with friends and didn't include her, she was livid. She asked him where the relationship was going, until he threw up his hands and said, "Nowhere."

The idea of giving Keith more time to allow things to happen between them gradually made Kristen uneasy. Her need to have a man adhere to her schedule for the relationship was about self-protection. Men who dated Kristen felt it wasn't love for them that made her want a commitment, but the need to control the relationship. They pulled away, feeling manipulated.

Terry, a twenty-seven-year-old architect, was in the midst of telling his girlfriend about an argument with his boss, when she said, "It sounds like a miscommunication."

He was bitter: "She's never supportive; she never listens to me." His girlfriend told a different story: "No matter what I say, it's never enough."

People like Terry want more and more validation. It's never enough because they're looking in the wrong place—there's an inner wound and they haven't yet learned how to handle it. They find it difficult to take the validation when it's given. They minimize people who validate them. They can't even take in a compliment.

Terry's parents failed to be adequate "mirrors" because they saw him as an extension of themselves. The result was little sense of who he was. He overloaded his relationships with his need for constant reassurance.

❧ *Don't make love a prison.* The belief, "We should always be close, we should do everything together," is a reaction to the unmet needs for bonding in childhood. Attracted to self-confident, distant people, you may find yourself caught in a familiar battle—one of you complains about wanting more freedom, one complains about wanting more intimacy. One of you feels desperately alone, the other feels possessed. If you are the one who always wants more closeness, paradoxically, you might also feel suffocated by your partner's demands.

Get yourself out of the game. What are you looking for in all that closeness? What do you need to develop in yourself?

❧ *Don't cling to freedom to the point you end up lonely in love.* Dolores, forty-eight, says, "When I was eleven, miniskirts were the thing. The first time I wore one I was sent back to my room to change. I'd walk a block away from the house on the way to school, unzip the zipper, and roll my skirt up three inches. On the way home, I'd roll it back down, praying that my mother wouldn't be cruising the neighborhood in her convertible hoping to catch me in that very act, which she did several times, and for which I did without the telephone, sometimes for a month. Rolling up that skirt and moving on became a metaphor for all of my relationships. I simply did what I had to do, behind someone's back. I smoked cigarettes out in the stairwell, rather than admit to the man I was living with that I smoked. When the sex wasn't good, I'd have affairs. I thought of this as 'having my freedom.' I was lonely in all of those relationships in the end. I kept looking for the one person whom I could really be myself with. But, you know, you're never going to find that if you don't have the courage to be yourself."

This woman took her freedom in very secret ways. Others are much more open about it.

You may look at your parents' relationship and believe that love is suffocating. You determine that you're going to do better. You organize your relationship so that each of you can still maintain your focus on yourselves, your careers, and your friends. Even married, you have separate bank accounts. You know exactly who contributed what to every piece of furniture, artwork, or appliance in your home. But by avoiding the risks of dependency, you hide your vulnerability, and you begin to feel lonely in love.

If you are a woman, you may have entered this relationship

under a false assumption that if you allowed your partner enough autonomy, intimacy would eventually come. Your man may not be interested in intimacy at all.

If you are a man, your false assumption may be that you can find safety in separateness. You may be protecting your personal freedom at the cost of intimacy. You're a candidate for the despair of having a competent, successful wife, a solid career, and a recurrent question that nags, *Is this all there is?*

The need for more freedom, more space, is often the hallmark of a person who doesn't know how to get his or her needs met, a person who has no idea how to negotiate with a member of the opposite sex. To get involved, the other person has to share every habit, every like and dislike. Differences are intolerable because they are afraid they'll end up being controlled: "She hates football; I'll never be able to watch it again."

At some point in their lives, this may have been true. A man named Scott, who married in his early twenties, comes to mind. Like his father before him, he struggled to give his family everything they wanted. But some of the things his wife set her mind on were impossible. "She bought clothes constantly, high-fashion, wild outfits. I was embarrassed to be out with her in public, but she'd just laugh at me. Then there were all the things she wanted for the house. There was always a room being painted or a wall being torn down. We went into debt.

"I was in love with the law in those days, as they say, and my practice was everything, so I pretty much let her have her way. The kids were as spoiled as she was. It was always, 'Daddy, what did you buy me?' Talk about never enough. She'd throw tantrums. She'd do it in front of my parents, our friends, my business associates. The divorce cost me a fortune. I always looked at it as money well spent."

But today when Scott goes out with a woman who doesn't like his car or can't name the starting lineup for the Bulls, he's out the door. He's never learned to get his needs met in a relationship, so he's terrified of being trapped again.

You don't build emotional muscle through avoiding conflict. Good relationships require honesty. They require both people to be current with their feelings, not stockpile them until the relationship is in tatters. Real freedom isn't always time alone. It's being able to be yourself.

❧ *Be active, instead of reactive.* Karla's date, Ray, left her at her door with a promise to call her the next day. When he finally called, three days later, and invited her to dinner, she said, "Forget it. I'm not going to go out with a man who doesn't call when he says he will."

Karla's one-strike-and-you're-out attitude was really a cover for a deep fear of being taken advantage of. But, fiery rages leave people feeling more powerless.

If you identify with Karla, chances are there were many times in the past when others didn't appreciate how upset you were. They didn't respond in a way that was helpful. You've come to think that no one will even notice you're upset unless you let them know it *loud.*

It gets you the opposite of what you want. You yell and make threats, and the other person gets defensive. You've given them ammunition. You went off. Now they have an excuse to avoid the entire issue: You made it bigger than it was. The argument now revolves around the fact that you overreacted, and the issue is buried.

❧ *Ask yourself if you have an unconscious investment in seeing to it that your relationships never work.* Emotional abandonment in childhood can lead us to repeat a scenario where we actually set things up so that other people leave us.

Think back about your relationships. Is there a familiar repeating pattern? As one client put it, "I never realized anything was up until I hit forty and thought of all the women I'd known. It was like there was this trail of dead bodies behind me."

This same man is in a wonderful relationship right now. More than any other factor, it was his determination to relinquish old worn-out patterns that caused it to happen. "One night, I decided to forget the games. Forget trying to hide how much I loved this woman. I told her, 'If something bad happens at work, or you feel depressed about something, I need you to tell me. I need to know what's going on with you. I need you to share what you really feel about work, about life, about me. I need us to be closer.'

"'We can do that,' she said. And, we did."

❧ ❧

Today I will look upon relationship difficulties as opportunities to see what I need to develop in myself.

❧ ❧

CHAPTER SEVEN

Why Do I Always End Up Getting Less Than I Give?

The Search for Control

How can anyone ever love you for who you are if you become someone else to be with them?

—STEPHEN C. PAUL

At 4 A.M. Barbara gets out of bed, goes into the living room, and turns on the television. Surprised to see Sally Jesse Raphael at this hour interviewing a Mormon who has six wives, she cranks up the volume. This is bad, but tossing and turning in bed praying for sleep is worse.

Barbara knows her trouble isn't a sleep disorder. What's spooking her is something she has to do at ten o'clock that morning: fire her assistant. That is, of course, if her assistant does her the favor of showing up for work today. The last four Mondays he's been too hungover to come in.

Why all of this angst over firing an employee so worthless that he's missed ten days of work in the last month? "I feel sorry for him. Jobs aren't easy to come by. I guess I always start thinking about what it would be like to be in the other guy's shoes, even when it's my shoes that are being stepped all over."

Craig was having a day from hell. For half an hour he was stuck on the phone with a patient who said she had a terrible toothache. She couldn't tell him which tooth hurt, whether the pain was sharp or dull, whether it was grating or agonizing, or whether this was an emergency or something that could wait.

Craig was philosophic: "I think there are people in the world who get out of bed in the morning and say, 'I'm bored; I need attention. Who can I complain to? I know! Let's call the dentist.'"

A patient arrived in the waiting room at a quarter past twelve screaming because there was a parade downtown and he had to pay five dollars to park his car in one of the city's lots. He paced around, terrorizing the other patients, screaming, "Are you going to fix my crown, or what?"

Craig was still trying to soothe him when Craig's receptionist hustled him out of the room.

"If you won't tell him to get lost, I will," she told him. "You don't have to take abuse from people, you know."

No, I don't know, Craig thought. If hard work and self-sacrifice were the key, Craig would be a millionaire. If honesty and flexibility made the ultimate lover, Craig would be Don Juan. Instead, he's a man recovering from a divorce, working a sixty-hour week to retain his place as a middle-of-the-road generalist, and wondering, *When is enough, enough?*

Recently he attended a high school reunion. All night long he met classmates who he remembered as nice, but limited, sensible but not exceptional, good but not gifted. All in all, a pretty mediocre bunch. "And they had money, deals, power, fame. It was absolutely galling. I mean, where did I go wrong?"

This chapter is about people who have good ideas but who aren't recognized for them. It's about people who work hard but find themselves underemployed or underpaid. It's about people whose talents are acknowledged but undervalued. It's about people who consistently give more than they get. In this chapter, we'll explore why they do it.

Why is it easy to give others the credit?

If you identified with Craig and Barbara, whose stories began this chapter, chances are when you think about your work and personal relationships you see yourself as a "giver." Being the "giver" doesn't necessarily mean that you are always buying things for other people, although it can. It means you are the one who ends up photcopying the 500-page report. You are the one who has to get on yet another plane to attend a meeting, when several other people in your department are just as qualified to go. You are the teacher with the largest class size and the worst students year after year. You are driving the car pool while your spouse has a leisurely cup of coffee.

You're frustrated, but you bite your tongue. You have your excuses for accepting these unpleasant circumstances: "I have no choice; they pay my salary; he works longer hours; my children need me."

These are certainly vital concerns and realities, but something more is often going on here. Why is it easy to give others so much credit and ourselves so little? Why are a few angry words enough to "shut us down" and rob us of our personal power? Why do we respond more to criticism than praise? Why do we feel guilty when others act irresponsibly and blame their problems on us? When certain people intimidate or manipulate us, why do we question our own thinking rather than theirs?

Our reasons generally fall into one of the following categories:

❧ *Fear of rejection.* Carole, thirty-eight, admits, "I'm a big peace-maker. I hate to upset anyone." Carole misinterprets the subtle manipulations of others who get "upset" and doesn't realize this is how people control her. She sees other people's anger as a rejection of herself and empowers people with the right to judge her. When the fear of rejection means you let others take advantage of you, you are the one doing the rejecting. You're rejecting yourself.

❧ *Fear of emotional independence.* We can feel that we are disloyal to our families or other people we love when we stop playing the role of "victim" or "compliant one." Two sisters come to mind, totally different in their temperaments—one a risk taker, the other shy. Their entire family, aunts, cousins, grandparents, thought of one of them as the good one, the other as the bad one. The "good one" grew up hearing, "Thank God you're not like your sister," a hundred times a week. And it wasn't because she was such an achiever, but because she was compliant with her mother's demands.

This compliance ended up having enormous costs almost everywhere else in her life—with men, with employers, with roommates, friends. Her manner of being light and pleasant but ultimately uninvolved, unwilling to share deep emotional feelings, was a habit, a way of getting appreciation that worked in her family. Now it was hard to have to follow that kind of implicit rule all the time, not to be able to say when something was bothering her, to have to be sweet and quiet, even when she felt angry or worried, and then to have to bear the consequences of other people's experience of that. A real and important part of her was caged up.

Some of us come from a long line of "victims" who confused suffering with sainthood and taught us that being powerless and depressed is the way to get love and attention. If we believe that being a victim will eventually get us what we want, we fail to develop other sources of power.

We can be quite comfortable feeling one down to everyone else if that is what we're used to. We may resist asserting our desires because we fear loss. As one woman put it, "Whenever I tell someone how I really feel, it causes an argument and I always lose." This had more to do with poor negotiation skills, weakened from lack of use, than from some irrevocable karma.

❧ *Fear of exposure.* The idea that if we let others really know us, as we are, they couldn't possibly accept us keeps many of us on our guard. We have a compulsion to hide what we perceive as personal failures or weaknesses. We may stretch the truth over shortcomings. Underneath is the fear that the real truth—the real self—is so awful, so unacceptable, that others will surely feel sorry for us, or worse, reject us.

A fear of exposing our thoughts and feelings to others almost guarantees that our relationships will be superficial. People sense that we haven't let them really see us as we are. Or they think that we're invulnerable and, therefore, unavailable. In either case, we're powerless in relationships in which we fear being fully ourselves.

Sometimes these fears are justified. There are, in fact, times when we assert ourselves that we do get rejected, or we do experience a loss of some kind. But often these fears are magnified, because we've been carrying around unresolved feelings from loss and rejection from the past.

The problem: A need for control

For many people, being the giver, the strong one, the willing one, the one who doesn't complain is an adaptation to life rather than a personality trait they're born with. It's almost always a stance that was set in motion years ago to solve or cope with a particular problem.

People who find that they often give more than they get generally share a common history: they were invalidated—made to feel as if their feelings, thoughts, and actions were unimportant or undesirable—by parents, family members, teachers, peers, or early employers.

Too much, too soon

"In my dream, my father is threatening to shoot our dog. He breaks down the door. I can't stop him, so I leap in front of the dog. My father shoots me."

The man who has this recurring nightmare is twenty-eight. He says that he finds this dream depressing, but somehow validating. It's the dream of the family hero—the long-suffering child who in his dreams is finally appreciated, only after he has given his life to save the family.

Having too many adult responsibilities in childhood creates the family hero, children who are familiar with the feeling of giving more than they get. These responsibilities include being a parent's "best friend" or confidant.

When children grow up in homes where there are serious problems—alcoholism, violence, poverty, illness, depression, and so on—they are in family systems that are often out of control. Their only rewards may come from never being a problem. By being helpful, by giving, by taking on other people's responsibilities, they try to restore control.

In such homes, children don't grow up with the assertiveness that springs from the inner knowledge that we're deserving of what we have, worthy of what we want, and important enough to ask for what we need. Alan, twenty-seven, would agree. His mother suffered from cancer during most of his childhood.

"One morning I was playing Monopoly at the kitchen table with two friends. My mother must have been calling for me, but we had the radio on and I didn't hear her. She came into the kitchen in her robe. While she got a glass of water, she made conversation with my friends. I saw them stare at her—the black and blue marks, the bald spots where her hair hadn't grown back. She started to pull a chair out, to sit down, and something inside of me snapped. I started yelling at her. I told her she was ruining our game.

"I just wanted her to go, you know? Later I found her in her room crying. 'I can't leave the house; people don't come to see me like they used to. Would it have been such a big deal if you let me talk to your friends?' I felt like The Beast. I've never gotten over it."

The helplessness, the anger, the fear, and the resentment Alan felt as his mother's disease progressed seemed insurmountable at times. In families where one person's illness or problem absorbs so much energy, there is no space for other people's agendas or needs. There is often no one to talk to; everyone is overwhelmed with their own fears.

There may be tremendous guilt over feeling angry at the sick person or the family member with the problem even though these feelings are inevitable. It is not unusual for a child who grows up in this type of situation to be ambivalent about expressing his or her own needs as an adult. Even though the problem that set everything in motion is long gone, self-expression is emotionally tied to guilt.

Given a history of looking for attention or recognition, and being frustrated over and over again, one learns an important lesson: A person with needs is emotionally dependent. Being the giver is safer. *The giver is always in control.*

The unconscious agenda in continuing this pattern today? "I'll make myself indispensable to you by being the good one. You'll be beholden. I'll get my needs met without having to ask."

Your home doesn't have to be highly dysfunctional to give you the message that the road to safety or rewards is through being the giver. For example, suppose you were an only child until just after your third birthday, when mother brought home your baby brother. When you try to crawl on Mother's lap, she pushes you off. She's tense and irritated by your demands for attention. She says, "You're not a baby anymore. Can't you see how tired I am after getting up all night with your brother? I need you to be helpful." So, you become helpful. The problem is, you don't always know when to step out of the helpful hero role or when it's too costly for you.

Teenage trauma and today's troubles

Sometimes it is a difficult adolescence rather than a troubled family life in the background of the person who continually gives more than he gets.

Think for a moment. How did you go about gaining acceptance and a sense of belonging when you were a teenager? What did it mean in those days to be a good friend? How did you make friends? How did you keep them?

Thirty-three-year-old Charles remembers a bad case of acne and growing to his height of six-foot-three almost overnight. "I was the scapegoat. I was the kid who was always fishing his book bag out of the garbage can. I was too awkward to fight anyone, too shy for revenge. I learned to laugh at myself when someone set me up. It was hard. One time they threw me, naked, out of the locker room into the hall and a female teacher let me back in. I was mortified. The basketball team laughed and applauded. I made it to the shower where the tears mixed with the water. But no one ever knew I cried. That was the most important thing."

It was a strategy that made him part of the group. Charles rode in cars with the rest of the guys, he went to parties, he made the yearbook staff. He had friends, if you could call them that.

Today the acne has cleared and what's left is a tall, powerful-looking man. "I'd like to be the person everyone else sees." But the shyness, the orientation toward pleasing everyone else even if it's at his own expense remains.

Another woman, Shelly, remembers being thirteen and learning the rules of popularity in the wealthy lakeside community where she grew up. "You gave everyone compliments; you praised clothes, boyfriends, hairstyles no matter what the truth was; you denied you were popular at all, compared to them; and you never, ever said what you really thought about anything, anymore than they ever said what they really thought about anything."

In eighth grade, the ultimate moment came. Girls were pairing off, buying friendship rings to announce their status as best friends. The most popular girl, Joanne, chose Shelly.

Their rings cost ten dollars, but the price, for Shelly, turned out to be enormous. "Joanne was so spoiled. She'd make fun of my clothes, or get me in trouble in class. She'd borrow money and then get mad at me if I asked her to pay me back."

It didn't take long for Shelly to realize that she was giving more than she got. "But if I stopped being friends with her, I'd have no friends. She was a total bitch, but everything in our group revolved around her, and there were plenty of girls willing to take my place."

Shelly's story illustrates so clearly the perks for being the giver. She earned instant status. By being Joanne's doormat, she thought she could fend off loss. When Joanne dropped her their freshman year, Shelly didn't question her strategy. She questioned herself.

Transference: The replay in adult relationships

The past is important to understand because we recycle it. At the heart of the problem is the phenomenon known as transference. Transference is an unconscious reflex reaction: We meet a person who has a characteristic or manner that unconsciously reminds us of someone in our past. Or, we become involved in a situation that is similar to one we experienced long ago. We react in the same manner we did in the past regardless of the current reality. We feel the same feelings. We expect the same outcome. At times, we set up the same problems. We transfer this experience into interactions with other people.

Transference can be positive. We can meet a person and immediately feel at ease. But the phenomenon of transference may also account for experiences such as those faced by Karen, a twenty-six-year-old account executive. "Basically, my job was to convince the feature writers at the newspapers to write a story about the city's annual Easter Parade," she explains. "I called the first reporter on the list and went into my pitch.

"'Look,' he yelled, cutting me off midsentence, 'there's some damn parade in this city every other week. Why are you bothering me with this?'

"I started feeling like an idiot. 'But, this is the Easter Parade,' I stammered. 'It's for charity.'

"'Big deal,' he said, hanging up.

"I know he was just a jerk, but I couldn't make another one of those phone calls the rest of the afternoon."

Karen heard a reporter raise his voice and she was immediately shut down. What shut Karen down was the feeling that she was "bothering" people. The trouble was, her entire career depended on bothering people—getting them to listen to her, making them agree to publicize her events.

We aren't born to feel guilty if we disturb another person for a good cause. Babies scream and thrash around and aren't the least bit concerned if it's the last minute of overtime in the Superbowl and it's time for a diaper change.

Where had Karen learned to feel this career-halting guilt over "bothering" people? "My sister has always been a mess. Drugs, shoplifting, anorexia—she wore my mother out. You didn't walk into the midst of chaos and ask for help with an algebra problem."

When she heard the reporter yell, "There's a damn parade in this city every minute," Karen went on automatic pilot. She immediately felt like that five-year-old girl in her family who had no right to voice her opinion or feelings, as if one more problem would throw the family into complete chaos. So she adapted by repressing her needs.

A woman with a different history might have said, "Give me one minute and I'll convince you that this one's worth an inch in your column. And I'll give you a ticket to the VIP tent where they're going to have great food and freebies for your kids no matter what you write."

Karen wasn't a failure at her career. She had the success of the kid who won't raise her hand in the lecture hall, but spends all night in the library figuring out what the professor was talking about. She did get reporters to publicize her events many times. She got it through memos and letters and follow-up calls. But the big hits—the talk shows, the top feature writers who you have to annoy for a good cause—eluded her.

Because of negative transference, some people and situations spell trouble for us at the start. In other words, these people and situations "plug us in" to childlike ways of thinking, feeling, and behaving. Brendan, a forty-five-year-old financial vice president, admits that when the chairman walks by he feels compelled to "look busy." "It's ridiculous to feel this way, and the idea that I have to prove anything when I put in sixty-five-hour weeks regularly is ludicrous." Brendan wonders why the chairman makes him feel "like a little kid, afraid of the school principal."

Phil, a thirty-nine-year-old chemical engineer, had a beautiful singing voice when he was a child. The vocal coach his parents hired was a man who hoped to see his dreams of stardom accomplished through Phil and would settle for nothing less. "I'd make a mistake, and he'd look at me in disgust and leave the room. I once told him that I thought he was wrong about something, and he put a hole through his own living room wall. I was terrified of him; so scared that I wouldn't even complain about him to my parents. I went to him twice a week for three years. Everyone just thought he was a good, tough coach."

Today when Phil competes with other people, they easily shut him down because he unconsciously equates the use of his competence with abandonment. "Someone will get the figures wrong during a meeting and I'll send a memo about it later, rather than say something at the time. Sometimes my supervisor tells my ideas as if they are her own. I never know what to do in these situations. I let it pass. You've heard the theory: Make the boss look good, make her job easier, and you'll get ahead."

But Phil isn't getting ahead. Other people on his team get better projects, larger raises, and Phil is frustrated. "I know I have to speak up because the situation is really getting to me." Intellectually, he knows that no one is going to kick down a wall if he corrects them during a meeting, but emotionally, it's a difficult pattern to break.

One can come from the most psychologically sound family, be surrounded by love and nurturing, and still be seduced into the hapless hero role. To want to give, to want to be warm and caring, to want to help others is laudable. It's easy to feel the cane around your neck when someone needs you. The challenge is balance. The objective is to know when you're simply being manipulated.

Evan says, "At my year-end review, I heard it all. Billings were lower than last year. The economy was off. He even threw in the fact that the rent on the office space was up from last year. In a confidential tone, he said his own earnings wouldn't be so hot this year, and it couldn't be worse for him because he was building a new house, and one of his kids needed surgery. The bottom line? A 3 percent raise was the most I could expect.

"But, I felt he'd really shared something with me by telling me his personal problems. It seemed callous to march back in and say, 'Sorry to hear about your troubles, but I've got some of my own.'"

You need an objective listener at a time like this, someone who doesn't feel those same emotional stirrings. In Evan's case, it was his wife. She told him, "For chrissakes, I can't believe you let him sit there and talk about the cost of office space. It's a bunch of garbage. He's a millionaire. He has health insurance. He just wants more money for himself. Talk to him again."

Are you giving because you want to, or because you have to?

We're not ruling out the possibility that someone will appreciate you for your giving nature. But how does one assess whether there are deeper needs operating here, primarily the need for control or the need to avoid responsibility?

There are many unconscious maneuvers people use in an attempt to gain control. These self-defeating maneuvers include trying to prove how good we are. Trying to show someone how much they have hurt us. Trying to be what we think will please another person.

Awareness is the first step. Suspect that the real issue is control or avoidance if you find yourself regularly engaged in these self-defeating behaviors:

♦ You apologize for being angry or having a different opinion. You take on other people's hurt feelings as your responsibility.

♦ You reward people for treating you badly. You make love after an argument to prove that you don't harbor bad feelings. You give the greater part of your attention to people who abuse or are indifferent to you.

♦ You don't ask people for what you want or need. You have a fear of being needy. You're likely to say, "Don't worry. I'll walk home from the airport."

♦ You make empty threats. Instead of feeling your power when you issue ultimatums, people roll their eyes.

♦ You give other people ammunition. You tell your boss, "I could be much more productive if you bought a new computer." You're shocked when the boss writes "below-average productivity" on your annual review.

♦ You become a chameleon. He likes jazz? Suddenly you own every Kenny G album. She runs marathons? You tape up your knee and join her on the track.

♦ You discount positive feedback. If people compliment you, you diminish them in your own mind, i.e., "What do they really know?"

♦ You're a screamer. You're always yelling, and people tune you out. Or they do what you want until your back is turned.

♦ You allow others to blame their problems on you until they drain you. You have little energy left to solve your own.

♦ You share too much of yourself. You tell all your secret insecurities. People give you a lot of attention at first. Eventually they pull away, exhausted, hoping someone else will help you pull yourself together.

♦ You let other people share too much of themselves. Everyone thinks you should be a therapist. Trouble is, some people reveal themselves to you too quickly. When they realize they've shared too much, they pull away from you and search for ways to diminish your power over them.

Why it will never be enough

It's called the Just World Theory: You give and you'll get back in return. Be nice enough, and the world will appreciate you. It's supposed to work.

True, there are people who find it deeply fulfilling to make a lifetime out of selfless giving. Mother Teresa and Gandhi come to mind. But do people like this constantly walk around dissatisfied, wondering when enough is enough? We doubt it.

You're the only one who can assess whether such a theory is working in your life. One wonders how often the curtain has to come down on this performance leaving us forever waiting for applause, until we heed the wake-up call. A hundred lifetimes?

What is, is. Your particular style is not satisfying for you, and it's time to face that squarely. Stop digging in the ashes. Please remember that people will take you at your word. If you act like it's okay, that you'll take on responsibilities that aren't really yours, people will let you.

As therapists, we rarely see two givers come together in a relationship. We see givers with procrastinators, manipulators, lost souls, and other emotionally unavailable people who are incapable of giving back. Seldom are these givers martyrs. Trouble is, when they finally get around to asking for what they want, they're too angry to be effective.

We recall one man, a father who had done everything in his power to help his teenage son who was causing havoc at school, experimenting with drugs, and verbally abusing the entire family. This father finally got so angry that he asked for what he wanted in no uncertain terms: "You don't want to go to school, you get a job, pay room and board, or get out." His teenager moved out. The trouble was, the father wasn't ready for such a heavy-handed solution. He wasn't emotionally prepared to go from the selfless father one moment to tyrant the next.

Unfortunately some of us never ask for what we want, regardless of how angry we get. "I wish my husband would bring me flowers once in a while," a client told us. "Ask him," we suggested. "Oh, no," she said vehemently. "If he can't think of it himself, what good is it?"

If you truly feel that if you have to ask for something, it isn't as good, then you may never feel satisfied. You probably aren't the type of person who attracts the mind reader type into your life.

RX: Your Prescription for Change

> *I don't know the key to success but the key to failure is trying to please everybody.*
>
> —BILL COSBY

What you need to understand about yourself

Given your history, it's easy to understand why you place others' needs above your own. But there are other ways you can achieve security in relationships.

The key questions

- Do I believe my needs are important?
- How much do I expect to get in life in return for being "good"?

Where you need to focus

- on validating your needs
- on building your personal power
- on tolerating disapproval
- on telling the truth

The cognitive shift

- I have to ask for what I want; no one is going to read my mind.
- Having needs doesn't make me needy.
- People don't automatically get what they deserve.
- I am not a victim; I can choose to say yes or no.

Thoughts and Exercises ❧❧❧❧❧❧❧❧❧❧❧❧❧❧❧❧❧❧❧❧❧❧❧❧❧❧❧❧❧❧❧

❧ *How much do you expect to get in life in return for being "good"?* What do you think you'll achieve by giving up your power to other people? Their affection? Their confidence? Their commitment to you?

Now ask yourself if you really achieve those goals via your present behavior. One woman who did this exercise wrote that the payoff for being the "perfect parent" and never asserting her own needs was supposed to be her children's love and confidence in her. However, by looking at her husband, she realized that his qualities as a parent were quite different from hers. He made mistakes. He lost his temper. He didn't back down. He made sure the children knew when he needed time alone. And the children adored him.

The problem with a lot of giving is that it doesn't spring from an open heart, but from a burning need. In that way, it's dishonest.

Your needs are important. You can be honest about them.

❧ *List your fears.* What is your greatest fear about using your personal power? That you'll be rejected? Humiliated? Abandoned?

Begin to test whether your fears are real or imagined. During the next week, express a negative feeling the moment you become aware of it. If your feelings are hurt, tell the other person how you feel rather than pouting, vowing to get even, or pretending you don't care. Was the other person's response what you expected? How did you feel after expressing your true feelings? If the other person became angry, how did you handle it?

❧ *Nurture yourself.* Marci, fifty-four, said, "I made a list of all the things I loved to do. Then I counted up how many hours I'd spent last month doing those things. Looking at the sheet of paper, I thought, *This is pathetic. No wonder you're miserable.* That was a start." You, too, can list your favorite activities and track how much time you've spent in the last week doing them.

Then, divide a sheet of paper in half. Label one side "My Excuses" and the other "My Rewards." List all of your excuses for not doing the things that make you feel good about yourself: "Court time is too expensive. . . . I can't leave my children with baby-sitters all of the time. . . . If I stop, I'll lose my train of thought. . . . We can't afford to go out."

Next, list your rewards for your excuses.

- *"I don't waste money on myself, so* _____."
  –"I'll be able to retire early."
  –"I'll never be accused of being careless or superficial."

- *"I never get angry, so* _____."
  –"Everyone will like me."
  –"People can never say I'm immature."

Take a closer look at those rewards. Do you actually receive them? Is the price too high?

❧ *Build your personal power in relationships through exercises that have helped hundreds of others.* Personal power-building exercises are based on using positive experiences in the past as your springboard. Dwelling on a problem *empowers* it. Focusing on negative events in our lives empowers those negative events. Much more is gained from focusing on the positive events in our lives—the experiences that made us feel strong.

Look for an experience in your life that contains the following elements:

- ◆ *A moment of personal power.* Think of a moment when you felt confident or strong inside, whether other people praised you at the time or not.

- ◆ *High potency.* On a scale of 1 to 10, the experience should rate at least an 8 in terms of your feelings of strength, joy, or confidence.

- ◆ *Emotional impact.* The feelings linked to the experience must be easily recalled. When you think of the experience, you should feel something. "When I finished singing, I didn't even need to hear the applause. It didn't matter. I knew I'd sung the best I ever had, and I felt wonderful. It was a moment I'll never forget."

♦ *Clear focus.* The experience must have a clear beginning and end. Short scenes work best.

♦ *Easy verbalization.* The experience should be one that you could easily write down.

To give you a jumping off point, here are some experiences our clients recalled when doing this exercise: One man's most power-provoking experience was bowling a 200 game in a tournament; a woman recalled the day she sold her clothing line to a major retail chain; a twenty-one-year-old man said he feels powerful when he recalls how he held onto his position at first base for three seasons of Little League amid stiff competition; a woman's most memorable moment was writing an award-winning poem; a middle-aged woman describes her most significant moment as, "The evening I threw my alcoholic husband out!"

If you have difficulty finding a moment in your life when you felt powerful, select a full-length picture of someone you would like to look, act, or feel like from a magazine or other source. List the qualities you imagine the person in the photograph has. Visualize how this person would react to troubling situations. Just as a "method actor" becomes the character, you can empower yourself with the qualities you would like to have and act as if you have them.

Visualize these experiences several times a day. The goal of this exercise is to reexperience feelings of inner power.

❧ *Invest in supportive people.* We feel most powerful when we're around people who live lifestyles we respect and who aren't personally threatened by choices or changes we make. When our energy is spent in negative relationships, we feel trapped. It's vital to build a network of support so that when we make changes in our lives there isn't a feeling of impending fear because of impending loss.

Practice being more honest about your feelings with people who aren't too self-absorbed to hear you. You can take the smallest step. When someone asks you how you are, instead of automatically saying, "Fine," tell the truth.

❦ *Stop the cat and mouse game.* You know the game. Acting hurt, but saying, "Nothing's wrong." Saying, "No, it doesn't matter." Hinting about what you want, hoping someone will get your hints.

You want the necklace with the silver chain? Tell him. You want her to do something different in bed? Ask her. This is also giving. It's giving another person the power to please you.

You may be depriving other people of the opportunity to have the joy of being helpful and giving by always having to go first, or by denying you have any needs at all. When you can openly receive as well as give, enough will be enough.

❦ ❦

Today I will give because I want to, not because I think I have to.

❦ ❦

CHAPTER EIGHT

Why Can't I Stop Comparing Myself To Other People?

The Search for Identity

The crazy person says, "I am Abraham Lincoln," and the neurotic says, "I wish I were Abraham Lincoln," and the healthy person says, "I am I and you are you."

—FRITZ PERLS

The restaurant opened a week ago, and the wait was two hours. By the time her reservation was called, Gail was famished.

Now, seated at the table with her friend Yvette, Gail pushed her Caesar salad around on her plate with an utter lack of appetite. Signaling the waiter for another glass of chardonnay, she wondered when, if ever, this evening would blessedly end.

"We leave for France on the fifteenth," Yvette was telling her, "and another little trip just got squeezed in. We're going to Bangkok—can you imagine? You know how every company is looking to get a foothold in Asia."

"What will you do in a hotel room all day, while Steve is working?" Gail asked. Her claws were out, but she couldn't help it.

Yvette looked at her, surprised. "I'm never in my room. I take tours. I hire a personal trainer and work out. Then I have to go with him to dinner, of course. Some of the people we have to entertain are boring, I guess, but it's all part of the gig."

They had started out together in the accounting department of a computer software company and held each other up through an avalanche of busy work, dashed hopes, and downsizing. Both were ambitious. Both saw the writing on the wall. Gail finally went back to school nights. But Yvette took a different route. She married quickly and efficiently, six months after meeting Steve through a coworker.

Gail wanted to be happy for her friend, but lately she went out of her way to avoid her. And the problem wasn't just Yvette. "With everyone I meet, I'm thinking, *I'm better, no I'm not as good; I'm better, no I'm not as good.* I'll see someone I know at the grocery store and I'll move into the next aisle, keeping my head down, hoping they didn't see me. I don't want to hear about their promotions, their new babies, their new condos. I can't stop comparing myself to other people."

It's safe to say that most people compare themselves to others. Yet, in all the interviewing we did for this book, this was one of the hardest subjects for people to talk about. Who wants to admit that they take surreptitious glances at another woman's body in the locker room, thinking, *Why can't I have her thighs?* That when they heard about a friend's promotion, they were so busy doing the math— *What's 8 percent after taxes in the 29 percent bracket, anyway? Not much!*—that they almost forgot to say congratulations. Who is comfortable admitting that they envy people they don't even know, or don't even like?

But there seems to be a cultural assault against our ever feeling that we're enough the way we are. One only needs to read the covers of major magazines: "Perfect Thighs in This Lifetime"; "Plastic Surgery Before 30"; "Hard, Firm Uplifting Tricks for a Tighter Derriere."

We're brought up to compare, to compete, and to win. The cultural bias is so strong that a recent study found that if economic conditions improve for everyone, there is sometimes a reduction in general satisfaction. Satisfaction with income depends more on comparisons with the incomes of others than on actual incomes— what people really want is to have more than other people!

Rampant competition in the workplace, a shake-up climate that has destroyed job security, and a slowdown in the economy have generated a new reality: We're not all going to have it all or be able to do it all. A man who moved rapidly along the fast track in the eighties told us recently, "The climate is so different today. I try to warn the younger men and women we hire. The truth is, they're going to be sitting and crunching numbers at a computer for the next five years. And it's not school. Not everyone can get an A. There's not enough spots opening up."

Yet every day someone wins out over the competition. Someone achieves fame. Someone gets a lucky break. It's only human to think, *Why not me, too?*

We're assaulted daily with stories about the best looking, the richest, the most talented, the newly famous. The illusion is that these people are the happiest. What's the truth?

One study of lottery winners found that after they absorb the exciting changes in their lives, their scale of emotions returns to normal. One hundred multimillionaires in the United States rated their emotions no differently than did one hundred average Americans chosen at random.

Still, many of us think, *Ah, but I'll be different. Give me the chance, give me the money, and I'll show you happy.*

Our cultural strength—a desire to do better and be better—is tied to our cultural weakness. It's never enough.

Those of us who constantly compare ourselves to others often feel a sense of shame about it. *Envy* is such an ugly word. It conjures up a childish drive to make it up to the top of the mountain and stand there alone in the smug satisfaction that you're better than everyone else.

But when we interviewed people who suffered from comparison thinking, a very different picture emerged. Many were completely ambivalent about making it to the top of the mountain. Some were there and didn't know it. Some were like the person who said, When you get there, there's no there, there.

Some of us will feel pangs of envy more acutely than others. In this chapter, we aren't going to admonish you if you compare yourself to other people. Rather, we're going to focus on why you do it. What drives you? Where did you learn it? What is the payoff?

The problem: An unclear sense of identity and the need for a reference point

We begin life in a symbiotic state where we see no differences. Mother is *me*. But soon we come to realize that there are differences. We learn where we end and others begin.

Comparisons help children gain a sense of autonomy: Your sister has dark hair, you have light hair. She's taller, you're thinner, and you're both unique. If no one ever used the word "better" to describe anyone else's attributes, comparing yourself to others would only give you information about who you are and a clearer sense of your identity. Unfortunately, this doesn't happen.

The family secret

Who am I? What do I really want? What do I really feel?

Richard, thirty-nine, is a man who often feels exhausted attempting to answer these questions. We met after a seminar we'd given to a group of people on the subject of developing personal power. Richard had organized the seminar. He'd achieved a huge turnout and an agenda that had gone like clockwork. He greeted us afterward with a handshake that was warm and firm, followed by an apology: "The room was so hot; I'm terribly sorry." We hadn't noticed, but he shrugged as if to say, *Of course you noticed; I know you're just trying to make me feel better.* We chatted for a few moments as the participants cleared the room. When we were alone, he said softly: "When you talked about all or nothing thinking, that really hit home."

As we walked outside, he told us his story. "I hate people who are victims," he began. "I can't stand it when people say, my life's a mess because my mother did this or my father did that. I know I had it bet ter growing up than a lot of people. I don't even like to talk about what happened, because what can I do about the past? You move on, right? I never thought I had any use for therapy. Not until recently.

"I grew up in a suburb of Chicago, in a little Jewish milieu, where every kid had the same kind of bicycle, the same Hebrew school classes, the same blue jeans. We moved there when I was ten, after my father remarried."

His parents' divorce had been a shock to Richard. "I was in my kindergarten class when the principal came to get me. My father and my aunt were in the office. My brother was already outside in the car. We went to a resort in Wisconsin. My father told me it was a vacation.

"They say I cried the whole time for my mother, but I don't remember it. I remember that my father took me to the barber and they cut off my long hair. What I remember was crying about my hair.

"A court order brought us back home. Rather than let my mother have custody of us, my father had kidnapped us. The first time I heard the word divorce was after it was over.

"I don't blame my father. Today it seems like every kid's parents are divorced, but in the sixties that wasn't the case. I didn't have one friend, one schoolmate, one person I could point to whose parents were divorced. My father couldn't go to a bookstore and buy a dozen books on how to cope. He felt he was doing the best thing to simply say, 'Adult problems are adult problems. You still have your home. You still have your friends. Nothing's changed so much.' Anyway, that's the explanation I got.

"The neighborhood was talking. It wasn't above some of the women sitting out on their porches on a warm summer evening to call my brother or me over and ask where our mother was. They looked at us strangely when we said she was in Florida. In fact, she was in the hospital, in what they call a detox ward today, although we didn't know it. I remember wondering why I didn't get any post-cards from Miami.

"*Don't ever tell anyone outside the family our family business.* I heard that one so many times I think I believed that if I told anyone my parents were divorced, I'd immediately turn into a stone or something. School forms were the worst. There, in black and white, you were supposed to admit that your parents weren't together, that you lived with your father, a stunning turn of events in those days. I'd lose the forms so many times that the teacher finally sent me to the principal.

"So I was thrilled when my father remarried and we moved. I was in fifth grade then.

"The first day of school I started the lie. I brought some kids home with me after school and introduced my stepmother as my mother.

"The problem was, I had a real mother. That's how I thought of it in those days—a real mother versus some kind of ersatz mother. My mother was remarried, trying to get her life together, rid herself of whatever devils. She was trying desperately to repair the damage in her relationship with us. My brother and I were frightened of her. Here was this person we barely knew, who tried so hard to please us, but who had these silent moods and the habit of sleeping for hours on the couch while my brother and I stared at the clock, waiting for the time when we could go home. She had weekend custody. I lied about where I went on weekends, why I could never attend parties.

"One day I was standing in line at the movies with my mother. A group of my friends came walking up. I tried to hide, but there was no place to go. Who was I going to say I was with?

"My mind was racing. My mother stood, unknowing and expectant, curious and happy to meet my friends, anxious to make me proud of her.

"'This is my aunt,' I mumbled.

"I thought I'd die at the look on my mother's face. There was shock in her eyes, followed by sudden comprehension. Then there was only hurt and shame.

"It's been years since I've thought of that moment. She never said a word about what happened. Maybe it would have been better if she had I never forgave myself.

"You see, I sacrificed any relationship I might have had with my mother because I couldn't stand being different. I wanted a normal family. I had no idea what normal was.

"There was never a moment when I wasn't afraid of being found out. There was a day when I was, but it came much later. It was a different environment then. People were talking openly about their childhood trauma. The self-help era was beginning. Suddenly it was in vogue to say you suffered, to share your suffering. I started telling my family secret to people I met at parties, over coffee on first dates. I thought I could milk some value out of it.

"But I never shared the truth. I never went to a meeting of any kind. I never admitted I was powerless over what happened. I simply used it to what I thought was my best advantage. *See how I'm a survivor. See all my achievements. See how my childhood hasn't even affected me.*

"I live in a high rise. There are many young people living in my building because it's near a law university. I saw two parents standing by the elevator the other night. They were holding a present. It had a bow on it, but it wasn't wrapped. It was a box of everyday dishes. They were checking out the lobby, making conversation with the doorman. It's a scene that's played out a hundred times a year in this building: two parents coming to visit their grown child in his or her first apartment, wanting to help. Two parents together. Suddenly I had a lump in my throat the size of a golf ball.

"I have always compared myself to other people. This one has a better job. That one has more money. I'm better off than her. I'm not doing as well as him. Just talking about it now makes me realize that I'm still that little kid, looking at other people, and fearing that I'm different, that they have something I lack. The funny thing is, I have no real conception of where I stand versus anyone else. People compliment me, and I can't take it in. There's no award so big or achievement so great, that doesn't make me say, 'Yeah but, look at him.' I think, if I can do something, anyone can do it. So all this comparing gets me nowhere. It's a no-win."

The fallout from feeling different

What, if anything, does Richard's story have to do with the problem of constantly comparing yourself to other people? In Richard's background there was a family secret: divorce and alcoholism. For some people the family secret is adoption, financial problems, depression, illness. We had one client whose family secret was that his father leased the family car because he couldn't afford to own one. It doesn't matter how big or how small the secret is. What matters is that it wasn't something you were supposed to talk about outside your family. You therefore feel a sense of shame about it.

The interesting thing about the family secret is that keeping it was supposed to protect you. There are parents who impose silence because they worry about how the secret will reflect on them. But there are many more parents who out of genuine, perhaps misguided, love impose the silence because they want you, their child, to be protected from their failures. Keep the secret and no one will know. No one will think you're different. No one will look down at you. You'll be able to compete with the others. You'll still have a chance.

Here's the crux of the issue: *You're just as good as the others.* Everything about this secret tells you that you're not as good. If Mom's alcoholism is so fine and dandy, then why is it a secret? If Dad lost his job and that's just a fact of life, then why can't I tell my best friend?

The family secret is isolating. Because you hold up your end of the family banner that says, "Everything's okay here, everything is fine," you survive your childhood. But you can't get too close to anyone. You can't pry too deeply into other people's affairs. They give you one of their secrets and now you have to give one of yours.

Happy experiences of being loved and cared for as children instill in us the belief that there is plenty to go around; the world will provide what we need. But people like Richard grow up with an overwhelming sense of being left out. This is where the comparison thinking begins, Other people have it easier. Other people don't have to cope with what you have to cope with. Other people seem born with silver spoons in their mouths. They don't have to work their way through school. They don't have to cope with an alcoholic mother, an emotionally frosty father. Others are getting more than their fair share. It's the beginning of a feeling of bitterness; the stirrings of feelings of envy.

Richard silently endured the isolation. What if he had spoken out? If he'd shared his secret, perhaps a friend would have said, "Gee, that's tough. I've got troubles, too. Let me tell you what's going on with my sister."

Isolation is only part of the fallout from feeling different at a time in our development when conforming to our peers meant everything. Perhaps the biggest lesson the family secret teaches us is a lesson we remember all our lives: Don't show your vulnerabilities to anyone or else. Because you can't be yourself, because you are often pretending to be someone else, you end up with a shaky sense of your real identity.

We had a client named Kathy. Kathy was a doctor, a brilliant competent woman who admits, "My practice is doing great, and I really love my work. This should be the happiest time of my life, but I'm miserable. I meet tons of men, but I just can't seem to connect with anyone."

What puzzles Kathy most is that the men she cares about leave just when the relationship appears to be meaningful to them both. "They tell me they're not ready for a relationship. Six months later I hear they're getting married to someone else."

Ron is a man who dated Kathy. He says, "She's a great lady, but something wasn't happening with us."

What was missing? "I just never felt she was really there when we were together. I never really understood what she wanted with me. Kathy was too perfect. Maybe this sounds silly, but I never thought of Kathy as someone I could cuddle with."

What Ron couldn't see in Kathy was her vulnerability. We tend to believe that others will love us if we present them with a flawless "package" of achievements. But admiration isn't love. Perfectionism doesn't make one person lovable to another. Although we find it hard to believe, it's the run in our stocking, the chronic mismanagement of our checkbooks, the way we break out in hives when we have to speak in front of a group of people, that makes us vulnerable, and therefore lovable.

Other roots of comparison thinking

School is a competitive environment. Grades and class ranks force us to look at where we stand next to some standard. Work is a competitive environment with its own hierarchies. But sometimes the greatest competition is in the home.

"My sister and I have different fathers," one man explains "which is why she looks like Christie Brinkley and I look like Danny DeVito. My parents were very careful not to compare us to each other. Trouble is, they couldn't control the rest of the world. Store clerks, the mailman, camp counselors—everyone who met my sister wanted to please her.

"At school she never worried about such small matters as homework; everyone was delighted to have her copy their papers. She only got nervous when it was final exam time. Then she'd go up to the teacher, her eyes would fill with tears. Her mind had been on personal problems, she'd explain. She couldn't concentrate. She'd flash a smile through her tears and even female teachers would thaw. She'd walk out with a C instead of a D, when I couldn't talk my way out of one missing homework assignment."

The biggest problem this man encountered wasn't his inability to ever be like his sister. It was growing up with no idea who he was. The constant focus on all of the things his sister was only showed him what he wasn't.

When we can't stop comparing ourselves to others, it's often because unconsciously we are seeking a mirror—something or someone to reflect us back to ourselves and tell us who we are. In childhood, we needed our parents to mirror us—to react to us in a way that was validating—in order to gain a sense of wholeness. If our parents could not or would not do this adequately, we may lack a strong definition of ourselves. With a shaky grasp on our identity, we seek a point of reference against others, to make us feel secure.

Today's parents are often wise to the dangers of comparing their children to each other or to their classmates. Sometimes sister and brother aren't a hard act to follow in any case. But what about Mom and Dad?

"You wouldn't recognize my father's name," a man tells us. "He pays a public relations firm to keep his name out of the papers. He still gets listed when they do those stories about the five hundred wealthiest Americans or whatever."

The man who is speaking is an attractive thirty-one-year-old. His clothes look well thought out, his demeanor is self-assured. His face shows only the slightest beginnings of the effects of life's stresses.

"What's Dad like? People tell me he's a great guy. My brother and I would agree, except for the fact that he ruined our lives and made it impossible for us to ever relax during this lifetime."

He grins then, and it's the smile of a man who understands the irony of having deep insights into ourselves and finding that not one of them helps.

"The man has a brain like a computer. He can look at a sheet of numbers, have no idea what they pertain to, and tell you which number is wrong. Yet he wouldn't help me with a calculus problem. He'd say, 'Figure it out. Pay more attention in class.' You know how it goes. He never got any help from his father, he grew up during the Depression, challenges build character, blah blah blah.

"My brother just dropped out. He figured he couldn't do it, so why bother? I made the mistake of following my father into the same industry. I spend the day making a grand effort not to remember who my father is."

Does he hate this career because he isn't suited for it? Or is it because it's become clear that he isn't going to achieve anywhere near what his father achieved? "It never occurred to me that I wouldn't surpass my father the way his father surpassed his grandfather. I know I face a whole different economic picture. Still, when people learn who my father is, they think I've had it easy all my life."

Like many high-achieving parents, this man's father never realized that his accomplishments would be a mixed bag for his children—a source of pride on one hand and a source of intimidation on the other. Raised to compete and surpass, it never occurred to this man that he wouldn't have the same interests, capabilities, or drive as his father did—and that being different would be okay.

We've had clients whose constant comparisons to their parents have been a persistent drain on their self-esteem. If you're falling short all the time, you need to find a solution to it. For some, it's to become driven, to never feel that enough is enough. For quite a number of people it's to fabricate and inflate themselves. It's a setup for future exposure. Worse, there's a sense of shame at not being able to be yourself.

The need to know, where do I really stand?

Several years ago, we were teaching a class at a local community college on how to overcome self-criticism. We had a hypothesis in those days. Surely the most critical people were the ones who had grown up being criticized by others, most significantly their parents. It only made sense.

In the first class our theory exploded. One student after another said, "I don't know why I'm so self-critical. My parents gave me everything. They always encouraged me. They told me I was the most wonderful person in the world." Those classes helped form the hypothesis for our first book, *When Parents Love Too Much*. You can, in fact, grow up with everything on a silver platter and become a pampered-deprived child.

Ann was a case in point. She had come to the class in the middle of a self-defeating relationship. "I don't know what attracts me to these men in the first place," she admitted.

Kent the man she was involved with, had been a blind date. She'd started the evening with low expectations and was surprised that they had a wonderful time. Kent was quick-minded, cocky, attractive. The second date was better than the first. During the third date, Kent told her that she was the best thing that had happened to him recently.

Then he stood her up. A mistake, he claimed. A simple mix-up. Baloney, she told him. There was too little remorse in his voice. She hung up on him. A week later he showed up at her door. "Still mad at me?" he said with a boyish grin.

"And I let him in. Can you believe it? We had another great evening and I haven't heard from him since."

Ann was puzzled. "The strange thing is I know he really liked me."

We pointed out that whether he liked her or not was a moot point. "There are men who really like you but are also irresponsible, careless, troubled, self-centered."

"Yes, but don't you think that there would be a woman who could change a man like that? I mean, couldn't the right person come along and make him act differently?"

It was clear that Ann wanted to be that right person. It's a common fantasy. Ann's friends who had met her boyfriend told her frankly that they found him obnoxious in his arrogance. She didn't argue. But she believed he had beautiful, wonderful things deep inside. All he needed was the right person to bring them out. If she could only do enough, be enough, she'd have the key.

"The funny thing is I have tons of men in my life who tell me I'm beautiful, I'm wonderful, I'm everything they ever wanted. I almost get angry. 'Get a life,' I want to say."

Which brought us to the main point: "You think these people who are accepting don't know anything? These people who are indifferent—they know?"

"Well, not exactly. I guess if I could get him to care, then I'd win."

Winning. Losing. It was Ann's own terminology that stood out like a red flag. As a therapist, the first place you tend to look when you hear a story like this is for a rejecting person in the past, someone who has always let the client down, who they want so badly to win over they keep playing the scenario out with other people. Where was this person in Ann's life?

"Not my parents. That's for sure. If anything they were the opposite."

Ann was the youngest of four sisters. In some homes there might have been enormous competition for attention. But Ann was clearly her father's favorite. "I always knew I was it in his eyes. I could do no wrong. We have old family movies. We sit around on holidays and we watch those movies and my sisters tease me because so many of the pictures are of me. It's because Dad had the camera. He photographed what he loved most."

Which is why high school was a rude awakening. "I got dumped by my first boyfriend. My father told me the guy must be stupid and he didn't want me with stupid guys. Well, Mr. Stupid turned out to be my only boyfriend through four years of high school. The popular guys never seemed interested in me."

It was the beginning of a life of comparing herself to other women. Why was this one such a magnet for men? Why couldn't her body look like that one's? Why couldn't she have this one's luck?

If you can identify with Ann, the most compelling questions in your life have to do with why you never feel you're enough when you've been told so often how special you are. Ann's parents let her know that she was special and deserving of constant attention in a way that had more to do with their own needs to have a special daughter than Ann's needs to have a clear picture of herself. As she met people outside of her family, she sadly realized that the rest of the world did not always share this view. Whom, then, could she trust? This basic core of mistrust was projected out into the world to create an even more threatening environment. She mistrusted people and opportunities, fearing criticism, rejection, and physical harm. Every man was a test. Was it true that she was special, or not? The more indifferent the man, the harder the test. In school, Ann's teachers assured her that the harder the test, the more realistic the assessment. Her parents taught her that what came easy was probably not true or real.

With the best of intentions, our parents sometimes love us too much. No one is as smart, no one is as beautiful. We grow up under a pile of expectations. We look into a distorted mirror. The reflection is ultimately as unreliable as it would be if our parents told us we were hopelessly stupid or we'd never amount to anything. You can really feel like the rug is pulled out from under you when you don't meet these impossible expectations. You can feel that there's something deeply wrong with you. You may spend your life minimizing the people who accept you or praise you. They remind you of your parents, and look where that went.

Self-esteem comes much easier to children who are told, "You studied hard, you did all your homework, and you've achieved your goal," than some global, "You're so smart; I've always known you would set the world on fire." It gets to the heart of the issue when a parent says, "Your stuff is all over the floors, your drawers are unorganized, and that's why you are having a hard time getting dressed in the morning," than saying, "You're such a slob; I'm embarrassed by your room." Children learn that their actions get results, and if they don't like the results, they can take different actions. They realize that they are the one rowing the boat, and they get a sense of their own personal power. Children are much more objective than adults realize. Tell them, "You're so smart," and they think, "Yeah, but Jimmy is smarter." Call their reading groups the Bulls and the Bears, but every child can tell you which group has the "smart kids."

What Ann eventually learned was that the other women she envied who seemed to have such a way with men weren't necessarily more attractive. It was simply that they had definite personalities. They made the best of their potential because they had a true sense of what that potential was. They didn't need to be perfect. People were drawn to their self-assurance, their comfort in being themselves. Ann was focused on trying to figure out where she really stood in life by trying to get someone indifferent to finally tell her that she was okay. What she eventually learned to focus on was finding herself.

Why it will never be enough

They say that every behavior has a purpose. Let's look at what we try to achieve by comparing ourselves to others, and why it doesn't work.

❦ *To motivate ourselves.* When the teacher said, "Why can't you hand in a neat paper like Mary's?" or your mother said, "You've got so much more going for you than your cousin Jimmy," they did it with a purpose. In the first case, you were supposed to be motivated to change your sloppy ways. In the second case, if your achievements were really better than cousin Jimmy's, you were supposed to feel proud of yourself. If they weren't, you were supposed to wake up.

Through a process psychologists call internalization, many of us are going through life with a voice in our heads that sounds alarmingly like our parents or teachers. What you hope to accomplish with all your comparing is to motivate yourself in the same way others once tried to motivate you.

The problem is, competition isn't always that motivating. Competing with others often hurts performance by keeping self-esteem low and making even the winners needy of more success. The best performance comes when we compete with ourselves and acknowledge ourselves when we've done our best.

❦ *To get a sense of safety by figuring out where we stand.* Many of our clients who constantly compare themselves don't do it because they are obsessed with becoming leaders of the pack. Rather they are looking for a safe place within that pack.

A young man recently spoke at length about a woman in his study group whom he was attracted to. He laughed when we suggested that he ask her out. "What, and get squashed like a bug? Listen, women like her don't look at guys like me and think, Here comes Mr. Right.'" He dates women who comparatively lack his education, his level of success. They disappoint him inevitably with the same qualities that attract him initially.

It's a setup for polarization. Such a person ends up in two kinds of relationships—those in which he or she feels inferior and people-pleases, and those in which he or she feels superior and attempts to control.

When we understand this fully, we're on the road to changing a style of relating that is ultimately rife with self-sabotage. "I have scores of friends, all of them depending on me for one thing or another," Sharon, thirty-four, realizes. "I'm always listening and giving advice. But do I really like any of these women? No!"

Today Sharon is forcing herself to take a closer look at the part she plays in these relationships. Make no mistake, it's very seductive to be the stronger one in relationships. You feel needed, superior. It's not easy to resist someone who makes you feel like such an authority. But for Sharon it went deeper. "I could avoid the risk of seeking out friends who had more to share than their troubles. Such people intimidated me. What could I possibly provide in those relationships? Troubled people were safer."

These types of codependent friendships benefit no one. The person you're helping eventually grows to resent you, even as he or she depends on you. This is why those stuck in these friendships complain bitterly that their friends never phone them when things are going well.

Comparing yourself to others feeds chronic dissatisfaction rather than protecting you from it. What you often seek through all of this comparison is a feeling of emotional safety so that you can connect. What you get is a feeling of separateness. You don't get a sense of belonging when you focus on differences, but when you seek out commonalities with others. Comparison-thinking keeps you focused on being special rather than *real*.

The people you've read about in this chapter who focused so relentlessly on others' attributes and achievements were fueled more by pervasive questions about their own identity than anything else. What they envied most was other people's abilities to use their full potential, to get the most out of themselves. You, too, can get the most out of yourself. To get out of the comparison trap requires a cognitive shift.

RX: Your Prescription for Change ᶠᶠᶠᶠᶠᶠᶠᶠᶠᶠᶠᶠᶠᶠᶠᶠᶠᶠᶠᶠᶠᶠᶠᶠᶠᶠᶠᶠᶠᶠᶠᶠ

> *Sometimes I wish I could be some-*
> *one else. Then I realize the only*
> *thing I haven't tried is being myself.*
> —ANNE WILSON SCHAEF

What you need to understand about yourself

Given your history, it's understandable that you may lack a true understanding of who you really are. But you aren't going to find it by concentrating on how you're different.

The key questions

- What would change in my life if I began to see that we're all essentially just like everyone else?
- If it was safe to be myself, completely, how would I be different?

Where you need to focus

- on strengthening your sense of identity
- on overcoming the habit of isolating
- on relieving yourself of the shame of the family secret

The cognitive shift

- We are all special and unique; therefore, none of us is special and unique.

Thoughts and Exercises ♪♪

❧ *Get back in touch with yourself.* Singer-songwriter Bruce Hornsby whose single, "That's Just the Way It Is," catapulted him to the top of the charts in 1986, was at a local bookstore in Chicago promoting his new album and the crowd was standing-room only. A man in the audience asked him for advice on achieving success as a musician. Although it's difficult to recall Hornsby's exact words, he spoke at length of the importance of developing your own sound. There is a time to study the masters, he said, but then there is a time to let go and create your own style of music. Imitations rarely become huge successes in the music industry.

Your own personality, whatever it is, is much more attractive, much more vital, than any you could try to assume. You don't need to be anyone else—you need to become more of yourself. Focusing on what others have and trying to achieve the same guarantees that we'll be imitations, at best.

Instead, do everything you can to learn about yourself. Here's one way that you can begin. The following fill-in-the-blank questionnaire has been very successful in helping our clients gain a clearer picture of who they are. Take a moment to answer these questions with whatever thought comes to mind:

♦ A talent I feel proud of is _____.

♦ One thing I would like to do more of is _____.

♦ One thing I would like to do less of is _____.

♦ Much of my free time is spent _____.

♦ I am happiest when _____.

♦ I get angry when _____.

♦ One thing I wish I had told my parents is _____.

♦ If I wasn't afraid to be myself, I might _____.

♦ I'm proud that I _____.

♦ Something I fear is _____.

♦ I relax when _____.

♦ My father thought I was _____.

♦ My mother thought I was _____.

♦ Ever since I was a child I _____.

♦ It's hard for me to admit I _____.

♦ My secret brag is _____.

♦ All my life I _____.

♦ One thing I could change about myself but I don't is _____.

♦ My friends are _____.

♦ Something my boss doesn't know about me is _____.

♦ The role I played in my family was _____.

♦ Something I'd like to start doing is _____.

Whether you like your answers or not, they are evidence of the fact that you do have an identity, one you can build on. Notice any resistance you might have to answering any of these questions. Ask yourself what that's about.

❧ *Ask someone you trust for some mirroring.* Some of our parents weren't very effective in giving us a clear picture of ourselves when we were growing up. But mirroring is a process vital to recognizing who we are. It doesn't stop in childhood.

One of our clients recently went through a bad period at work. He felt that he was merely drifting, that he was afraid to take the kind of risks that would lead to a more fulfilling career.

"Do you see me like that?" he asked a close friend. His friend went on to tell him how he had always admired him. "You're not impulsive.

You think things out. The things you do don't seem like risks because you really understand what you're doing and why you're doing it. I've always wished I had your patience."

It was a new way of seeing himself that allowed him to recognize his "drifting" as having a purpose.

❦ *Trust your intuition.* In each of us there is a voice that is connected with our higher truth; however, we must look inward to hear it. It may appear as a hunch or a feeling.

Take fifteen to twenty minutes daily to close your eyes and ask for inner guidance on what you need to know about yourself.

❦ *Take a closer look at what you envy.* We recall a client who was depressed when all of her friends got married and began to have children. At every baby shower she'd find herself growing more and more self-critical. "I want a baby, and I don't even have a boyfriend. By the time I meet someone, it's going to be too late."

It's five years later and this woman is completing her master's thesis. Having a baby is the furthest thing from her mind, even though she recently met someone and marriage is suddenly an option. "I thought I wanted a baby, but the truth is I wanted to have some purpose in my life. My pregnant friends knew exactly what they were going to be doing in the coming years and I had no idea. My boyfriend sometimes refers to my master's project as my baby. He doesn't know how right he is."

Make a list of all of the things you want, right now, that you don't have. When you compare yourself to other people, what is it that they have that you wish you had?

Now consider that there might be more to each of those things you've listed. For example, the top thing on one of our client's lists was: "I wish I was young. I hate turning forty. I never realized how much I'd hate it. When I look at the twenty-five-year-old women at work, I want to die."

Unlike wanting more money or a nicer apartment, this client felt completely hopeless because being young again was something she could never have.

But working through this issue gave her insight. "I realized that I also hated being twenty-five. At that point in my life I was insecure; I never knew what I wanted. What I really envied about the younger women was that they had opportunities. I didn't need another jar of alpha-hydroxy cream. I needed to recover a sense of hope."

❧ *Ask yourself, Is the real problem that I'm stuck?* Part of the distress of the whole comparison game is realizing that we're stuck, while others seem to have the courage to move forward. Envy is a passive emotion. It drains energy and saps courage. On the one hand, we can't accept ourselves as we are. On the other, we can't make the effort to change.

Chances are, you are dissatisfied today because you haven't realized your ambitions. You may be troubled by feelings of failure. You may be suffering from depression or be unable to take much pleasure from your life right now. What you need to do is revive those unfulfilled dreams.

If you're envious of someone who is constantly outperforming you, try to analyze exactly what it is that person is doing right. Realize that the reason for your envy lies in your similarities—most of us don't spend our time envying Prince Charles. Study that person you envy. What can you learn to expand on your own techniques? Chances are, you're closer than you think.

❧ *Stop isolating yourself.* Terry Mandell is the author of *Power Schmoozing.* She teaches seminars in Los Angeles on learning to network. She tells a roomful of strangers to look around the room and find someone who intimidates them. Then she tells them to go up and talk to that person.

People are as surprised to find out that they intimidate others as they are to find out that most people aren't intimidating at all once you get to know them.

Certainly you are going to find many people in your life who have things that you wish you had. But the illusion that these things or qualities automatically equal happiness is sometimes a product of our own isolation. Isolation doesn't really protect us. It just perpetuates more myths. One woman says, "I joined a health club that had always intimidated me because of its reputation for having the most wealthy, successful members in the city. I got to know some of those people very well, and I'll tell you this: You can't imagine what's behind the lives of people you think of as the perfect couple. You can't imagine the cost some people have paid for their success. I don't idealize these people anymore."

❧ *Bring that family secret into the light.* John Bradshaw touched the hearts of millions of people in *Healing the Shame That Binds You* when he spoke of the effects of holding on to that shame and the necessity of externalizing it. He offers many suggestions for doing this in his book. Our clients have had particular success writing their feelings out, either as an autobiography or in letters to people in their past. Sometimes just the experience of telling your story is enough.

Group therapy is a setting where we bring together men and women of different ages and backgrounds to work through issues where they feel stuck. Initially, people see others as different based on appearances and their public presentation. However, over time as people reveal their private selves, it becomes clear that we are more the same than different.

One day in one of our groups a client took a risk and said, "I feel like I'm the only one who grew up in a family with no love." Immediately four members chimed in simultaneously and said, "I feel exactly the same way!"

You couldn't do anything about your childhood, but you aren't powerless now. You can discover how your childhood has affected your perceptions, and you can change those perceptions.

❧ ❧

Today I will stop looking to other people to tell me I'm enough.

❧ ❧

CHAPTER NINE

Why Do I Always Want the One Thing I Can't Have?

The Search for Safety

Life is what happens when you are making other plans.

—JOHN LENNON

Emily stood crunched in the crowd by the bar, impatiently shifting her jacket from one arm to the other. As she turned toward the door, she saw a tall man in a khaki sport coat heading toward her.

Emily caught her breath sharply. "It's Brad," she thought, her heart starting to race. "What if he comes up to me? What if he's with his fiancée?"

She was ready to dash to the ladies' room, when the man turned. It wasn't Brad. It was just another guy who looked like him.

Emily barely made it out of the restaurant and into a cab before the tears came. It all rushed back—the way Brad looked on that day so long ago, how she found out he'd met someone else. "It's been over a year," she admits, "but nights like that I wonder, *Why do I go out? Why bother? I'm never going to get over him.*"

Seven years ago Emily, college freshman, was anxiously riding her bicycle through the campus quadrangle, glancing around for a familiar landmark that would tell her where she was. The one place she wasn't looking was directly in front of her. Suddenly she was on the ground, her Schwinn on top of her. A tall guy wearing a faded chambray shirt was standing over her, alarmed, his own bicycle lying on its side, wheels spinning. It was Brad. "He apologized to me, like it was his fault," Emily remembers, with a smile.

It was the beginning of a friendship that was to last all through college. It was Brad who taught her to write a term paper, who found her a ride home over Christmas break, who dried her tears when she didn't get invited to pledge at the sorority she had her heart set on.

"'Is that your boyfriend?' That's what everyone we met wanted to know. I never thought of Brad that way. We were buddies, friends. And of course, then I met Warren, and I wasn't thinking about other guys."

It should have been a tip-off that the night Emily met Warren at a party, he was on a date with another girl. Still, he flirted with Emily the entire night while his date got progressively drunk and ended up crying in the bathroom. "I knew the girl, too, and I felt guilty. But Warren was overpowering. His kind of good looks make everyone stare. I couldn't believe he was attracted to me."

Warren hated Brad from the moment they met in Emily's dorm room, and the feeling was mutual. "I wasn't going to give up a friendship just because he was jealous, but it made things difficult."

Warren became an obsession. "I never knew where I stood with him. Once I went home for the weekend. When I came back I rushed to Warren's dorm, and he hugged me like he really missed me. He pushed me down on his bed, kissing me, and there was the unmistakable smell of another girl's perfume. He denied it. I didn't press. I was frantic at the thought I was losing him."

Summer came and without the day-to-day contact with Warren, Emily felt the relationship slipping through her fingers. "'Just be yourself, Em,' Brad would tell me. 'If he doesn't realize how special you are, it's his loss.' But I never felt special around Warren."

Over the next two years of college, Warren and Emily broke up and went back together many times. "Brad used to shake his head in disgust. 'You know what that guy needs, Em? A new shirt, a shave, and a new attitude. When are you going to wise up?'"

When Warren graduated and went to work at an accounting firm in the Midwest, it was the beginning of a year of unendurable anxiety for Emily. "After a weekend back home with Warren, I'd return to college and call Brad and beg him to come over. One night that spring I cried so hard I thought something inside of me would break. 'Brad, tell me the truth. Do you think I'm being paranoid? He tells me he's going to Las Vegas with this girl from work for a week. When I asked him why they were staying through the weekend if it was just business, do you know what he did? He slapped twenty dollars down on the table and walked out of the restaurant, leaving me sitting there. Do you believe it?'

"'I believe it,' Brad said, and he walked into the kitchen and I could hear him opening a bottle of wine. When he returned with two glasses, I thought for the hundredth time, *Why can't I fall in love with someone like him? Why am I always attracted to jerks like Warren?*

"That night Brad and I took a long walk. We sat on a park bench. We could see the whole campus lit up and it was beautiful. There were three weeks until graduation. Maybe that was it. The nostalgia, the sense of all we would lose in the coming weeks. He kissed me. It stirred me more than I would have imagined. I was in his arms and I felt this tide of warmth come over me. I wanted to run my hands through his hair, wrap myself around him. *It's almost like I'm in love with him,* I thought. *But I can't be. I'm in love with Warren.*

"'Why are we doing this?' I whispered. 'Don't you know? Don't you see?' he whispered back, kissing me again and again. I broke away. I was so confused. I left him sitting on that park bench."

Brad called the next day and apologized. Emily didn't know what to say. Before she could respond, she heard a knock on the door. Warren stood in her hallway holding a silly graduation gift, half drunk and wanting sex. "I used to think Warren was so passionate. He used to say things to me, embarrassing things, while we made love, and tell me I was uptight if I got turned off. That night I bit my cheek hard, listening to him. I wouldn't laugh. I couldn't. But it was just so funny. He sensed I wasn't with it. We never even finished.

"Back home after graduation I landed a position with an advertising firm. Warren said, 'Let's move in together. With what you're making and what I'm making, we'll have it made.' I would have died to hear him say that a month before. We were out celebrating at an expensive restaurant, but I could barely eat. All I could think about was Brad. Brad, who hadn't called me since that night on the park bench over two months ago. I told Warren I thought I was coming down with the flu and when I watched him drive away, all I felt was relief.

"Brad was in his bathrobe when I got to his apartment. He went out to pay the cab, and when he returned he sat on the couch waiting for me to speak. But when I started to talk, to explain how I had suddenly realized I loved him, had probably loved him for years and just been too stupid to know it, he stopped me. 'It's too late,' he said. Then he told me he'd met someone.

"I couldn't believe it. 'You care about her more than you care about me?'

"'It's not about more, Em. I'm not like you. I'm not always looking for more. She loves me. She knows what she wants. It's too late for you and me.'

"Something in my voice sounded like begging, and I hated myself. But I had to make him see. Finally he said, 'Let it go, Em. It isn't going to be.'"

And it wasn't. After months of crying nightly and berating herself, Emily sincerely wants to move on. But somehow she can't forget him. "He's never coming back, but there's never a day that I don't wake up wanting him. I just can't get over this."

Futile attractions

Emily found herself in therapy because she wanted something she couldn't have and had no idea how to stop wanting it. She discovered that it was a familiar theme that had permeated most of her life. She came to realize that Warren was most attractive to her when he didn't want her. When Brad pulled away from her emotionally after their disastrous night on the park bench, she was suddenly drawn to him in a way she had never experienced before.

To a certain extent, most of us long for what we don't have. It's human to want what we lack. There are disappointments and limitations all of us have to live with and accept. But for some of us, such longing has made our lives miserable and unmanageable. It isn't a simple wish for more, but a driving fixation on one special thing we can't obtain or accomplish that robs us of happiness and leads to years of discontent and frustration.

Wanting what one can't have isn't something reserved solely for star-crossed lovers. Says one man: "My father is obsessed with my brother, Jack. Jack is abusive to him, he neglects him, he uses him for his money, but if Jack suddenly calls him, it's like the sun comes out. Last Christmas he spent the evening in his bathrobe, too depressed to get dressed, because Jack wasn't coming. My two sisters, my mother, and seven grandchildren were there, but it didn't matter."

Wanting the one thing you can never have may mean wanting someone—your parents, your stepdaughter, your boss, your husband—to change. It can mean feeling you can't be happy until they do. Or it may mean wanting a change in yourself—to be a powerhouse of assertiveness instead of the shy, reflective person you are. To be small boned and thin, rather than tall and large.

When wanting what you don't have means you spend your life inexplicably drawn to people who are indifferent to you, pursuing careers you have no talent for, throwing time and money at the problems of your children who don't want their problems solved, waking up each morning depressed by thoughts of "If only this, if only that," something much more significant and destructive than the fact that the grass always seems greener on the other side is operating.

The problem: We attach fantasies to whatever it is we want

People who are obsessed with achieving the one goal that eludes them spend hours fantasizing. As one woman, involved in a tortuous relationship with a married man, tells it: "He would get dressed at midnight and go home to his wife. Of course, he'd always shower. I'd go to sleep holding the towel he used. It smelled like him. I'd think about him going home and missing me, waking up and finally realizing that I was the person he wanted to spend his life with. I imagined it all—our wedding day, the home we'd have. I spent hours laying in my bed, and it was like a movie where I kept adding new scenes."

But these fantasies often have a goal that goes beyond captivating the married man, making the million dollars, turning the underachieving child into an academic success.

✿ *The liberation fantasy.* Sean is a twenty-one-year-old actor whose credits include several commercials and a bit part in a television show. He is frank about his yearning to be famous, which has little to do with wanting acknowledgment for his effort. Sean was teased mercilessly by several male classmates throughout high school because he was overweight and sensitive. He admits, "I'd like to do something someday, and they'd hear about it. I'd be someone special, and they'd still be pumping gas."

Emily, the college student who fell in love with her best friend, also came to see that her "love" for men who were indifferent to her held out the hope of liberation. Liberation from a shaky self-esteem. Liberation from doubts about whether or not she was really desirable.

When I'm rich, they'll be sorry. When I'm married, they'll see I was lovable. When my stepdaughter appreciates me as she does her own mother, I'll know I'm important. The liberation fantasy is about having control over other people's sense of our value through some accomplishment.

✿ *The gratification fantasy.* Robert, a thirty-five-year-old human resource specialist, tells a story which illustrates how achieving a dream can lead to disappointment when the dream isn't based on what we really need but what we need to prove.

Robert was formerly a high school teacher who absorbed his

wife's and society's negative perceptions of the teaching profession. "People would remark that I only worked nine months of the year, as if that made me lazy. My wife said, 'Anyone can teach,' like I had nothing special. The business world seemed to hold out this promise of respect.

"Trouble is, when I was teaching I used to feel I was contributing something to the world. Next to that, rewriting employee benefits manuals seems meaningless."

At the heart of the gratification fantasy is the belief that by achieving this one thing we will finally be happy. Unfortunately, happiness, like any other feeling, is transient. The person wrapped up in the gratification fantasy has the hope that by achieving some goal, happiness will be his or hers once and for all.

Let's look at how these fantasies might work in tandem. At forty-three, Cindy wanted one thing more than anything in the world: For her twenty-four-year-old son, Jeremy, to be a responsible, motivated, stable human being. She was beginning to believe it was the one thing she could never have. She was struggling with a dilemma: Should she rescue Jeremy from bankruptcy?

It was far from the first warning that Jeremy was irresponsible, Cindy admits. "After two months in a junior college, Jeremy flunked out and decided he wanted to backpack across the country. For a woman like me—always planned, always organized—the prospect of my son drifting around the country was impossible. I wanted to know, 'Where will you eat? You have no money.' He shrugged. 'Aw, Mom, I'll eat at happy hours along the road.' It was incomprehensible to me that anyone would cross the country living on hors d'oeuvres. I lectured, begged, and screamed until I was so exhausted I could barely move. I even tried to enlist my ex's help. 'See what you've caused now,' he said. And of course, a part of me believed that. And I was so bitter. He still had the power to hurt me. My ex had never wanted to settle down. I got pregnant with Jeremy accidentally, a month after we were married, and he wanted me to get an abortion. It always hung in the air, between us, every time we had a problem with Jeremy.

"The night before Jeremy left, I threw a party for him. Can you believe mothers do these things? I mean, I actually planned and threw a party.

"Once Jeremy moved out, he could completely avoid me, and he did. So why didn't I just say, 'Adios, Amigo. You're old enough to be on your own?' Why didn't I get on with my own life? After all, Jeremy wasn't committing murder. My friends would say, 'Cindy, you're still young. Why don't you go out, meet somebody?' But Jeremy consumed all of my energy."

It was a call from a bill collector that finally made Cindy see how desperate the situation had become. Jeremy had debts in excess of $30,000. "I flew out to Arizona, determined to take some control. Jeremy was shocked when I ended up at his door. 'Mom, you're making such a thing about this. It's no big deal.' In the end, I forced Jeremy to take money that he didn't want to take. Why? I kept hoping he'd change. I kept praying he'd grow up. I kept thinking I could do something right, say something right, give him a clean slate, and he'd change into the person I knew he could be. He was my son. I couldn't just give up."

There's an old saying that goes, When you're ready to learn the lesson, the teacher will appear. Two months later, Cindy was interviewing a young man for a position in her department. "At that time, our firm still sent job candidates for lie detector tests. I asked the man if there was anything special about his resumé, which was a nice way of saying, Tell me whatever it is now, before it comes out in the lie detector test. He told me that five years ago, he had declared bankruptcy. I practically pumped him for information, finally confessing that I had a son who almost suffered the same fate. 'Didn't your parents help you?' I asked. 'They never had that kind of money,' he admitted. 'I owed ten thousand dollars.'

"Here was this young man, so mature, so together. He suffered the consequences of his actions and learned from them because he didn't have parents wealthy enough to bail him out. I felt a sense of shame pour over me.

"He looked at me as if he was measuring me. Finally he said, 'I don't know your son, but I think you should realize something. It was drugs or gambling or bad business deals that got him into this. It always is. For me, it was the racetrack. I haven't been at the track for five years. Look around his apartment. Do you see anything worth $30,000?'

"Suddenly, I wished with all my heart that I had allowed Jeremy to declare bankruptcy."

For so many of us, action is a defense against pain. Rather than feel our despair, we have to do something, anything. Cindy, reeling from the pain of her divorce, refused to acknowledge her despair and guilt and became a doer and a giver. She never allowed herself to grieve her loss. Instead, she fought to exert power in her son's life. She tried to replace the agony she couldn't control with agony she thought she could.

She made Jeremy her life. She made solving his problems her major goal—a gratification fantasy of finally being appreciated, finally being in control, and a liberation fantasy of finally proving that she could overcome the defeat of her marriage. She could show that she was worthy, she was important, she was needed, by being the perfect mother.

Jeremy had all of the qualities Cindy feared and buried in herself. He had spontaneity. He feared nothing. On an unconscious level, Cindy envied his liberation from everything that had been such a burden in her own life. She would have loved to have one moment in her life where she felt safe. She would have loved to have a person come and rescue her from her own mistakes. She unconsciously gave Jeremy what she lacked in life: a stronger person who would really care.

We learn in therapy that the stronger person who is going to come and rescue us and make everything feel safe is *ourselves*.

Until that realization hits us, we have little sense of our own value. We are tied up in knots, obsessed with these fantasies of someone else giving us the signal that we are okay or offering so much security that we never doubt ourselves again. We are attracted to what we can't have, and even when it's making us miserable, we can't let go. Therefore, the woman captivated by a married man tells an attractive single man who pursues her at work that she's busy and spends the holidays in loneliness and bitterness. The family with the six-figure income feels poor. The person who loses twenty pounds is devastated because the last five just won't come off.

The interesting thing about these fantasies is their all-or-nothing quality. Cindy, for example, had so many other opportunities to be of value. She had reassurances from her career, from her friendships, that she was important and lovable. It fell around her like so much rain. *This and only this will result in liberation or gratification. If I can only get my son to change, he will become everything I need him to be, and I'll have everything I've wanted all my life.*

The question is, do we really want to be liberated from our pain? When we get what we think we want, will it finally be enough? Do we really want the gratification of knowing we're important? Given our history, maybe not.

Your probable history

Sometimes we only see it later:

- ♦ "I realize now that I fell so hard for her because she was a challenge. She was a little wild, selfish, insensitive. It drew me like a magnet."

- ♦ "I saw the writing on the wall the day I interviewed for the job. They sent me out to lunch with a man who told me confidentially that four people had left that position, most within three months, because no one could work with the man who would be my supervisor. I thought, *No, it will be different for me. I'll be the one person who can handle him.*

♦ "My expectations were always ridiculously high. If it came easy, I didn't want it."

It's no accident that we're drawn to goals that will ultimately elude us. No one becomes a person who is consistently drawn to the insurmountable, then beats himself up over what he can't accomplish by accident. In your soul, you believe that one thing and only one thing will banish all of your despair. Given a certain history, this is understandable.

Ellen, twenty-four, is a case in point. She has dyslexia. Throughout her childhood her parents could barely drag her away from her books to play, so desperately did she want to learn to read. As she grew older, she came to understand her learning disability, but never to accept the finality of it. "My parents were very supportive. My father would say, 'You're just like anyone else.' My mother helped me with schoolwork every night, telling me that she believed in me, that I could do it. But it wasn't true. Every day I saw that I wasn't like everyone else. But I wanted to believe them. I know that they were trying to help, but in the end it might have been better if they'd just told me the truth."

With tutors and special programs she made it through high school and college, even though an assignment that might have taken her classmates fifteen minutes would take her two hours. Recently, she was accepted to law school. She is a woman with ragged cuticles, deep circles under her eyes, and a stomach constantly churning with anxiety from a punishing routine. She is also a woman with many other strengths. In fact, about the only thing Ellen doesn't do easily is read—but it's all she wants to do.

You may be saying to yourself at this point, "But isn't it good not to be a quitter? Isn't it just human nature to want what you can't have?"

It may seem natural to you, but consider this: People who come from backgrounds where there was enough empathy, where there was attention, approval, and validation of their truest selves, where they weren't constantly pitting themselves against challenges too steep, aren't drawn into situations where they have to consistently wring admiration or attention from others. They aren't drawn to situations where they consistently feel like failures. These situations don't feel so familiar to them. Such people aren't drawn to overcoming the impossible or making others see the light. They are accustomed to promoting their own well-being. If a situation doesn't feel good, that's enough of a reason to move on. They give wide berth to people who make them feel insecure, rather than concluding that they are unlovable and should try harder to prove themselves. Indifferent people, impossible circumstances aren't something to be pursued, but avoided. If a relationship is unfulfilling, a career unrewarding, the situation becomes disagreeable, not compelling. Giving up isn't something one does because one is a quitter, but because one has simple emotional common sense and doesn't always need to feel he or she is to blame.

There's an interesting fact about blaming oneself which explains why so many people are so willing to take it on. If one is at fault, then one can always do better. As long as one is responsible, one always has hope.

❧ *Magical thinking.* "This will be different. This will make everything all right." In normal childhood development all of us pass through a stage of magical thinking. We believe we control other people's actions through our thoughts.

But in a dysfunctional family, we stay or fixate on this type of thinking to avoid the pain and fear of confrontation. Those who keep obsessing bitterly about the one thing they can never have suffer from an addiction to hope. In a dysfunctional family, the goal is always to become something more so that something we wish for will happen. Our parents will stop fighting, our father will stop drinking, our mother will stop being depressed.

Brian is a man who works as a claims adjuster during the day and then works at a men's clothing store two evenings a week and every other weekend. He has three children, a second mortgage, and a stack of bills he never gets to the bottom of. His wife, seeing his exhaustion and frightened by his depression, has offered to go back to work, to move to a smaller house, but those conversations anger him in a way he can't explain. After a particularly grueling week, he'll wander into an electronics store and come out with a new television or a computer. "We don't need this; we can't afford this," his wife will tell him, and the arguments that follow will be bitter. The strain on their marriage is overwhelming. Money is all they discuss, argue about, dream about, and despair about. But Brian won't allow any one to remove his burden.

There's something very understandable about a man wanting to provide for his family and his willingness to go to many lengths to achieve it. But Brian's background makes such a quest to overcome the odds even more understandable. The need to take on a challenge was great from the start.

Brian's strongest memories of his childhood are the many times he comforted his mother, a woman who was often in tears over the passive-aggressive behavior of his father. "My mother would invite ten people to a dinner party. My father would go to take a bath before the guests arrived and then stay in the bathtub the entire evening and never come out. Ten people would try to eat and make conversation, and the whole time they could hear the water running and know he was in there."

In another home, this might have meant war. But Brian's mother sunk into deeper depression and hopelessness, so terrified was she of taking a stand against her husband, so frightened of being alone.

Can a twelve-year-old child fix a parent's empty marriage? No. But he can be one terrific Band-Aid. Unfortunately, a twelve-year-old child doesn't sit himself down and say, "My father's an emotionally limited, passively aggressive person and my mother is weak and scared, and none of the despair in this home is something I can do anything about so I'll look elsewhere for support and accept what I can't change." Brian felt his mother's anger and frustration keenly, and he found himself in the role of his mother's confidant. He heard many things in that role, and not one of them made him feel anything but anxious and insecure. He learned to force himself to listen with compassion to details of his parents' sexual life, their financial picture, their secrets. He protected his mother at the expense of himself. He never complained that his own right to have a childhood was overlooked. This is where magical thinking developed in his life for the first time. If he could be helpful enough, if he could be strong enough, if he could be no burden at all to anyone, he could solve the problem in his family. He could overcome the odds.

People like Brian become used to challenges, impossible situations. Difficult childhoods spawn magical thinking because magic is a child's only hope for power in a situation over which he or she is completely powerless.

Your difficult experiences may have had nothing to do with your family. They may have involved trouble in school. You may have felt excluded by your peers. Your early dating experiences might have been painful. There may have been financial problems, loss. There may have been another sibling so gifted, so talented, that you felt unable to compete. Perhaps your parents were there for you through it all; but if there were elements in those experiences you could do little about, you may still be blaming yourself. You may be drawn to situations where you can once again attempt to prove yourself. The more difficult it is for you to let go of this one unrealistic hope or dream that is making you miserable, the more elements of the past struggle it contains.

❧ *Attachment hunger.* In *How to Break Your Addiction to a Person,* Dr. Howard M. Halpern writes of his work with clients who remained in bad relationships, but could not end them even though they knew the relationships were bad for them. "The basic illusion, which is itself a distortion of reality, is, 'If I can be connected to this one person and make it good, my life will be wonderful, and if I can't my life will be horrible, empty, and unhappy.' It is based on the unconscious wish to recapture the experience of a blissful connection with

Mother in the very early years and/or a special and exciting connection with Father a little later."

In other words, we are hungry for a powerful sense of connection that eludes us. While most people hunger for a sense of attachment, some of us are literally starving for it, perhaps because we never experienced a deep enough or lasting enough attachment during the early period of life. According to Halpern, such hunger may make us cling to the illusions such as: "The mother or father to whom you looked to make you feel good, secure, and strong exists in the person with whom you are now involved; therefore, if you can get that person to love you, everything will be okay."

Although Halpern's advice is for those who want the one relationship they can never have, it makes equal sense for people who find themselves focused on whatever it is they can't accomplish. This thing, this person, this goal appears to promise more than a sense of accomplishment. The tip-off that attachment hunger may be at work, according to Halpern, is when we tell ourselves that we must have one and only one thing to make us happy.

❧ *The need to avoid our real feelings.* By fixating on this one thing we can't have, by blaming everything that goes wrong on the fact that we don't have it, we may be attempting to avoid a deeper anguish and despair. We keep an underlying depression at bay by fixating on chaotic but stimulating interactions of pursuing our goal. It's not that our marriage is empty—it's that we can't lose twenty pounds. The diet books, the meetings, the exercise programs keep our minds well occupied. The obsession with the unaffectionate man, the child who won't do his homework, the deal we can't close is like a drug that helps us avoid our pain, emptiness, or anger. The more impossible it is, the more of a distraction it provides.

To be without the dream is to be without hope, to be left to confront the real pain. This, we think will be worse than the day-to-day pain of the longing for what we can't have.

Carl, fifty-three, admits, "It never occurred to me that I had no sense of purpose at work, that the whole trouble boiled down to that. I decided my college major when I was seventeen on the basis that someone told me that accountants make money. My whole life I've been frustrated because I don't make enough money. There was never a moment that I thought that I could be happy without a lot of money."

In *Real Magic,* Dr. Wayne W. Dyer, points out that you can never get enough of what you don't want. "The alcoholic despises the alcohol that consumes his life, yet he can never get enough of it. So too the drug addict. The person who is argumentative and full of rage despises the anger in him, yet never seems able to resist the invitation to argue. The overweight person hates the food that he craves and yet never has enough. So many of us disdain the money that seems to run our lives and the need to chase it, yet we never seem to get enough of it."

We want it, we can't have it, and we are always in crisis. What we don't realize is that we may actually *need* the crisis in order to function. Something in our past has made us crisis addicts. We were confronted with the inconceivable, the unendurable, the painful, and we put aside our feelings about it and endured. We got a lot of applause from this endurance. In fact, this might be the entire foundation of our self-esteem—we made it despite the lack of empathy, the lack of support, the lack of love, because we refused to feel our feelings. Without the stress, without the desperate situation to manage, buried childhood feelings of being overwhelmed would surface.

When we're dreaming of all the things we can do, the phone calls we can make, the diets we can try, the words we can say, there's no panic, no pain. There's only the hope of relief. *We can never get enough of what we don't want.* What promises relief weighs us down and feeds our discontent at the same time.

Why it will never be enough

You know this. Before we say it, you know it. But we'll say it anyway: When you get what you think you want, you won't want it. It won't look as good to you. It won't be enough.

You know this is true because you've had the experience of getting what you wanted before. You sense it because when you get close to what you want, you know in your heart of hearts that you've sabotaged it. Or you found a new crisis to obsess about, another reason why you can't be happy.

You are not alone. We once asked a client, "If we could give you a pill, and this pill would mean that you would no longer want to pursue this path that is making you so unhappy, would you take it?" Silence. "I don't know," she finally said, staring down at her shoes. The answer was clear.

Insight isn't curative. Although you may identify with many of the people in this chapter, and conclude that you, too, are drawn to difficult situations, you may be ultimately unwilling to let go. The most prevalent reason is that this entire struggle makes you feel safe. How so? Consider the following:

❧ *In mysterious ways, the fantasy provides you with a sense of fulfillment that can sap your motivation for anything real.* Fantasies about unavailable people or situations actually provide a sense of being in an exciting relationship. *Why bother with that resumé; if I sell my screenplay I'll have so much money, I won't have to work.* You lay down on your bed, fantasize, and feel stimulated. The unconscious mind has no time frame. You get an exhilarating high, as if you're having those experiences.

Such fantasies provide love without commitment, intimacy without involvement, comfort without being vulnerable. Suppose you get what you've been dreaming of. Now you are faced with fears of commitment. Now you will struggle with the challenges of intimacy. You will be vulnerable. You may suddenly be face to face with whatever you've tried so hard to avoid.

❧ *Giving up may leave a big, black hole in your life, which you have no idea how to fill.* You're involved in this quest, worrying, and wondering, what if. It gives you an illusion of an enormous sense of purpose.

What will you have left, you wonder, if you let go? It may be more comfortable to wait for someone else to change than it is to do the work of changing yourself.

❧ *You may become so fixated on or comforted by your fantasy, that you no longer question it.* It's possible that what's keeping you hooked isn't this thing or person you think you can't be happy without, but something else. George, thirty-two, realized, "It wasn't Lori I couldn't get over. It was four years at the University of Illinois. I felt an emotion in those days I just can't get in the nineties. Lori was tied to all the things I can't recapture about those days."

If George gets Lori, will he be eighteen again? Or will he piece together the fragments of whatever was broken, try to live with the new whole, and see the broken pieces whenever he looks too hard?

You get to avoid risk. If you send those poems into a publisher and they're published, what then? Worse, what if they're rejected? Agonize over why they're never good enough to send out and paralyze yourself, and you never have to know. You never have to give up the comforting dream. Stay in a tortuous relationship where you'll never get enough, and you'll never confront your fears of intimacy. Pursue the unfulfilling career that frustrates you but pays the bills, and you never have to face a future that's uncertain. But it's taking those very risks that will provide a real sense of safety, rather than a house of cards.

RX: Your Prescription for Change

> *A little of something is better than a lot of nothing.*
>
> —DAN MILLMAN

What you most need to understand about yourself

Given your history, it's understandable that you are drawn to challenges, but you may be avoiding the real risks you should be taking.

The key questions

- What scares me so much in the present that I focus on the past or the future to avoid it?
- If I had only one more month to live, what would I be doing differently?
- What is the payoff for never succeeding?
- What purpose do I have in life if I put an end to this fantasy?

Where you need to focus

- on the here and now
- on diminishing denial as a defense
- on figuring out what you're attempting to avoid in the present
- on finding stimulation in reality instead of in fantasy

The cognitive shift

- Thinking about real situations can be more fulfilling than being preoccupied with exaggerated dreams.
- I can feel afraid and take action anyway.

Thoughts and Exercises

❦ *You are the only person who can assess whether you have a goal or a fantasy.* You are the only person who can count the costs of pursuing that dream and decide when enough is enough. Make an assessment. How long have you been trying to get this one thing you can't have? Have there been any changes, any real evidence that you should go on hoping? Do any of your efforts make the situation better? Are you really making sincere efforts to move forward? How long has this quest been making you unhappy? Does the cost outweigh the benefits?

If you're always attracted to the losing cause, now is the moment to figure out why. Now is the moment to look at the central issue— your self-esteem. Your belief that you are deserving of happiness. You don't have to earn it. You don't have to wring appreciation out of indifferent people to believe you are worthwhile.

We were giving a lecture a year ago when a woman came up to us and said, "I really identify with what you're saying about trying to make up for the past. But I really did mess up. I really have hurt my parents. I did things that were terrible."

There's an old biblical saying: Go forth and sin no more. Every one of us messes up. Every one of us disappoints other people. And every one of us had a reason. You don't have to accomplish the impossible to say you're sorry. Just say you're sorry. And mean it. Make amends where you can, but don't feel you have to dedicate your life to overcoming childhood flaws, righting wrongs, or proving you were right.

❧ *Ask yourself what you're avoiding by continuing your focus on this one thing you can't achieve.* For instance, if your struggle is with a relationship that you cannot set right no matter how much you try, ask yourself what you might be avoiding by continuing to try. Being single again? Rejection? Confronting your own high expectations? A sense of failure? A Saturday night alone? Whatever it is, write it down and look at it squarely.

Take an inventory of your relationship and see what the payoffs are. Possible payoffs are safe sex, companionship, financial support, knowing someone cares. What are yours?

Take a closer look at what happened each time you attempted to break off the relationship. What drew you back into it?

Most important, ask yourself: *If this relationship is the same way ten or fifteen years from now, will I be glad I stayed?*

❧ *You may come closer to getting what you want when you let go than when you chase after it.* Many clients have told us stories which point to the power of letting go:

For five years my boyfriend and I went back and forth about whether or not we should get married. Finally, we set a date. All of a sudden I could feel him pulling away from me. After all this, was he backing out? What would I do? I started to panic. Then I heard this very reasonable voice in my mind say, *You can move back to LA.* I thought of my friends there. One of my girlfriends was going through a divorce, herself. I could stay with her. We could help each other get past it all. It seemed a very real, viable choice. I knew in that moment that if he left me I'd be devastated but not destroyed. I'd be opening the door to who knows what, and it didn't feel scary as much as exciting. I wanted him, but I didn't need him to survive. What I was thinking showed in my eyes and he saw it. We got married two weeks later, and we've been happy ever since.

When I stopped worrying about money, it suddenly flowed into my life. I stopped thinking about what I was supposed to say, and I said what I thought. I stopped thinking about how I was supposed to invest, and I did what I wanted. I stopped thinking about how my company had to change so I could be happy, and I started thinking about how I could change so I could express myself. It meant risk. It meant that I had to control my anxiety over the future by concentrating on here and now. I started to ask, *What would I be doing with my life today, if I was not worrying about my finances?* When I started to feel panic, I looked for ways to deal with my anxiety, rather than why I wasn't making enough money.

I stopped dieting when I was looking through an old photo album and I saw a picture of myself in my twenties. I weighed

109 then. But I looked at that woman in the picture and I remembered how I still thought my thighs were too big. People and opportunities didn't fall on my doorstep. Why did I keep thinking being thin was the answer to my problems now? So I gained seven more pounds, but I was no longer obsessed with a list of what I could eat, what I shouldn't eat. I was no longer thinking about dinner when I was eating breakfast. A month later, I noticed that a pair of pants I hadn't fit into in a year actually fit. No, I wasn't 109, but I was losing weight without even thinking about it. When I was hungry I ate what I wanted, and I found that I didn't want it as much once I knew I could have it. I suppose I'll take that pill that makes you lose weight automatically if they ever put it on the market. Until then, I have other things on my mind.

I think that when you can't bear it, when you believe that your adult children's plans, dreams, and lives are impossibly misguided, when you've talked yourself blue in the face, it's time to let go. Just let go. Accept. Trust that you've done the best you could do and that doing more at this point speaks to your own needs rather than their needs. I refused to pay my daughter's parking tickets. If I told you how much time, energy, and money has been spent on this child, how difficult it was for me to say no, you wouldn't believe it. My self-esteem slipped an extra notch every time my help didn't solve her problems. She ended up getting a loan from her credit union, and she complains that it means that she'll have to stay with that job a little longer. That, to me, is a bonus.

These people didn't come to these insights without help and support. Letting go isn't something we should be doing with clenched teeth and white knuckles. When this is the only stance we can take, it's a signal. We may be trying to change our behavior without changing the underlying beliefs that support it.

Your attitude has to change as well as your actions. To truly let go, you have to believe that this is a positive step for you. And you have to realize that it is a step-at-a-time process. You don't walk away from something you've given years of energy to with a shrug.

One mother gives this advice to parents: "Start with the little things. Big issues like your son's drug addiction aren't the first thing you tackle when you're trying to let go. I started letting go by not jumping up to look for my son's car keys every time he couldn't find them. Sounds ridiculous? Believe me, the small steps lead to the bigger ones."

❦ *Address the real issue.* The starting point is to treat ourselves with enough respect to realize that if there are goals that elude us, there are excellent, if not immediately apparent, reasons why. Those reasons are inside yourself. Do you really want it? Are you trying to pit yourself against formidable odds to prove something to someone? What do you need to prove to yourself? Is your inability to let go of what isn't succeeding in your life a fear of the unknown?

❦ *Eliminate the worlds "wish" and "hope" from your vocabulary.* The cardinal rule is, What you see is what you get. Yes, there are many people who finally achieved the impossible after years of struggle and misery; however, there are millions of people who will tell you that they wasted years hoping for something they never got.

❦ ❦

Today I will commit to going after what I want, or I will let it go.

❦ ❦

CHAPTER TEN

Saying Enough Is Enough

The Search for Satisfaction

Our dilemma is that we hate change, but we love it at the same time. What we want is for things to remain the same, but get better.

—SIDNEY HARRIS

Is anyone ever satisfied? What intrigued us when we began our research was discovering people who felt satisfied in spite of their failures, conflicts, and problems. How do they do it? What did they know that the rest of us should know?

Some of the people whose interviews follow gained their insight from overcoming great disappointments. Others came to understand that their dissatisfaction was self-created. Although the details of the stories differ, certain themes emerge:

♦ The importance of pursuing personal growth as well as achievements

♦ The importance of building a "family of choice"—a support network of people who allow one to change without fearing abandonment

♦ The need for a clearer perception of how much success one has actually attained relative to others

♦ The importance of fully accepting all parts of the self

♦ The changes that happen quickly when one stops digging in the ashes and says, "How am I setting myself up for dissatisfaction?"

Dan C.: "I had to be the best."

"I was a kid who grew up more privileged than most. I would drive to school in my father's Mercedes. I felt a sense of specialness because of that. I must admit that I flaunted it on occasion for my own gain, but what went with that was a sense of shame that I was flaunting something that had to do with my father's success. I learned that some people would just use me for the fact that my family had money.

"My father was a perfectionist and driven. My mother was controlling and what they call codependent. I've always felt that what I did wasn't good enough. I've always had to become the best. I got into golf, and I had to become the best golfer. I had to be Jack Nicklaus. I got into music, and I wanted to become Bruce Springsteen.

"I never wanted to be myself. I always wanted to be like someone else. I wanted to be famous. I wanted the adulation of a tremendous crowd. I wanted to hear, 'You are the greatest!'

"If I didn't get that, nothing else was enough. I didn't believe I could feel satisfied with less. And so I worked at it; however, the amount of work that it would entail for me to get to the levels I aspired to were too difficult for me to stay with. I didn't become a professional golfer, although I'm a good golfer. I didn't become a professional musician, although I can compose some good music. And I really had to struggle with a sense of failure at not being able to accomplish what were my dreams. I quit a lot because it got too hard. It was almost like I was unable to attain the dream, and that made me less.

"The bottom came in Florida when I was planning to become a professional golfer and didn't make the golf team. I didn't measure up. With a perfectionistic father and my own perfectionism it was very hard for me to accept failure. I tried to rationalize, 'Oh, it's not that important. I'll just do something different.' At that point, marijuana came into my life. So I began sedating myself and getting into music, drowning my sorrows in song and pot.

"I left Florida and went to Washington, D.C., to major in music because that was now my new American Dream. My new illusion was becoming a rock star like Bruce Springsteen. Again the goal was to be somebody else. If I could be just like him, then I'd be good enough. Short story: That didn't work out because I wasn't disciplined enough to follow the music curriculum. I just wanted to compose my own stuff. So again, another shock to my system. I wasn't the fantasy big star with the frigging contract putting out albums and having a tour. Once again drugs seemed to be around my life. Again I drowned my sorrows.

"As I look back on it from where I'm at now I realize that all these events were moments of chipping away at my illusions, at my need to prove to everybody that I'm something special, to be seen, to be noticed. I had to be noticed by a lot of people; it couldn't just be one or two. It had to be on a big scale.

"At this point, I've come to accept a smaller scale. All the stuff that had to be so big, had to do with my own feelings of not being good enough, my own issues of shame. So if a whole bunch of people could acknowledge me for my talents, then I'd be okay.

"I think what basically happened to me was that I didn't feel really heard. I grew up with loving parents, but like in your book *When Parents Love Too Much,* I grew up with parents who did too much and stamped out my own capacity so that I didn't trust my capacity. And I replaced my own self-trust with someone else's notion of the right way to do it, which wasn't really my way but became my way.

"I began to understand my defenses, like when I would expose my shortcomings before someone else would. If they criticized me first, I would be so vulnerable and caught in that experience of shame. At least there was some small victory in being first, in bringing it upon myself. I would have control over the intensity of it. That insight pointed me in the direction of understanding myself at a very deep level.

"So now my eyes aren't so focused on what everybody else sees. I'm not so preoccupied with everybody else's perception of me. I've started to go in to discover myself. And understanding my sense of shame was the bridge that connected me with all my inner strivings that had to do with not really being seen in the way I needed to be seen. I thought I had to become bigger than life to be seen. I've been able to give up that dream of being somebody big, to some degree, and scale my desires down to a more manageable level that doesn't have to do with always proving myself.

"Now, years later, I'm a therapist and I really value the fact that I'm not a musician. I am a composer—a half-assed composer, but a composer. And I can compose my own stuff and it comes from me. I can take pride in it. And I can golf on a Saturday morning and enjoy the game more than the score. And no matter how good I am, or how out of tempo, it comes from my true self. It's enough."

They say that the most famous of us all are driven by the deepest deprivation. They are overcoming something in their past, so it goes, and that's what drives them. Your guess is as good as ours as to how much truth there is in this theory. What you find when you talk to people who have failed to accomplish their dream is that many of them didn't want that dream in the first place. It was more about proving themselves than about being themselves. Watch Olympic skaters and you'll see the result of children who grew up loving to skate. Talk to successful musicians, and you'll find people who loved to play their instruments and whose real goal is to play with other great players.

Those of us who are driven by the need to compensate for what we feel we lack in ourselves seem to end up telling the same story Dan does. We want to be spectacular because we want to be loved. We want success to be loud because we have had so much difficulty finding someone to hear us, to listen to our soft, insistent voice. We stopped listening to that voice ourselves. But the fact that people don't hear us may have more to do with our choice of audience than anything else.

When Dan listened to his voice, it didn't lead him where he thought he wanted to be but where he needed to be. His life ended up making sense. He talks about a smaller scale, because something in him has yet to get the real point of this struggle. He is a man who may yet achieve the big audience, but he'll do it by being himself and believing in himself. He'll do it through a profession that draws on his strengths more than his illusions.

You, too, have that soft, insistent voice. When motivation disappears, it isn't always a sign that we are lazy. There's an old saying: People vote with their feet.

Don't be so hard on yourself when you fail. Perhaps you didn't really want that achievement so badly in the first place. What you want might not be the same thing as what you need.

Leslie R.—"To put it simply, I wanted to have so much money I'd never have to worry again."

"'I'm going to be a millionaire before I'm forty.' My father said that a hundred times when I was growing up. My sister says she never heard him say it once. We grew up in the same household and came out with totally different memories.

"Did you ever watch that old TV show, 'Garfield Goose'? Every time I watched 'Garfield Goose' I'd fight with my grandmother. There were photographs planted on the top of the TV set of my late grandfather. It was like a shrine. He looked exactly like Frazier Thomas. 'Grandma, you have to call the station. Grandpa isn't dead. There he is! He's Frazier Thomas!'

"A therapist once analyzed this for me: I gave up on the living and was hoping someone would come back from the grave to fix my family.

"My grandparents lost their money during the Depression. All anyone in the family ever obsessed about was money. They were cheap with me; they were cheap with themselves. People died in the family, and everyone would go to the lawyer's office to hear the will. Suddenly no one was speaking. 'They're fighting over Bubba's pennies,' my sister would tell me.

"In my family, everyone worked hard, but no one got ahead of the bills, even for a moment. Everyone was dissatisfied because they weren't rich.

"I got my first job baby-sitting when I was eleven. I baby-sat for a rabbi's three kids. I pulled down thirty dollars a week by the time I was twelve. My father used to borrow money from me before he left the house.

"I got my first real job at fourteen. I went to work at McDonald's by forging my birth certificate. In those days, a Big Mac, fries, and a Coke were one dollar. So kids used to take the dollar and just put it in the drawer without ringing it up. They'd line up pennies to remember how many dollars they'd put in the drawer. At the end of the night, they'd pocket all of those dollars. I knew the scam, but I was too scared.

"I moved on to work at a department store. The kids who worked there would stick clothes, bras, makeup down their pants and walk out looking like they were nine months pregnant.

"They would take orders for stuff from their friends. I know people who outfitted themselves for college that way. I was once standing in a store meeting. While the boss was speaking, I looked over at a girl who worked in my department, and I could see something creeping down her leg. She'd stuffed an order of bras and matching panties down her pantyhose, and they were leaking out, climbing down her leg. I could see a bra strap at her knee.

"Some of those boys and girls are lawyers, accountants, politicians in pretty high places. They put those practices to good use. You can thank the baby boom generation for all those security devices and tags that ring when you walk out the door. It was the American Way. Talk honesty, peace, and equal rights over dinner, then walk out of the restaurant with the silverware in your purse.

"My father died while I was in high school. My aunt always said the bills killed him. He died $40,000 in debt. I went to college on student loans—the family curse of buy now, pay later. I vowed that I would never die in debt the way my father did.

"Like him, all I ever thought of was money and how I didn't have enough of it. All I thought of was how unfair it was that I worked so hard and never got ahead. I was always working about two jobs at a time. My top salary was $30,000.

"About five years ago, I was having lunch with a very wealthy friend. I was complaining again about money, how hard I worked, how little I made. She turned to me and said, 'You want money? That's crazy! You run from money.'

"'No, it's just that they don't pay teachers a decent salary,' I argued.

"'My point exactly. Who told you to become a teacher?'

"The truth is, everyone had told me not to, that I wouldn't make any money.

"I've learned something very important. I thought I was trying to win the struggle my father had lost. In fact, all I was doing was re-creating the drama I had grown up with.

"I started to see the truth of my career history, past the myth that I worked so hard and never got paid my worth. I spent ten years as a special education teacher, hating every minute of it, being paid about $25,000 a year. I did the job well, I did it with honors, and just when I might have made it out of the classroom into a position that might have made me any real money, I quit. My reasons seemed valid at the time. Now I know the truth.

"I decided what I needed was an MBA. These were the people making money. I got that MBA with honors. So guess what I majored in? Communications. One would think that someone as obsessed with money as I was would have interviewed some people in this field and learned that they make the absolute least of all their business school counterparts. My salary? Twenty thousand a year. My rationale—you have to start somewhere when you're starting over.

"When I divorced my first husband, he was at the pinnacle of his career. My lawyer said, 'I don't think I can help you.' He said that because I shook my head to reconstructive maintenance, alimony, anything reasonable he suggested was my right at the time. I reasoned that I was the one who wanted out, so why make my ex-husband pay? I didn't realize that he had much to do with the reason I wanted out as I did. I didn't see that I had married a man as obsessed with money issues as I was.

"You run from money. How does a person decide that they need this and only this to make themselves happy, and then throw it away with both hands at every opportunity?

"We're drawn to what we're familiar with. I had been repeating my father's life. Within a year after figuring that one out, I doubled my salary. I quit a job I hated but that I had spent so much energy trying to hang on to. I humbled myself enough to ask someone who had a few connections to make a call for me and get me an interview. Am I satisfied? Well, I'm no millionaire, but I'm finally seeing rewards. Suddenly money isn't such an issue in my life. I started to have enough when I finally realized I deserved to be happy."

Leslie was more acquainted with the thirst than the water, as they say. Unconsciously, many of us choose environments and situations that will call on the well-honed skills and attitudes we learned in a difficult childhood—self-sacrifice, disappointment, perseverance, frustration, defeat. We're often drawn to what we're familiar with. Leslie was familiar with hard work and struggle but not well acquainted with fulfillment and joy.

Leslie, like many people, set herself up for disappointment. When her hard work didn't pay off, she got a second job. When she began to get close to her dream, she froze. She sabotaged herself.

Leslie's payoff for a frustrating work life was an illusion of close-ness with the father she had lost. She shared his dream and she shared his failure. She wanted money as much as she was ambivalent about having it.

Leslie learned one of the most important lessons of her life. If the way you are proceeding isn't working, don't keep doing the same thing louder and harder. If you have a goal and you can't attain it, ask yourself, *Do I really want it? Am I afraid of it?* You can deal with those fears and overcome them, but first you need to know they are there.

Jim.—"There was every reason to be happy but the one that made sense."

"The issue for me has never been a lack of opportunities or choices, but the struggle to really enjoy anything.

"I grew up in the suburbs in a traditional middle-class family. Like many of our neighbors, we seemed to paint a picture of a perfect family. Trimmed lawns and cute kids were the norm in this quiet community.

"I really don't remember a lot of details from my childhood, but I do remember one thing that stands out. The way my family acted inside our four walls was different from how they were around the neighbors. It seemed important to present some sort of image to the public. I got the message that how people looked seemed to be of so much more value than how they felt. This was underscored many evenings when in the middle of a family fight the phone would ring. In a split second, my mother's rage shifted to a bright tone as she spoke into the phone: 'Oh, Mary! I'm wonderful, and you?'

"I was a trouble-free kid. I got good grades, played on a sports team, and was well liked in school. As someone once put it, I showed well.

"In the years that followed I graduated from high school and college, followed the appropriate path, never made waves. No great highs or lows. I just sort of existed.

"In my twenties and early thirties, I dated a number of women. The relationships were short-lived. Most of the time I ended it. Women told me from time to time that I seemed distant.

"It was not until I was thirty-five that I realized that I had a problem. I started to notice that the lows were lasting longer and the highs (which were never that high) were getting nonexistent.

"With one ulcer under my belt and a more and more ever-present feeling of depression, I finally accepted the fact that something was wrong. I thought therapy was for people with terrible childhoods or compulsions and things like that. Despite my reluctance, my symptoms enrolled me into therapy. What was a guy with the perfect childhood doing in therapy? In the next year and a half, I began to understand why.

"I was encouraged to enter into a program of individual and group therapy. The former provided a supportive environment in which a female therapist listened attentively and periodically offered little gems of insight that helped me make sense of this whole mess. I don't quite know what happened, but I started to feel better. I started to remember things in my childhood that weren't so perfect.

"The dinner hour stands out. I can still see traces of my mother's anger and disappointment. My rebellious sisters and brothers seemed to provoke her into some sort of nightly drama around school problems or disrespectful talk. At least once a week someone stormed off in some sort of rage. Nothing ever got resolved, only recycled.

"My mother always encouraged conversation. She would center it around politics or community affairs. Participation was encouraged, but I always passed. I listened but never participated.

"But I couldn't avoid that inevitable moment when my mother turned to me and said, 'What did you do today?' All eyes turned to me. She always prodded, asking question after question, but I held my ground. I became a master of the one word response—yes, no, nothing, fine, okay. Eventually she got frustrated and moved on.

"Where was my dad in all of this? You know the type. The classic breadwinner of the 1950s. He arrived home at six, tired. He rarely added to the conflict, but he never did anything to stop it.

"From time to time my therapist would say things like, 'From what you went through at home it is understandable that you might keep a distance from women,' or 'I can understand why you choose not to say much in your family given all the criticism you heard.'

"While individual therapy was a mostly supportive experience, group therapy was a real trip. They told me at the start that it would re-create my family. It would give me an opportunity to learn new ways of dealing with it. Well, to put it mildly, it did.

"By my second group session it was clear that I was again the quiet one, attentively listening, figuring out ways to be a good client. I patiently waited my turn and intellectually described my problems.

"Sometimes things bothered me during the group, but I said nothing and waited patiently for someone to ask me what was wrong (as my mother had done so many countless times).

"When they didn't stop to ask I got mad, in the usual way, feeling like a victim. I suffered silently and resentfully, waiting for someone to notice.

"When they didn't seem to notice, I figured they were insensitive jerks and decided to show them by quitting. I announced this to my individual therapist and she asked calmly if I had told them how I felt. She explained that I didn't have to express myself with my mother who was always monitoring me, but in the real world people will not be that invested in reading my mind. It was so obvious but nothing that had ever occurred to me before.

"In my family I was a master at avoiding communication, but in group, where honesty and emotional expression were valued, this became an impossible task. With my walls up initially I managed to stay 'in my head' and intellectualize everything. I guess the therapist determined it was time for more drastic measures. One day when I was carefully injecting a well-planned comment, he said, 'Shut up, you little twerp!'

"I was stunned. I completely lost my voice and did shut up—for the rest of the night. Seething and humiliated inside I once again vowed to quit.

"After group I talked to another member who suggested I tell the therapist where to stick it. I felt validated and agreed; however, it was easier said than done. It was like telling Dad where to stick it—you can't do that. Or can you?

"Hesitantly, I finally told the therapist, 'I don't want you to talk to me that way—I'm angry; it wasn't fair.' To my amazement, he said, 'Okay, it's good to hear your feelings.' This was amazing to me. In my family, standing up for yourself was always an invitation to a feud or tears or anger, never to communication or resolution.

"But gradually over the next few months I was given certain 'assignments' to reconnect with my feelings. The easiest feeling for me was anger because actually I had been pissed off most of my life. The vulnerable emotions were much harder—sadness, hurt, fear— as it is for most guys. However, these too appeared with time, support, and safety.

"Another assignment was to play out the 'victim' part of my personality. I would tell the group things like, 'No one understands me' or 'Poor me' or 'If only I had been treated better.' The interesting thing was that when I 'owned' this part, it was so much harder to act it out in real life. It almost seemed kind of silly. I started to feel that it was now really my responsibility to turn things around and to shape my life.

"At this point of my life, I still have an occasional bout with depression. Falling asleep is still sometimes an aggravating and tedious task. And, yes, my parents do get under my skin from time to time. But I'm not going through life numb, unsatisfied but uncomplaining. I feel alive. I married an incredible women (the love of my life); I have a meaningful and satisfying career, a few good friends, and can actually enjoy quite a bit of it."

Jim's story is a common one. He grew up in a family that functioned well on a material level (house in the suburbs, all the right appearances), but was unavailable on any emotional level. The message was, "We provided all of this for you, kids—now go and be happy." Jim was punished when he wasn't happy and couldn't pretend. His mother punished him with her depression and disappointment. Jim paid her back with his withdrawal.

How many times have you heard, "You should be happy, look at all you have." When you hear this as many times as Jim did, you feel a sense of confusion and shame as if you don't have a right to feel what you feel. Jim learned to half-heartedly agree. He felt he "should have" been happy. He went through life half alive. In the end, he couldn't hide the truth from himself.

Jim's parents probably had the best of intentions but were unable to teach what they didn't know themselves. They had experienced the Depression of the 1930s, which had placed a great value on survival. As Abraham Maslow suggests in his hierarchy of needs, we are not able to deal with the higher levels of self-actualization until the basic needs for safety and security are met. Jim's parents were still addressing these basic needs from their families of origin.

Unfortunately, therapy or personal growth was not in the value system of most of Jim's parents' generation. And when these unresolved issues are not addressed, they repeat.

For Jim, the hardest step was going to therapy because he had to admit he wasn't happy, which was not in keeping with his family's rules. The thrust of his personal growth was getting in touch with his feelings. His natural defense mechanisms of denial, intellectualization, and rationalization kept him "in his head." He had no models for addressing or communicating these feelings. Because Jim had been emotionally discounted in his childhood, he learned to discount himself.

Paradoxically, Jim's solutions (isolating, intellectualizing, pretending) became his greatest problems. When we disguise our actual feelings, we are living a lie. There's an old saying that goes, You can't heal what you don't feel. Jim's unexpressed feelings came back at him in the form of depression.

The lessons are simple: Express yourself. Be honest about what you feel.

Jim isn't a satisfied person today because he has more. It's because he feels more. He responds more. He's simply more alive.

Gary S.—"You've got to have perspective."

"I don't want many changes in my life. I'm happy with the way things are. But at the same time, I continue to grow and change.

"I think satisfaction is a state of mind where you don't need to make compulsive changes. You're pretty okay with things. It's a general sense of well-being. Problems do occur, but you are able to see them in perspective. An overall good feeling inside all the time, an inner peace of tranquility—that's what I think it means to be satisfied.

"My life continues to bring problems and challenges. For example, my wife has MS and uses a wheelchair. It's not easy to find any positive aspects of that other than trying to make her the happiest person in a wheelchair in the United States.

"I have no control over her condition. The control I do have goes to help eliminate that negativity, if I can. I do feel bad when I take business trips that bring me to fancy resorts to talk about my work and I cannot bring my wife. But if I were to dwell on that, I wouldn't be able to get any joy out of that trip at all.

"I accept it for what it is. We do the best we can. I have the best time possible on these trips, keeping the guilt at bay, and I give her a complete report, take pictures, bring her back a gift, share with her as much of the experience as I can and then try to compensate by going somewhere she can go.

"It does bring me down at the moment when I'm traveling with my wife and I find out that nothing is handicap accessible there. This makes me feel bad, but if I stayed in that state I would have a problem.

"What I do is face it, see the ugliness in it. I feel badly about it, we talk about it, and then it goes away. If I didn't allow myself to feel those feelings there would be a problem. We both put it into perspective and move on.

"When I moved out West, I had lots of heavy bills to pay. But I only worried about it when it came down to paying the bills. Once a week for about an hour we agonized about the bills. The rest of the time it really wasn't on my mind.

"I could not dwell on the dissatisfaction while I was out in nature, looking at the tide pools, visiting beaches, skiing, and doing things that didn't cost much money. If I dwelled on the ugly things, I could have been doing it twenty-four hours a day.

"If you dwell on dissatisfaction, it's hard to achieve satisfaction. You've got to compartmentalize your misery. Feel it for that time, but let it go. The more fully you feel it, the quicker it goes and lets you spend time seeing life for all its positives."

Many of us are like Jack. We have challenges in our lives, disappointments. We have problems that won't disappear through effort on our part. There are things we can't control, can't fix, can't make better. Denying those situations, burying our heartbreak or rage isn't the answer. Jack allowed himself to feel his feelings rather than block them. Then he was able to let them go and move forward.

Don't dwell on your dissatisfaction. But don't suppress it either. Suppressing feeling preserves it. Grief will run its natural course if we don't get in the way. Worry will run out of steam if we don't try to bury it or deny it.

Janet J.—"I told myself I'd be satisfied if I had a better marriage, and that wasn't going to happen if he kept letting his children manipulate him."

"I knew Sarah was in trouble. I also knew I was only her stepmother. But I couldn't just sit there passively and say nothing. The whole situation was starting to affect my health.

"I remember the first time I met Sam's children. We took them out for a ride to get ice cream. Sarah and Rebecca sat in the backseat, checking me out, and Sarah said, 'You know, my father has lots of girlfriends.' Sam laughed, but I didn't think it was funny at all.

"I married Sam knowing that I'd be living with his two children. I was looking forward to us all being a family.

"After our honeymoon, we had a family meeting. Sam made it clear that it was now my house, too. I set some rules right away.

"Something I could never understand was that Sam never told his children the truth about their mother. She's an alcoholic, which is why Sam had custody. I'd watch his wife every week from the window when she drove over to pick up the kids for the weekend. She'd sit in her car, smoking cigarettes, and flicking the ashes out the window. Every time the kids came home, they smelled like smoke. But Sam used to warn me, 'Never say anything bad about their mother to them. I don't want them to grow up feeling ashamed.' I thought this was ludicrous. Why shouldn't they know what their mother was?

"They'd come home from visits with their mother, excited about all of the places they'd been with her, and it would really burn me up. Everything I did, I did for Sam's kids. I used my paycheck to buy them clothes. I was the one who drove them to school. I was the one they came to when they needed something, not their mother.

"One day Sarah, Rebecca, and I were having a heart-to-heart talk. Sarah said that she was worried about her mother because when they visited her, she slept on the couch all day long. Sarah was studying about cancer in school. She thought her mother had cancer.

"I told them the truth. 'Your mother is an alcoholic. That's why your father divorced her. That's why you live with us.'

"Later I told Sam how well the children took the truth. Sarah had cried and gone to her room, but I'd gone up afterwards and held her, and it was okay. I felt so close to her that night. Sam wasn't happy that I'd told them, but he could see that maybe it was time.

"About a year after that I started to get really worried about Sarah. She was a good student, but her teachers told me that she was constantly talking to the boys in class, writing them notes, and things like that. She was popular, whatever that means in eighth grade, and the leader of a big group of kids. I tried to talk to her. I set stricter limits about curfew, using the telephone, things like that. Sam told me to back off. I told him Sarah was manipulating him.

"My marriage was in bad shape. Talk about never feeling satisfied. Then the bottom fell out. I was putting something away in Sarah's drawers when I saw her diary. I know that parents shouldn't read their children's diaries, but I was concerned about Sarah. I wanted to understand her. I knew she must be in trouble because she was so quiet and guarded all of the time. Too many parents wait until it's too late.

"I opened her diary and it fell open to a page where she'd pressed so hard with her pen, that the writing on the paper was indented. What she wrote over and over again was: 'I hate Janet! I wish she'd die!'

"I was crushed. We'd had our arguments, but this? All I'd ever done was try to help and guide this child.

"This is hard for me to admit, but when we all went for family counseling, what I really wanted was for the counselor to tell my whole family how ungrateful they were and to tell Sam that he should stop taking his children's side about everything. Instead, he met with me alone the following week. He asked me a question I resented at first: 'Why do you think it's so difficult for you to come second?'

"I think he looked at my perfectly manicured nails, my put-together outfit, the long hair that was never out of place, and saw right through me. I know his question eventually saved my marriage. It was the root of the whole battle. As stepparents, we waver between the boundaries of legal relationships and the feeling that we nonetheless act and love as true parents. When we aren't respected and appreciated as such, we feel out of control.

"When I would look out the window at Sarah's mother, I would think, 'She doesn't deserve these children's love. I'm the one who is really raising them.'

"Maybe I was right and maybe I was wrong. But I couldn't change a fact. All those rules I set, which made the kids resent me, really had to do with establishing myself as a parent. Being number one.

"The counselor told me it was significant that everything I came into his office talking about had to do with Sarah's problems. I never talked about myself. I never spoke about my own fears and doubts about what was going on with Sam. I think I thought that if I could make Sam's kids accept me, I'd be that much more valuable to Sam. I had a lot of work to do on my marriage.

"I've learned to take a step back with these kids. I've attempted to reconcile the amount I'm willing to give with what I'm going to receive in return. I've learned a lot about love. In spite of how much you love or give others, you aren't guaranteed love and appreciation in return. You have to love as an act of faith, not as an act of control.

"I also learned to be more realistic about my role as a stepparent. I knew other people had a hard time, but I thought I was different, that I knew better. Again, I was going to be number one. Talking to other stepparents, I realize that I'm doing as well or even better than most. So, you have to give up your fantasies.

"What I've learned is that there are plenty of satisfactions that come from being a stepparent. I've got a unique role to play in the children's lives, and it's a role no one else can have.

"Sarah and I are becoming friends. I no longer feel as competitive with Sarah's mother. Now I hope we can both give Sarah something that will help her grow and become the best person she can be. I stopped wearing myself out trying to be the perfect mother. I don't cook hot meals every night. I don't leave the office early every time one of the kids needs a ride. I'm more at peace and more satisfied than I've ever felt in my life because I did the simplest thing. I decided to forgive."

Many people have what we call "If, then" fantasies. *If I give enough, then people will love me back. If I work hard enough, then people will appreciate me.* Unfortunately, other people don't always live up to their end of the bargain. They don't even know the bargain exists.

Janet wanted nothing more than to love her new family and be loved in return. Unfortunately, Janet's stepchildren were emotionally unavailable in many ways for reasons that had little to do with Janet. They struggled with their allegiance to their mother who appeared to be cast out of the family for little reason—an illusion enhanced by their father's reluctance to be more honest with them. To protect their mother, they defended themselves against their natural affection for the woman who cared for them daily.

Janet sensed this emotional unavailability on an unconscious level. Her mistake was thinking that damaging her stepchildren's illusion of their mother with truth about her alcoholism would bind them more closely to her. Instead, it only made their need to protect their mother—and deny Janet—more intense.

The pain of loving and getting little back in return cannot be minimized, and it's a major cause for dissatisfaction in many people's lives. In the desperate hope that our efforts will be rewarded, some of us keep giving, and love even harder.

Janet became bent on changing Sarah, which pushed her stepdaughter further away. If we demand children give more than they are ready to, they withdraw in self-defense. In desperation, Janet searched for evidence that if Sarah didn't love her enough, it was because she had a problem. Janet unconsciously wanted Sarah to have a problem, because it would be easier to think there was a reason that Sarah pulled away from her, other than anything Janet might have contributed to the situation.

It's okay to feel competitive with a natural parent. It's okay to feel angry over the past. It's okay to feel out of control in a situation where we're suddenly handed two teenagers to raise. Loving Sarah "more" by setting rigid limits wasn't the answer. Janet got much more by letting go, backing off, and allowing Sarah to come to her.

For those of us who are feeling a great deal of dissatisfaction because someone close to us won't change or give us what we want, Janet's story contains a lesson: Let go. Build a support network outside of the family. If we're overinvolved with others, we're underinvolved with ourselves.

Perhaps it is not so strange that we all want more, and we want it most from people and situations that don't give it to us. How we go about getting it is often strange.

Janet decided to forgive. She wasn't the perfect stepmother and her children weren't perfect either.

You, too, may need to forgive. But don't do it in little pieces. Forgiveness isn't any good if we do it in little drips and drabs. Don't say, "I'll forgive you this but not that." Do it all at once, and be done with it. Or decide you can't do it and move on.

Eric K.—"No pain, no gain."

"As far back as I can remember life was serious business. My father and mother got divorced when I was about five years old. My father kind of just disappeared, so it was always me and Mom. I had to learn to take care of things. She called me the 'little man of the house.'

"Mom would cry a lot. I didn't know what to do. I never felt like I was doing enough. I still feel that way most of the time.

"I grew up with a lot of responsibilities other kids didn't have. I don't regret them, but I don't deny their impact. I wish I had a dollar for every time someone said to me, 'You're too hard on yourself.' People don't seem to understand what it's really like for me.

"I've always recognized that I have a hard time having fun. I'd play tennis, and every point was filled with self-evaluation, critiques, and an obsession to win. I've huffed off the court in total disgust, either at myself for playing badly or at my partner for winning.

"So, I was going through life this depressed, very uptight person, when I decided to sign up for singing lessons. It ended up being therapy in disguise.

"The vocal instructor was a very laid-back guy who stressed taking it slow and easy. This was hard to understand because I always thought that to improve at something you must push yourself to the limit. I would strain to reach the high notes. I wanted be able to sing like Paul McCartney, a tenor, not wanting to accept that my range was more like Dean Martin, a baritone. Half my problem was singing in keys that were too high for my voice. Yet the voice in my head kept saying, 'Push harder and you will get it.'

"Once I looked at my throat in a mirror when I was singing. I couldn't feel it, but now I could see it. The strain. The tension. Still, I resisted my teacher's instinct to take it slow and relax my body. How could you quickly progress without pushing? He said that the strain in my throat was only blocking the natural sound of my voice.

"It felt like a regression to slow down and relax. Yet over the next two years I began to do just that, and magically my voice improved.

"In the time since, I have often thought about how parallel these voice lessons were to how I ran my life. Always pushing. Seeking more, but getting in my own way. I eventually learned a great truth. Less is sometimes more. As I relaxed and let go, the natural sound of my voice began to emerge.

"Now I'm in my early forties and really starting to make a change. More than ever I sing for the joy of connecting with others about the music. I still compare myself with the Paul McCartneys, but less so than ever. I'm starting to play tennis again, but with a different mind-set. My goal is not about refinement, but about getting in touch with movement and being gentle with myself. As the Zen gurus suggest, I try more to be in the moment."

Eric's story is of a lost childhood. The attraction he felt toward tennis and singing lies in the potential of those activities to re-create the childhood struggle. Life had never been much fun, and Eric knew nothing else than how to survive with little and pit yourself against formidable odds. So it wasn't enough to sing. He had to be Paul McCartney.

What's your attraction to whatever it is that frustrates you? Achievement? Or compensation?

You, too, have a relaxed voice that is clear and unique and better than any voice you could try to assume. You, too, have a moment that is yours to live fully. You have your mentors, and you have the capacity to be a mentor. There are things you know that no one else knows because you have a unique experience, a take on the world. No one else knows what you know because no one else is exactly like you. Only you can do what you can do.

※ ※

CHAPTER ELEVEN

Reaching Satisfaction

Guidelines for Change and Growth

*We're so engaged in doing things to achieve purposes of
outer value that we forget that the inner value, the rapture
that is associated with being alive, is what it's all about.*

—JOSEPH CAMPBELL

Feeling alive. Feeling content. Waking with a sense of well-being.
Believing that your life has meaning. These need not be goals you
can't attain, but a natural part of your life. These feelings can be
experienced by anyone who is motivated to break free from self-
defeating life patterns.

Throughout this book we have shared the steps that countless
people have used to achieve greater satisfaction and fulfillment in
their lives. To help you on your journey, in this chapter we have sum-
marized the key points.

1. What is, is. Accept what is true for you.

*I never feel good enough. . . . I'm angry at my parents. . . . I feel like
a victim of my job. . . . I isolate myself because I don't feel safe. . . . I
don't trust people. . . . I think women are manipulative and controlling.
. . . I think men use women. . . . I play up my problems to get attention.
. . . I'm afraid of succeeding. . . .*

Most would rather jump off a cliff than be this honest. Is it hard to say what's really true for you? It may be the one thing standing in the way of your happiness. Changes begin to happen rapidly in our lives when we begin to accept the truth.

In *Gestalt Therapy Now,* Arnold Beisser defined what he calls the "Paradoxical Theory of Change." Briefly stated, it is this: Change occurs when one becomes what he or she is, not when he or she tries to become what he or she is not. By fully identifying and "owning" a stuck part of ourselves, we break an inner power struggle and free up energy for change.

Nothing changes until it is fully experienced for what it is. What does this mean for you if you're dissatisfied with your life?

It means you stop telling yourself you should be satisfied. It means you learn to recognize and express what you really think and feel. As you begin to do this, you will be accepting and appreciating who you really are and come home to your true self.

2. See how your symptoms serve you.

All self-defeating behavior is protective. If we grow up in families that do not validate our needs and emotions, we learn to adapt. Recall that we learn early on that our needs for safety and survival are far more important than our needs for expression and understanding.

Here is a table of the symptoms we've explored in this book, the underlying issues, and the protective function each symptom serves.

Symptom	Underlying Issues	Protective Function
Can't stay happy for long	• Guilt • Superstitions • Dysthymia • Need for affirmation	• Avoid dissapoint-ment • Criticize yourself before others do • Avoid emotions through depression • "Ward off evil"

Symptom	Underlying Issues	Protective Function
Wanting what one can't have	• Gratification and liberation fantasies • Fear of the present • Overcompensation	• Avoid rejection • Comfort oneself • Try to find magical solutions to problems • Keep hope alive • Avoid risk
Can't relax	• Anxiety • Compulsive self-reliance • Fear of letting go of control • Diminished sense of trust • Too many responsibilities in childhood	• Protect self through scanning and hypervigilance • Avoid hurt • Avoid dependency
Comparing oneself to others	• Feeling unsafe • Early deprivation • Unclear sense of identity • Number two-ness • Depression • Sense of being "stuck"	• Attempt self-improvement • Attempt to understand and define self • Avoid responsibility
Not following through	• Self-sabotage • Wishful thinking • Fear of abandonment	• Avoid criticism and rejection • Keep hope alive
Getting less than you give	• Need for control in relationships • Fear of confrontation • Disregard of one's true needs • Fear of exposure	• Attempt to enlist love • To avoid disappointment • Protect by not revealing self

Symptom	Underlying Issues	Protective Function
Bored and restless	• Shaky sense of competence • Pampered deprivation • Passivity • Disregard for real talents • Out of touch with true self	• Avoid exposure • Enlist caretakers for rescue • Avoid risk
Can't find the right person	• Shaky sense of personal competence • Fear of intimacy • Financial fears • Overloading relationships • Search for a "provider" or mirror	• To manage fears of intimacy • To maintain control • To complete oneself • To avoid risks of self-development

What is required if you want to give up the illusion of protection and gain more satisfaction in your life? First, you see every complaint, every habit, every weakness, as a creative solution that once protected you. You look at how it still serves you today. You say, "How does it serve me to feel stuck? How does it serve me to feel nothing is enough? That no one understands? What do I get out of this?"

Once you've identified how your symptoms protect you, you will need to find a healthier way to address these problems. For example, if I ensure safety by avoiding all risk or avoiding criticism, I must learn new ways to take care of myself. This may require building an empathic support system and practicing new communication skills to build a sense of competence.

Or, if I try to attract love by being a caretaker, I will want to clarify my true needs and choose people who are available to fulfill them. When you find more self-affirming ways to meet these needs, enough will be enough.

3. Use your life as a mirror of your inner belief system.

Shakti Gawain, author of *Living in the Light,* popularized the concept that the world is our mirror. If we project the fact that we feel different, alienated, or not good enough, we get back a response from others that is often indifferent, detached, or resentful. This response will occur regardless of the magnitude of our achievements.

If I feel unlovable, I will surely fend off the admiration of one who finds me loving. If I fear success at work, I will find ways to validate that belief through self-sabotaging behavior. If I feel victimized by life events, I will act out this role in my relationships, by rejecting responsibility.

There is a cliché in the therapy world: You cannot change others, but you can change yourself. To do this, you must first turn the mirror on yourself.

The eastern culture has known for centuries what we in the West are just starting to learn. Change and satisfaction come from within. Inner peace comes from within. Self-acceptance and understanding come from within. So how do we get in touch with this land inside our minds?

Many of us have spent a lifetime trying to stay away from our inner lives and feelings. We hide from ourselves for fear of encountering our unresolved emotions.

Going within will ultimately bring the opposite of our fears. It will bring inner healing, self-love, and a profound sense of relaxation. Looking inward is another way of paying attention to what matters The intention is not to do anything, but to be with yourself in a calm way. For many of us doers, this will initially feel like a waste of time. We feel that if there is no action, there is no substance, no change. The opposite can be true. As we tune inward, we can access our real experience.

See life events as reflections of unresolved issues within you. If you can't find love in your life, it may reflect back that you feel unlovable. Trouble reaching success may reflect back a fear of success.

Know that change always comes from within as you change your beliefs and, subsequently, your actions.

4. Understand that what you want may be different from what you need.

Whatever we fantasize will finally make us happy—getting that job, buying that car, earning that raise, losing that weight, finding that person—may not make the revolutionary difference we imagine. Countless people we interviewed in the course of this book found that what they want often had little to do with what they need.

In order to exchange a true search for purpose in one's life for the frustration of constant striving, you have to connect with what you care about most deeply.

We ask clients, "What do you really need in a relationship?" and they talk about safety, empathy, trust. They mention nurturing, autonomy, a sense of independence. When we ask, "What do you need in work?" they talk about a sense of purpose, a sense of validation, a sense of connection with others. This is the same process you must work through yourself. Begin making some lists: What do I need from my job? My relationship? My marriage? My children?

You may have the right goal, but the wrong way of achieving it. Or you have unmet needs that are vital to you, and no real sense of what they are.

This cognitive shift will require a lot from you. First, you need to realize that your best thinking got you here and stop digging in the ashes. Go off your goals for a week or two. You need to give yourself a vacation from your goal-setting or "To Do" lists.

Ask yourself some key questions: *What did I have to do to please my parents? Which actions received the most praise? The most criticism?* How much of your dissatisfaction today is related to feeling compelled to act in ways that are alien to your true nature?

Ask, *What am I trying to talk myself into in my life? What feelings do I experience when I'm offered a job that I know I won't really like? When someone calls to ask me out and I know the relationship will never work? Do I tell myself there might never be a better opportunity?*

There is a voice within you that holds the answers. Many people have not learned to trust this messenger. As you learn to tune inward, slow down, and listen, you will find that this voice will always lead you in the right direction—toward your true needs and sense of meaning.

Think about the times in your life when you were happiest. What was it about those experiences that made them so satisfying?

Listen to what your procrastination is trying to tell you. It's a shout from the unconscious, a signal that something is out of adjustment. Are you putting things off because you sense at a deeper level that something is intrinsically wrong with the project or goal? Is this something you want, or something you think you should want?

5. Express your voice.

Learning to say, "This is who I am, this is what I need, this is what I feel, this is what I think," is the most important thing you can ever do for yourself.

What this requires is realizing that each of us has our own unique take on the world. Expressing and sharing it is our highest purpose.

If you knew you couldn't fail, what would you really do with your life? If you knew people would listen without judgment, what would you really say?

Most of us find that the more creative the idea we have, the more doubt we have about expressing it. We need to learn to manage the creative process. Creative thinking, the use of our imagination, naturally leads to moments of self-doubt, of worry that ideas won't pan out, or that they won't be accepted. Going toward these doubts can often prevent them from destroying the creative process. How do you do this? Many creative writers swear by journaling. They write out their fears before they sit down to do their work, and once expressed, the fears no longer seem to carry such an emotional charge. Visualization is another way of managing the creative process. One visualizes succeeding through pleasant imagery.

Your vision must be followed by action to make it real. Yet most of us who grew up in unsupportive families fear change. Make it a priority to find people who share your vision and who will help you process your fears. Make your goals small and attainable. Self-esteem is built on these small, but very real, successes.

6. Be empathetic.

To be empathetic requires one to listen without judgment, to be there for someone without a need to make it better, change what is, or give advice. True empathy causes an emotional release.

Have you ever asked people who were clearly upset how they were doing and heard them respond, "Fine"? If you really want to understand where these people are coming from, look closely. Notice how you feel when you look deeply into their eyes. Can you feel that overwhelming sadness written on their faces? Or perhaps the anger in their clenched knuckles? Do the wrinkles on their brow show years of worry and anxiety?

Why is what they say so different from what they seem to feel? Perhaps it was the unempathic responses in their childhood. Maybe it wasn't safe to express their truth.

Now look in the mirror at yourself. Spend a few minutes. What does your face tell you? Do you see the years of worry, disappointment, or anger that you may be afraid to express or even acknowledge? Have compassion for yourself as well.

7. Find balance—within and without.

There is an Indian belief that everyone is a house of four rooms: a physical, a mental, an emotional, and a spiritual room. Most of us tend to live in one room most of the time, but unless we go into every room every day, even if only to keep it aired, we are not complete.

Rumor Goddan

In these fast-paced times, it is harder than ever for most of us to create balance in our lives. We work hard and forget to play. We think intensely and ignore our feelings. We exercise our minds and not our bodies. We relate to concepts and not to people. As we strive for position, power, and money, we often neglect our basic needs of connection, love, and inner peace.

If you find your life has a singular focus, take a four-sided approach to creating satisfaction. Spend some time each day in each of these four "rooms": mental, emotional, spiritual, physical.

8. Take a leap of faith.

Many of us have grown up in a world that has become cynical about spirituality. We have seen instances of spiritual leaders exposed for unholy deeds. We are confused as to why bad things happen to good people. We are suspect to things that cannot be proved by science.

Yet this disconnection with anything larger than ourselves creates a feeling of emptiness in our lives. We turned to achievement and power as a way of managing our emptiness. Spiritually bankrupt, some of us turned to drugs, food, or alcohol.

Spirituality looks different for each of us. For some, it's taking a walk in the forest. For others, it's sitting quietly for twenty minutes, looking inward. For others, it's going to church.

Why is this important for the never-enough thinker? Because spirituality is a source of power. It is the beginning of feeling you are never alone. It is a source of connection with others, a source of purpose, and a source of serenity.

Like anything of value, contentment doesn't come easy. Yet, the suggestions in this chapter can help you stretch toward greater satisfaction in your life.

What will it feel like when enough becomes enough? You will still want some things you don't presently have. You will still have goals. But these goals will fill you with a sense of energy and purpose, rather than an obsessiveness that exhausts you.

What you want and what you need will no longer be two vastly different things. You will be empathic with yourself enough to be honest about who you are and where you are. You will think for yourself.

You may still see the glass as half empty. But when you do, it's a message that you're ready to move forward; it's not a hopeless, superstitious habit that makes you bitter.

When you catch yourself running in circles, you no longer run faster and harder. You pause and deal with the underlying issue. If you can't relax, you focus on learning to trust. You work through whatever in the past made you distrustful, and a day comes when you can finally let it go.

If you are bored and restless, you search for ways to feel a greater sense of competence.

If you can't find the right person, you focus on becoming the right person.

In other words, you get out of your own way. Will life be better? It will definitely feel better. And this won't be because you've learned to settle for less than you hoped for. It's because you're no longer tied to the past or living for the future. Time will become a friend rather than a measuring stick against which you feel inadequate. It won't be too late, because it's never too late to say enough is enough. Satisfaction may be closer than you think.

❦ ❦

Basch, Michael Franz. *Doing Brief Psychotherapy.* New York: Basic Books, 1995.

Bloomfield, Harold, and Peter McWilliams. *How to Heal Depression.* Los Angeles: Prelude Press, 1994.

Bradshaw, John. *Bradshaw On: The Family.* Deerfield Beach, Fla.: Health Communications Inc., 1988.

Cameron, Julia. *The Artist's Way.* New York: Tarcher, 1992.

Covey, Stephan. *The 7 Habits of Highly Effective People.* New York: Simon and Schuster, 1989.

De Angelis, Barbara. *How to Make Love All the Time.* New York: Dell, 1987.

Dowling, Colette. *Perfect Women.* New York: Summit Books, 1988.

Gawain, Shakti. *The Path of Transformation.* Mill Valley, Calif: Nataraj Publishing, 1993.

Jampolski, Gerald. *Love Is Letting Go of Fear.* New York: Bantam Books, 1979.

Miller, Alice. *Drama of the Gifted Child.* New York: Basic Books, 1981.

Paul, Stephen. *Illuminations.* New York: HarperCollins, 1991.

Robbins, Anthony. *Giant Steps.* New York: Simon and Schuster, 1994.

Shapiro, David. *Neurotic Styles.* New York: Basic Books, 1965.

Sills, Judith. *Excess Baggage.* New York: Viking, 1993.

Viorst, Judith. *Necessary Losses.* New York: Fawcett Crest, 1986.

Williamson, Marianne. *A Return to Love.* New York: HarperCollins, 1992.

Reaching Satisfaction

This book is part of an ongoing effort to study personal satisfaction and to encourage others to search for it in their lives. If you would like further information or would like to share your personal experience, please contact us.

For a brochure on our tapes, books, and services, or to let us know your reactions to *When Is Enough, Enough?* write or e-mail

Mitch Meyerson or Laurie Ashner
875 Dearborn, Suite 204
Chicago, IL 60610
(312) 440-0815

e-mail *MitchM2000@aol.com.*
LaurieA1@aol.com.

or visit our web site
http://members.aol.com/mitchm2000

Laurie Ashner and Mitch Meyerson are the authors of *When Parents Love Too Much* and monthly columnists for *Chicago Life* magazine. Mitch Meyerson is a psychotherapist who specializes in the areas of chronic discontent, dysthymia, and relationship difficulties. Laurie Ashner is a writer, teacher, and therapist; she is the co-author of *Resonance: The New Chemistry of Love.* Between them they have appeared on "The Oprah Winfrey Show," "The Tom Snyder Show," "The Jenny Jones Show," and many other television and radio programs. They reside in Chicago.